ROOTED IN DUST

Rural America

Hal S. Barron
David L. Brown
Kathleen Neils Conzen
Cornelia Butler Flora
Donald Worster

Series Editors

ROOTED IN DUST

Surviving Drought and Depression
in Southwestern Kansas

Pamela Riney-Kehrberg

 UNIVERSITY PRESS OF KANSAS

© 1994 by the University Press of Kansas
All rights reserved

Maps by Jill Freund Thomas

Data for maps on pages 13 and 39 from U.S. Department of Commerce, Bureau of the Census, Fourteenth, Fifteenth, and Sixteenth Censuses.

Published by the University Press of Kansas (Lawrence, Kansas 66049), which was organized by the Kansas Board of Regents and is operated and funded by Emporia State University, Fort Hays State University, Kansas State University, Pittsburg State University, the University of Kansas, and Wichita State University

Library of Congress Cataloging-in-Publication Data

Riney-Kehrberg, Pamela.
    Rooted in dust : surviving drought and depression in southwestern
Kansas / Pamela Riney-Kehrberg.
        p.   cm.—(Rural America)
    Includes bibliographical references and index.
    ISBN 0-7006-0644-0 (cloth : alk. paper)
    1. Depressions—1929—Kansas. 2. Droughts—Kansas—History—20th
century. 3. Kansas—Economic conditions. 4. Kansas—Social
conditions. I. Title. II. Series: Rural America (Lawrence, Kan.)
HB3717 1929.R56 1994
330.9781'4032—dc20   94-11032

British Library Cataloguing in Publication Data is available.

Printed in the United States of America
10 9 8 7 6 5 4 3 2 1

The paper used in this publication meets the minimum requirements of the American National Standard for Permanence of Paper for Printed Library Materials Z39.48-1984.

For my grandmothers

MARGARET COLLIER THOMPSON BARNES

and

ELSIE SWAFFORD RINEY

CONTENTS

ILLUSTRATIONS, MAPS, AND TABLES

Maps

Tables

ACKNOWLEDGMENTS

In writing this book, I have accumulated debts too numerous to mention. Nevertheless, at this point in my work, I would like to make an attempt to thank those who have made this project possible.

For research support I wish to thank the State Historical Society of Wisconsin, which provided an Alice E. Smith Fellowship. I would also like to acknowledge the Madison chapter of the AAUW, which awarded me their Martha L. Edwards Fellowship. The Kansas State Historical Society supported a research trip to their facilities with an Alfred M. Landon Historical Research Grant. While at Illinois State University, I have been the recipient of a University Research Grant, which aided in the revision of this work, as well as a Travel to Collections Fellowship from the National Endowment for the Humanities.

For aid in my research I am greatly indebted to the staffs of the State Historical Society of Wisconsin and especially the Kansas State Historical Society. Both facilities are indeed first-class research institutions. I also wish to thank Joyce Boswell, fellow researcher at the Kansas State Historical Society and more-than-helpful archivist at the Central Plains Branch of the National Archives. David Haury, then archivist at the Mennonite Library and Archives, Bethel College, was also a great help. There are individuals too numerous to mention who gave freely of their time and expertise in a multitude of county libraries and historical societies across southwestern Kansas. I am particularly grateful to the many survivors of the Dust Bowl who completed questionnaires, gave interviews, and mailed bits of information, many of which are included in this book.

Last, but not least, are personal debts of gratitude for support rendered during this project. The book began as my doctoral dissertation, and the direction I received while at the University of Wisconsin–Madison was superb. My academic advisors were truly wise and patient. I especially thank Allan G. Bogue, who allowed me to embark on this project and insisted that I perform to the best of my abilities, Diane Lindstrom, who listened to it all, and Bob Ostergren, whose classes inspired a good bit of the early research on this topic. Also, thanks to the other members of my committee, Margaret Beattie Bogue and Stanley Schultz. The graduate students in the History Department of the University of Wisconsin were willing to listen to years of musings about the Dust Bowl; I particularly thank the members of the American caucus dissertators' group. Cynthia Miller, Editor-in-Chief of the University Press of Kansas, has provided enormously useful advice.

My family, and people whom I have come to think of as family, have been tremendously helpful. I owe a special debt of gratitude to my grand-mothers, Margaret Collier Thompson Barnes and Elsie Swafford Riney, who inspired this project and who each, in her own way, supported my work. I dedicate this book to them. I thank the many people who took me in while I researched—my aunt and uncle, Sandra and Rod Williams of Elkhart, George and Laurie Copeland of Ness City, and particularly the Hiller-Briggs family (Karen, Glenn, Bryan, Michael, and Neil) of Topeka. You each made my research trips easier. My parents, Norm and Mary Riney, and brother, Scott Riney, have always believed in me and have been ever so patient.

But most of all, I wish to thank my husband and partner, Richard Kehrberg. He now knows more and has seen more of southwestern Kansas than he ever cared to discover and has hardly complained. Bless you.

INTRODUCTION

The thing that impressed me the most was probably not the dust storms but the devastation on the land. . . . There would just not be any vegetation at all on the land for maybe half a mile in any direction. . . . I don't know how anyone survived.

I suppose it was living one day at a time. We never had all of the, I call them, luxuries. We had nice homes, but it was nothing fancy. Carpet sweepers and our washing machines was the kind that takes manpower. I think getting the washing done was a major operation. To get them dry before they got dust, because we hung them out on the line. . . . It was rough.

We knew there wasn't anything going on but another dust storm. It would come from one direction one day, and then the next day it seemed like it came back from the other direction. People got so they knew just about what part of Kansas the dirt storm was coming from by the color of the dirt.[1]

The 1930s were grimly memorable years for the people of the United States. The decade was marked by economic collapse, resulting in bank failures, staggeringly high unemployment, and widespread, persistent poverty of a type previously unknown in the history of the United States. The Great Depression plunged many an individual, family, and community into despair. Although the depression's impact was variable, affecting families and communities with different severity, no state or region remained untouched.

Throughout the nation's heartland, the problems of the 1930s took on a particular urgency. As if the Great Depression were not hardship enough, a prolonged drought also afflicted the Great Plains. Year after year, the rains failed to come, and farmers watched their crops wither.

The drought, accompanied by high winds and unusually high temperatures, desiccated the soil, driving it into the air in enormous, seething clouds of dust. The choking, all-pervading dust wreaked havoc on agricultural communities already staggering from conditions almost too difficult to bear. The residents of the plains, in a broad swath from western North Dakota south through west Texas, suffered the indignity of the worst sustained environmental and economic disaster ever to affect the United States. The people of sixteen southwestern Kansas counties were trapped in the heart of the Dust Bowl.[2]

When the story of the Dust Bowl is told, it is most often the story of those who left—the impoverished and discouraged multitudes who departed for California, Oregon, and Washington in the darkest days of the 1930s. Hoping for jobs and opportunities outside the region, many residents of the farms and towns of southwestern Kansas quit waiting for the rain to fall. By the late 1930s a significant number of the area's population were searching for new homes. Their story captured the imagination of the American public, in part because of the stirring writings of John Steinbeck, particularly The Grapes of Wrath. The Joad family, although not true Dust Bowl refugees, came to represent all of the Americans displaced by the economic and environmental dislocations of the thirties.[3] The loss of their rented farm, their difficult journey to the unwelcoming West Coast, and the poverty and humiliation of migratory farm labor stirred the hearts of many readers. This was the most common Dust Bowl story and the one with which most Americans were familiar.

The migrants' story, however, is only a small part of the larger history of the Dust Bowl. While a quarter of the population of southwestern Kansas joined the Dust Bowl migration, fully three-quarters of the area's residents struggled on.[4] While migrants faced the painful task of creating a life in a new location, those who remained behind faced the equally difficult problem of survival, pitting their stubbornness and ingenuity against both economic depression and environmental collapse, as well as the unsympathetic response of many observers—not an easy task.

The lives of those who endured the decade in southwestern Kansas were unique and individual, but many bore the stamp of endurance and determination. Opal Musselman Burdett was in her teens when dust pneumonia took her father's life. She and her sisters had no choice but to let the bank repossess the family farm. For her, the thirties were years of hard work, exchanging her housekeeping skills for room and board and working for the National Youth Administration, which provided jobs to hard-pressed students. Hers was not an ideal childhood, but one filled with hard work, a common denominator in the lives of many of those who grew up during the thirties.[5]

George and Laurie Copeland married in 1931, determined to make a success of farming. After several years on George's father's farm, they purchased their own in 1934 with the aid of the Federal Land Bank. Keeping their farm enterprise afloat was a struggle. Crops failed, and those that did not brought poor prices in the marketplace. Their cattle had to be sent to the eastern part of the state for pasture. Laurie taught school for three years to supplement their meager farm income, in addition to raising and preserving food and sewing clothing. They lost a baby, and Laurie endured a serious illness. Nevertheless, they held onto their farm and eventually made it into a paying enterprise.[6]

Ona Libertus was a married woman with children when the Dust Bowl and depression struck. She was also a landowner, who in 1913 had homesteaded her own claim in Hamilton County. On 160 acres, she and her husband grew broomcorn and other crops. The family of seven lived in a sod house, built over their original dugout. They papered the interior with newspapers. In 1935, she ceased to be a farmer when circumstances forced the family to sell the land for only $300. As she said, they essentially "gave it away." It was a bitter disappointment. The Libertus family was forced to begin again in a home of their own construction in Coolidge, only sixteen miles south of the farm they had lost. They, like many other Dust Bowl families, had to start over in their own backyards, rather than migrating to greener lands farther to the west.[7]

Unfortunately, little has been written about the ways in which individuals and families such as these adapted to the challenges of the 1930s. Other historians have focused on federal policy, agricultural practices, and environmental considerations, leaving largely untold the history of the individuals, families, and communities that survived this economic and environmental crisis.[8]

The circumstances of the decade thoroughly disrupted and altered the pattern of life for thousands of individuals and their communities. The drought, depression, and dirt storms created a kind of poverty and hopelessness previously unknown to the people of the region, except perhaps during the shorter period of drought and depression during the 1890s. The Dust Bowl also altered the relationship between humans and the land, when the soil that they depended upon refused to support them. Although the Dust Bowl years were but a decade in the history of the southern Great Plains, that decade reshaped life for the residents of south-western Kansas and prompted them to reshape the land to meet their desire for stability and continuity in the face of recurring environmental desolation.

An important factor in this story was the recent settlement of the region. Although the area had experienced depopulation during the 1890s, farming families and other settlers flooded into the area in the years following the turn of the century, particularly during and after World War I. Many of the newcomers had little or no experience with the vicissitudes of the western Kansas climate. Often they had formed very few attachments to their localities. The cooperation and mutuality that strengthened many older agricultural communities during the Great Depression was in its formative phases throughout much of the Dust Bowl. Those who had developed this spirit benefited enormously; those who had yet to discover the virtues of neighborliness suffered seriously from the decade's blows, often succumbing to the urge to migrate.[9]

This story is about those who chose to stay, despite the hard times, and the accommodations they made to the problems of the decade. The townspeople also had to adjust to diminished incomes, due to loss of trade with the area farmers. Conditions forced city and county administrators to find ways to create a relief network that would allow people to feed and clothe themselves. These administrators often discovered that these costs meant bankruptcy for their counties, a problem that remained through the decade's end. The farmers, who formed the basis of this society, had to devise the means of saving their land, in spite of terrific hardships. Without government aid, very few would have been able to remain farmers throughout the decade.

Success or failure at meeting these challenges shaped the migration of the 1930s. Larger towns, which were able to garner large government aid packages and attract business from outlying towns, were better able to retain their populations and reach the year 1940 with their populations and economic importance to the region relatively intact. Farmers who were able to draw upon the resources available within families, such as emotional and financial support, and who were unable or unwilling to sell their land survived to enjoy the bounty of the Second World War. But before they could reap the rewards of their endurance, the southwestern Kansans who had been such enthusiastic settlers in the early years of the twentieth century were tested in ways that they could hardly have imagined during the boom times following the turn of the century.

1. HARDLY A CLOUD
IN THE SKY

The people of southwestern Kansas began the 1930s optimistically. Although many areas of the country were feeling the onset of the Great Depression, its effects had not yet reached this corner of the southern Great Plains, where many believed the nation's problems would be slow to arrive or would hardly touch at all. These communities were young, relatively prosperous, and had been undergoing tremendous development during the first thirty years of the century. Wheat farming, begun in earnest in this region during the First World War, had treated the area's farmers kindly. While many of the nation's agricultural communities had suffered from a depression during the 1920s, those of southwestern Kansas had done well by comparison.

A number of factors made the farmers of southwestern Kansas successful in the period following the First World War. Fertile land, freshly broken to the plow, enough moisture, and the newest of agricultural technology, the tractor, helped farmers to produce bumper crops and earn more than adequate incomes. In 1934, the Gray County agricultural extension agent recalled the twenties as "a period of plenty." Application of new farm technology had turned "the idle acres of Gray County . . . into a sea of wheat."[1] In fact, residents on the far western border of the state claimed that their counties had only reached their peak of agricultural production and expansion in 1931, the year that the agricultural economy of the region disintegrated. Southwestern Kansas began the 1930s as a scattered group of small but rapidly growing communities. The settlement history and successes of the very early years of the twentieth century explained the optimism that southwestern Kansans felt, even at the onset of the Great Depression.

Settlers had arrived in southwestern Kansas fairly late in the total

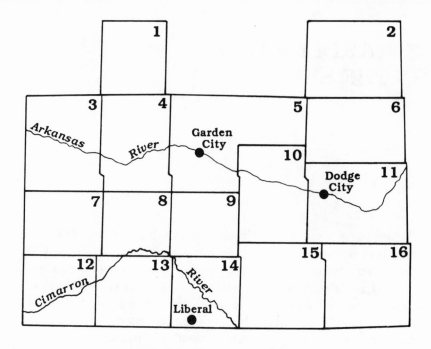

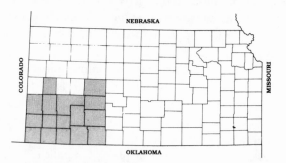

Map 1.1. Study counties: 1. Wichita; 2. Ness; 3. Hamilton; 4. Kearny; 5. Finney; 6. Hodgeman; 7. Stanton; 8. Grant; 9. Haskell; 10. Gray; 11. Ford; 12. Morton; 13. Stevens; 14. Seward; 15. Meade; 16. Clark.

process of westward expansion. The 1880 census showed that the first trickle of pioneers had moved into the area, but their numbers were quite small. Although more than three thousand people lived in Ness and Ford counties, the areas that were to become Stanton and Wichita counties boasted five and fourteen residents, respectively.[2] In fact, most of the territory remained unsurveyed and unorganized at the time the census-takers arrived. Enough newcomers made their way west during the 1880s, however, to push the so-called "frontier line" back nearly to the Colorado border. The 1890 census, which sparked such concern about the close of the American frontier, declared all of southwestern Kansas except Morton County settled, since more than two people to the square mile resided there.

The counties were composed mainly of scattered agricultural holdings interspersed with small, rough frontier towns. Dodge City, the oldest and largest of these towns, was home to 1,763 people in 1890, followed by Garden City, with a population of 1,490. Despite the smallness of the towns, the residents had big dreams and high hopes for the future. Consequently, they fought major skirmishes with each other over any and all possible opportunities for development—railroads, land offices, and county seats. Some county seat wars, such as those in Wichita, Ness, and Stevens counties, went to such bloody excesses that they received comment in the *New York Times*.[3] Business boomed, and settlers flowed into southwestern Kansas.

An item in the 1885 report of the Commissioner of the General Land Office illustrates the headlong pace at which homesteaders settled the land. The register of the land office at Garden City reported: "The rush for land in this section of Kansas is unprecedented. Every train brings in a crowd of land seekers. For more than an hour before the office opens a mass of humanity throngs the doorway, and it is a remarkable sight to see the press and excitement." He concluded by saying that in their "heedless rush" to settle the land, homesteaders failed to understand their obligation to the government. He also implied that they did not understand the difficulty of the task. These concerns were borne out by the events of the 1890s.[4]

The settlers' initial enthusiasm for southwestern Kansas did not last. Between 1890 and 1900, the population stampeded east once more, overwhelmed by drought and an agricultural depression. Proud frontier towns, buffeted by county seat fights and often left high and dry by railroad companies, could not withstand the general exodus of the decade. Appomatox, Kendall, Hartland, and Woodsdale, booming towns in 1890, were too small for the census-taker to notice in 1900. Hartland, for example, had been a fairly substantial town, home to approximately one thousand people and numerous businesses: three hotels, two newspapers, a bank, three hardware stores, and five lumberyards, among others.[5] By

1900, Hartland no longer existed. Other communities such as Old Ulysses, Santa Fe, and Coronado died lingering deaths, disappearing completely by 1910. Residents of nearby towns such as Coolidge and Richfield could point to the 1890s as the beginning of their towns' descent from importance to inconsequence.[6] The frontier line actually receded.[7]

Residents found that their land, which had been so valuable in the boom years, was now virtually worthless. Homesteaders who had not yet patented their claims allowed their holdings to revert to the government when they left. A flood of failed settlers headed to points east, with "In God We Trusted, In Kansas We Busted" emblazoned on their wagons. Others, unable to pay their mortgages, lost their land to foreclosure or signed it over to the bank. Speculators found that they were unable to make a profit. In 1887, for example, the agents of an English firm acquired approximately 51,840 acres of land in Kearny County. They intended to create an irrigation company, the Amity Land Company, and to sell irrigated farms to settlers. They soon discovered that it was impractical to irrigate the land, a realization that coincided with the drought and depression of the 1890s. The speculators found a market for their holdings after the turn of the century, but at $2.50 an acre and less, far short of the $6.00 an acre they had invested. In the course of the 1890s, much of the land of southwestern Kansas passed into the hands of nonresident owners and speculators, who bided their time, expecting both farmers and profits to return.[8]

The disastrous 1890s gave way to more hopeful times following the turn of the century. Farmers poured into the region, rebuilding decimated communities. The families that came formed a fairly homogeneous population, largely of white, old American stock, with a few scattered German and Mennonite communities, and an even thinner population of African American farmers. They created rural communities that supported a considerable network of schools and churches. The farmers, for the most part, prospered, reaping the benefits of greater than average precipitation and reasonable grain prices.

The farmers supported a growing network of small towns and cities that existed primarily to serve their needs. A more heterogeneous population lived in the towns and cities, with small but visible African American and Mexican communities located in both Garden City and Dodge City. Most city dwellers were, however, white and native born. The residents of these isolated towns soon developed businesses and institutions designed to meet the needs of both town and country. Townspeople founded their own

As late as 1911, rural Hamilton County south of Syracuse was essentially undeveloped and unsettled. (Kansas State Historical Society)

schools and churches, complementing similar rural facilities. They operated banks, hardware stores, and groceries that were largely dependent
upon the patronage of the rural population. Only in Garden City, Dodge
City, and Liberal, which each had a small base of manufacturing, did
business owners have the luxury of catering to a preponderantly urban
population.

A tremendous burst of population growth fueled these developments.
Although the Census Bureau had declared the frontier closed in 1890, it
still existed in southwestern Kansas well into the twentieth century. From
1900 to 1910, the counties of southwestern Kansas were quite obviously
still experiencing frontier rates of population growth—in rural areas far
above 20 percent.[9] During the first decade of the twentieth century, the
rate of total rural increase exceeded 100 percent. By 1920, this dramatic
growth appeared to have ended. In only seven counties did the rural
populations grow at a rate exceeding 20 percent during the years from
1910 to 1920, and the average rural rate of total increase for these sixteen
counties was only 17 percent. Southwestern Kansas seemed to have
passed its frontier stage.

But settlers streamed into southwestern Kansas again in the 1920s. Ten
of the sixteen counties showed rates of total rural increase over 20 per-

cent, even though some of these had actually lost population in the 1910s (see Table A.1). Only Clark County lost farmers during the 1920s. As the Grant County agricultural extension agent could attest, the area was rough and undeveloped and experiencing tremendous change. He and others like him had great confidence, however, in the ability of the farming population to transform hastily erected dwellings and newly broken fields into prosperous farms.[10]

A large number of tenants operated farms in southwestern Kansas. In 1930, close to 50 percent of all farm operators in Dust Bowl counties were tenants; even most landowners did not own all of the land they farmed, renting at least part of their total acreage, often from nonresidents who had made purchases in the years immediately following the turn of the century.[11] Tenancy was not generally an indication of poverty—usually the case in other regions such as the rural South. For farmers in semiarid regions, tenancy provided a means of managing risk. Tenants would not be forced to make mortgage payments or pay taxes on unprofitable acres during dry years. Instead of sinking capital into land which might be drought-stricken and unprofitable one out of every five years, farmers could invest their money in items that they normally could not rent, such as machinery that could be moved from farm to farm with relative ease. Renters did not commit themselves to the costly upkeep of hundreds or thousands of acres of land.[12] The practice was potentially hazardous to the health of the land: Tenants, with little or no long-term stake in the land they farmed, were less likely to take costly and time-consuming conservation measures. But the financial risks of area farmers were thus minimized.

Changes in farming practices accompanied this dramatic expansion in farm population. Although farmers grew a number of different cash, subsistence, and forage crops and raised pigs, chickens, dairy cows, and beef cattle, wheat became the predominant cash crop. Nonresident farmers engaged in large-scale wheat farming in the area during and after the First World War, and by 1933, local farmers were showing an interest in wheat nearly equal to that of these "suitcase farmers."[13] The number of acres all farmers, resident and nonresident, devoted to wheat grew tremendously after the turn of the century. The census-taker counted 441 acres of wheat land in Clark County in 1900. By 1930, farmers there planted 153,160 acres of wheat. Stevens County topped the list in 1930 with 2,060,409 acres seeded to wheat.[14] The promise of highly profitable wheat agri-

In 1917, the Jessie J. Henry family of Stanton County called this claim home. (Kansas State Historical Society)

culture attracted ever-increasing numbers of farmers to southwestern Kansas.

Thus, people who were generally inexperienced in agriculture on the semiarid southern plains propelled southwestern Kansas into this experiment with large-scale wheat farming. During the years of expansion, these farmers were fairly recent arrivals, learning a new craft—large-scale, mechanized wheat farming.[15] What they did not know was that the lessons they learned were based upon an unusually favorable set of climatic conditions. (In the long run, average normal rainfall for these counties was 18.09 inches per year, but average rainfall during the 1920s was 19.97 inches per year, a small but important increase in total rainfall.)[16]

Although some years between 1921 and 1930 were less profitable than others, farmers in four southwestern Kansas counties (Gray, Grant, Meade, and Morton) harvested 78.3 percent of their planted acres and earned incomes averaging $4,231.11 per year for each 640 acres planted.[17] These numbers closely corresponded to the actual income of the area's farms, since the average farmer in these four counties either owned or rented approximately 660 acres in 1930. These were good times, and the memory of the 1920s, not the hard, drought-ridden times of the 1890s, shaped people's expectations of the rewards of farming in southwestern Kansas. Earl Owens, a longtime resident of Seward County, explained the experiences of farmers during the 1920s. "Boom, all you had to do was plant, and you had a crop. It was just no problem. In the 1920s . . . it was a cinch. You put the grain in the ground, and it grew."[18] The Kansas these farmers knew was a generous land.

The region's cities and towns grew along with the farm population. Fifteen new towns appeared after the turn of the century, ten during the 1920s. Existing towns expanded at tremendous rates.[19] The people of Dodge City numbered less than 2,000 in 1900; by 1930, more than 10,000 people made their homes there. Residents of all the area's county seat towns could report similar growth, if on a smaller scale. A reporter for the *Hugoton Hermes* was supremely confident that the development his town had experienced during the 1920s would continue in the 1930s. Although the census enumerator counted 2,200 residents, the writer advised that "if you are asked as to Hugoton's population a year from now the answer correctly given would be 5,000."[20] The editor of the *Grant County Republican* was equally optimistic, believing that the census enumerator's report for his county revealed "what has become of some of the population missing in the eastern part of the state."[21] While the rural population of Kansas as a whole declined from 1910 to 1930, gains in the total population of western Kansas, both rural and urban, often compensated for the losses in eastern and central Kansas and kept the population of Kansas more or less stable (see Map 1.2 and Table A.2).[22]

While towns sprouted above ground, developments underground encouraged southwestern Kansans as well. Oil and gas exploration uncovered vast reserves on the southern plains immediately after the turn of the century. Wells in Texas, Oklahoma, and New Mexico yielded oil prior to the First World War, bringing reasonable profits to investors. Encouraged by successes throughout the southern plains, developers began work in southwestern Kansas in 1919, drilling three wells near Liberal. By the mid-1920s, companies were conducting tests all over the area.[23] With the discovery of an enormous natural gas field near Hugoton came a flurry of activity, and companies initiated several large-scale projects. Panhandle Eastern Pipeline Company planned and began construction of a pipeline to carry natural gas from Kansas to Indiana. The company also constructed a compressor station near Liberal, beginning work in 1930.[24] Developments undertaken by Panhandle Eastern, the Argus Gas Com-

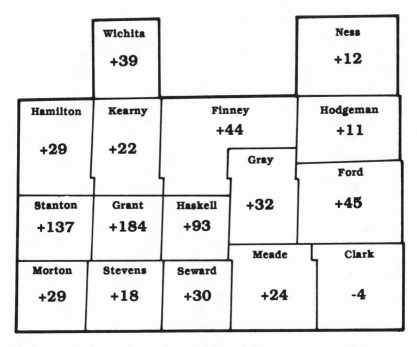

Map 1.2. Study counties, showing percentage increases in population, 1920–1930. *Source:* U.S. Department of Commerce, Bureau of the Census, Fourteenth and Fifteenth Censuses.

pany, and Northern Natural Gas inspired celebrations throughout the region. In 1929, the people of Dodge City organized an area-wide party in honor of oil and gas development, and Gov. Clyde M. Reed officially declared Hugoton the Gas Capital of the Southwest.[25]

The rejoicing was warranted: The discoveries and their consequent exploitation brought business into area towns. Residents saw their streets filled with incoming laborers. One observer of developments in Clark County wrote that "it looks like boom days ahead for Ashland. . . . like harvest times in the days before the combine when men by the hundreds used to flock in for work."[26] People in the "Gas Capital of the Southwest" were equally cheerful. "Without the discovery of gas we were entitled to grow into a city of 2,000 people. With the discovery of gas and the strong possibilities of oil being found later on we should be 'sitting on top of the world.'"[27] Oil and gas development was the latest good fortune for an area already blessed by agricultural abundance. Sages predicted an even greater burst of population growth and development, not just based on farming, but also on the industries that they hoped would be attracted by the inexpensive and abundant energy available in the natural gas fields.

The frenzied activity of the 1920s provided the resources for tremendous development. Everywhere southwestern Kansans saw concrete evidence of this boom in new building projects, increased business volume, considerable municipal improvements, and the creation of new social institutions. Both the quantity of business and the quality of life were improving. Opportunities appeared on every side.

One of the clearest indications of the increased volume of business was the growth in the number of both home and office buildings in towns throughout the region. Between September of 1929 and September of 1930, contractors built 152 new residences in the city of Hugoton, and 30 new business blocks. Even so, there was a waiting list of prospective tenants. This construction represented a million dollars in investments and, from the perspective of the local newspaper publisher, "permanency" for Hugoton.[28] Other towns experienced similar building booms. Between 1926 and the end of 1929, the population of Ulysses, in Grant County, grew from 300 to 1,300. In 1929, builders met the needs of newcomers with fifty new houses and nine new office buildings. Residents of Ashland, in Clark County, saw more than a dozen new business structures erected in the last three years of the decade and fifteen new houses built in its last three months. Despite all of this construction, the city suffered a housing shortage into the winter of 1931. Families building new residences in Stanton County in 1929 spent $100,000 in the process.[29] The people of southwestern Kansas were witnessing a tremendous burst of development unmatched since the earliest days of the area's settlement.

A writer for the *Liberal News* predicted: "The individual who bets on this city by investing his money here will make no mistake. . . . covering a term of ten years or longer there is no question as to the wisdom and practicability of owning one's home in Liberal. It will pay."[30] From the vantage point of 1930, it was hard to imagine that within a few short years the area would be dotted with abandoned homes and homes that families could not sell and that buyers would actually move homes from towns such as Elkhart to be occupied by families elsewhere.

The construction of new homes and businesses throughout southwestern Kansas during the twenties reflected underlying increases in economic activity throughout the area. The *Hugoton Hermes* found that rail shipments of all items both into and out of Hugoton had increased substantially since the beginning of gas exploration. Wheat shipments had increased by 260 percent. The number of agricultural implements received by local retailers had increased by 480 percent. Over a five-year period, the number of automobiles shipped into the county had grown by 180 percent. Even shipments of coal accelerated, which was surprising since nearly all city residents and many farm families had replaced coal with natural gas.[31] Stevens County's reserves of natural gas brought business and economic development that the people of Hugoton could not have imagined prior to the 1920s.

In 1930, economic growth was not isolated to Stevens County. Residents of Liberal, the third largest town in the area, celebrated the completion of the Liberal-Amarillo link of the Rock Island Railroad, as well as the building of the Wheatland Hotel, and began planning construction of a $50,900 airport. Liberal business people bragged about their successes: "Business Is Good: Everything As Good As Last Year: Trade Is Better Now Than Every [sic] Before: We Can't Kick a Bit: Picking Up All the Time: No Slump for Us Yet."[32] Even the post offices were doing well. Receipts at the Johnson post office doubled in 1929, and those at the Hugoton post office increased by 33 percent.[33] Gambling on business in a rough, rural area was, for the time being, paying off for local entrepreneurs.

The economic returns from doing business in southwestern Kansas were great enough to convince many residents that they were indeed blessed and living in one of the most prosperous areas of the country. Local newspaper editors kept a close eye on *Nation's Business* and its monthly maps showing business conditions throughout the country. They could hardly contain themselves when they saw that the maps for January and February of 1930 confirmed what they already knew—that southwestern Kansas was one of the most prosperous areas of the country, while much of the rest of the country was experiencing only fair or quiet business conditions.[34] One editor at the *Garden City Daily Telegram* wrote that "it is not hard to understand why people like to live in Kansas. It's a great old state and growing better every year." The maps were front-page news and elicited considerable comment. The *Garden City Daily Telegram* proclaimed that the area should "congratulate itself, sit tight, not rock the boat, keep investments inside the safety zone and the business depression which is affecting other sections of the country will not be seriously felt here."[35] However, by the end of 1931, local newspapers were no longer publishing the *Nation's Business* maps. They had become embarrassing.[36]

But in the late 1920s and into 1930 increased business activity brought

The Map of the Nation's Business

By FRANK GREENE

Managing Editor, Bradstreet's

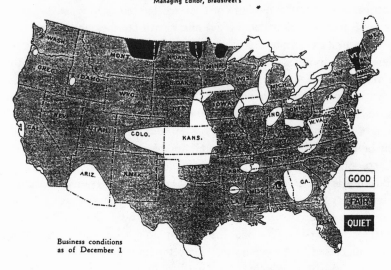

Business conditions
as of December 1

GOOD
FAIR
QUIET

A BRIGHT DAWN FOR 1930

This January 1930 map from Nation's Business *illustrates the economic strength that persisted in southwestern Kansas even after the onset of hard times. (By permission of* Nation's Business, *January 1930, © 1930, U.S. Chamber of Commerce)*

greater amenities to people who had been living in a fairly rugged environment. Natural gas discoveries paved the way for gas lighting and heat for the people of Hugoton, beginning in 1928. During 1930, Ness City completed a waterworks system and a sewer system and paved many city and county roads. Stanton County also installed a waterworks and began building a new rural high school. The editor of the *Liberal News* encouraged the people in his community to build a new high school, as well as a new junior high and several new grade schools, based on population projections for the coming year.[37] The voters of the cities and counties willingly approved bond issues to improve the physical quality of life throughout the area.

Gas lighting, waterworks, and expanded school systems were not the only amenities available in the towns; they were developing as social centers as well. During the late twenties and early thirties, individuals organized a number of churches, as well as social and occupational clubs. Congregants in Ulysses founded the Patterson Avenue Church of God in 1929 and the First Baptist Church of Ulysses in 1930, and those in Meade organized the Pilgrim Holiness Church in 1930 and an Apostolic church in 1932. County agents and farm women created extension homemakers units in many of these counties for the first time during the early years of the 1930s. Members of the Lion's Club of Liberal traveled to Hugoton to help form a new chapter, and Hugoton's women created a Business and Professional Women's Club. The people of Johnson went through an amazing period of activity between 1930 and 1932, reorganizing their chapter of the Red Cross, defunct since 1924, and organizing for the first time a Parent-Teacher Association, an Odd Fellows Lodge, a chapter of the Rebekah Lodge, and a Lion's Club. Perhaps most astonishing was Liberal's Country Club, whose organizers completed a membership drive in January 1930 and planned a $17,000 clubhouse on the land that the

The Map of the Nation's Business

By FRANK GREENE

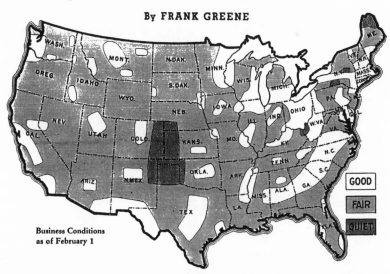

Business Conditions
as of February 1

As this 1935 map shows, the Dust Bowl was seriously affecting the economic fortunes of the southern Great Plains. (By permission of Nation's Business, March 1935, © 1935, U.S. Chamber of Commerce)

club owned adjacent to the existing golf course. These developments helped to make southwestern Kansas' communities more appealing places to live, adding the comfort of new social institutions to the economic advantages.

Still, the cities and towns of southwestern Kansas would have appeared primitive to eastern eyes. Residents could not attend symphonies or visit museums, but they could see the latest movies, attend school plays and community picnics, and read locally produced newspapers. The radio connected them with the outside world, and the residents were in the process of founding the churches, clubs, and service organizations that made these isolated towns a place to call home.

In the midst of all this optimism and development, doubts did persist in a few observers' minds. As 1930 wore on, it became evident that the depression might not resolve itself quickly, and a few writers cautiously drew parallels to the 1890s. Would the decade bring the same sort of ruin to the area as had that previous depression? But many writers assured their readers and themselves that the good times of the 1920s and the first year of the 1930s were real and lasting. The *Hugoton Hermes* reproduced the following item from a forty-year-old paper: "Stevens County Commissioners make an appeal to Eastern Kansas people for food supplies, fuel, clothing and feed, in order to carry the people of that county through the results of total crop failure." After noting that young residents and newcomers would find this item impossible to believe, the writer went on to explain that the situation could never recur. "Modern methods of soil preparation," better seeds, and the ideal soil and climate conditions of Stevens County guaranteed continued success, no matter what hardships the coming decade might bring.[38] The editor of the *Garden City Daily Telegram* was equally confident, believing that the quality of the new residents of southwestern Kansas would ensure a better outcome for them than their forebears had suffered in the 1890s:

The 1930 newcomers are composed of two classes chiefly: successful farmers who have wearied of high priced lands, high taxes and low yields farther east, who know agriculture from A to Z. . . . The second class, consists of business and professional men who have been successful in other locations but are looking to the future and casting their lots where prosperity is apparent. We may look for different results, than those of the eighties.[39]

People remained optimistic into the spring of 1931, even though the price of wheat fell lower and lower as harvest approached. They assured themselves that experience would tell, and the area would not have another exodus if the "boom busted"; southwestern Kansas would not go "back to sod" again.[40]

Civic and regional pride permeated discussions of the area's recent past and promising future. On New Year's Day 1930, anything seemed possible. Even a year later the people of southwestern Kansas maintained much of their optimism. As far as the local boosters were concerned, southwestern Kansas had recovered from past troubles, and the local economy had developed in ways that ensured both prosperity and security. The *Liberal News* boasted that "the government will not be called upon to take care of this part of the United States for some time, at least."[41] Staying out of the poorhouse, however, was not all that the people of the area expected from their future. "The more we learn of the achievements of science, of the force of economic pressure, and the spirit of the pioneer, the less inclined we are to assert that anything is impossible."[42] These twentieth-century pioneers believed that new technology, in concert with continued growth and optimism, ensured their success.

If a prophet of doom had wandered into Dodge City, Garden City, or any of the small communities across southwestern Kansas in 1930, he would have been laughed out of town. Although homesteading on the southern plains had ended in disaster in the 1890s, no one truly anticipated the problems of the 1930s. Although people could have been a bit more realistic about the local impact of poor business conditions in other parts of the United States, there was little to foretell the extreme hardships to come. The population of southwestern Kansas had grown tremendously, and westward-moving farmers had brought prosperity with them. Freshly broken lands yielded abundantly. Oil and gas discoveries diversified the area's economic base. The profits from these ventures made their way into the small cities and towns of the area, funding housing booms, municipal improvements, and business expansion. New churches and new clubs made the towns more pleasant places to live. Intense pride in the accomplishments of the preceding thirty years informed the residents' sense of place and sense of self. They believed that they lived in the best communities in the world and farmed the richest and most productive lands in the nation. They had mastered the elements and achieved success where skeptics said it could not be done. In the words of a local writer, "The old argument that the western third of Kansas was over enthusiastic will no longer hold."[43] Of course, the Great Depression had yet to intrude seriously on the lives of residents, the dust had yet to blow, and in terms of total production, their most bounteous wheat crop to date had yet to be harvested. There was hardly a cloud in the sky. Unfortunately, the coming decade would bring little but trouble to the people of southwestern Kansas.

2. TRIALS, TESTS, AND HARD TIMES

In the spring of 1931, the good times ended abruptly. That year should have been a banner year for the people of southwestern Kansas—Kansas farmers harvested their most bountiful crop of winter wheat to date. But the prices for which they sold their grain were inadequate to cover the costs of production and the region's already dry climate became much drier. The years of drought began just after harvest in 1931 and lasted through the growing season in 1939 as farmers watched their parched fields take to the air in huge, rolling clouds of dust. Deprived of birds, flowers, and growing crops, people recognized the arrival of each spring in the first dust storms of the year. That three-quarters of the population hung on through the decade seems remarkable.

Kansas agriculturalists raised a tremendous winter wheat crop in 1931. From 1920 to 1929, yields statewide averaged 13.1 bushels per acre. Yields per acre in 1930 were slightly higher, with farmers harvesting 13.7 bushels to the acre. In 1931, in cooperation with the weather, farmers completely outdid themselves, raising 17.7 bushels to the acre. The results were astounding. Kansans harvested 223,000,000 bushels of winter wheat, outstripping both their record harvest of 1927 and the five-year average harvest for 1925 to 1929 by a considerable margin. Not only was the grain plentiful, but it was the best quality wheat harvested in the United States that year.[1] Harvest time, 1931, should have been a time of rejoicing.

Wheat prices had been falling since the agricultural depression at the end of World War I but fell sharply in 1931 with the collapse of international markets for wheat and in response to the Great Plains bumper crop. By September 1931, wheat prices had fallen to an all-time low. Kansas farmers who had collected 70 cents a bushel at the elevator for their winter wheat in 1930 received only 28 cents in 1931, if they tried to sell it at all. By contrast, it cost farmers 56 cents to raise each bushel of wheat.[2] One Meade County farmer fed wheat to the fish in his lake.[3] On January 1, 1932, a commentator on the agricultural situation reviewed the results of the 1931 growing season and harvest and thought the year might best be forgotten. He wrote that "the year 1931 will be remembered long and unfavorably by farmers. It was a reasonably productive season but was marked by another staggering decline in prices."[4]

In fact, due to the bumper crop, prices received by farmers in Kansas were the lowest in the nation. As a result, the analysts at the Bureau of Agricultural Economics of the U.S. Department of Agriculture (USDA) reported that "farm holdings at this date are probably the greatest ever, not only in actual bushels but as a percentage of production as well. Much wheat will be fed to livestock again this year."[5] In anticipation of this response to falling wheat prices, the Columbian Steel Tank Company of Kansas City began manufacturing and marketing enormous steel grain bins, holding five thousand bushels of wheat or more.[6] Farmers had little hope of selling their grain for what they thought was a fair price, and many planned to store the wheat until prices rose.

This determination led to concerted action by a group of farmers. Led by George Rooney of Minneola, agriculturalists all across the southern plains staged a "wheat strike" in 1931. Just before harvest, Rooney began an effort to convince farmers to leave their land fallow until they received a dollar per bushel for the wheat they had on hand. If the price of wheat did not rise, Rooney urged the farmers to plant no crops for 1932.[7]

In May, farmers from Kansas, Oklahoma, Texas, Colorado, and New Mexico held an organizational meeting in Minneola. They published a two-sentence platform in newspapers throughout the area: "Hold all wheat until the price reaches the $1 per bushel mark. If it does not reach this mark by seeding time, do not sow an acre."[8] Charles Trostle, one of the largest farmers in Stanton County (he owned thirty-three quarter sections), showed his support by cutting his acreage for 1932 and agreeing to hold most of his 135,000 bushels of wheat until the price rose. Trostle told a newspaper reporter that large landholders, like himself, would not plant out of principle, while the small holders would plant less for 1932 because they could not afford to plant a large crop. A writer for the *Johnson Pioneer* estimated that wheat farmers in Stanton County planned to cut their winter wheat acreage by 35 to 40 percent.[9]

The farmers did hold much of their wheat off the market and planted fewer acres for the coming year, but "nation-wide notoriety" was all they received for their pains. Although Rooney proclaimed that his organization represented "a determined and definite revolt of the agricultural interests," the wheat strike did not produce the desired results. The price of wheat remained well below a dollar a bushel.[10] Out of disgust, one Ford County farmer hauled a load of wheat into Bucklin and dumped it in the middle of Main Street. That act haunted some Bucklin residents as the year wore on and people realized that farmers would harvest very little wheat in 1932.[11]

Southwestern Kansans found themselves in a deteriorating situation. It was just as well that farmers planted fewer acres in the fall of 1931 because the drought was already becoming serious. A few counties, such as Clark County, had begun to feel the pinch of drought conditions as early as 1930. By the late spring of 1931, farmers and ranchers throughout the area were suffering. Although normal average rainfall for these counties was just over 18 inches per year, rainfall for western Kansas between 1930 and 1940 averaged only 15.25 inches per year, with the lowest rainfall in 1934 and 1937 (11.14 and 14.19 inches, respectively).[12]

The amount of rain that Dust Bowl farmers expected under normal conditions varied by location. In general, farmers needed at least 18 inches of well-timed rain to grow wheat. On the eastern border of the Dust Bowl, in Ford County, farmers could reasonably expect about 20 inches of rain a year. Those in Stanton County, on the Colorado border, had to make do with just over 15 inches of moisture a year. Ford County received less than its usual 20 inches of rain every growing season between 1931 and 1940. In Stanton County, residents limped along on less than 10 inches of rain for four years of the decade—in Morton County, directly to the south, for five years. In an area where rainfall was normally barely sufficient for a wheat crop, this drought meant disaster.[13]

Eventually, people stopped looking for rain, since they had been "fooled so much that we dont think we'l get it."[14] They also endured many years without seeing snow. Iman Wiatt, a farmer in Kearny County, noted this in his diary in February 1937. "I think most of the wheat is doomed as we have had no snow so far. In fact we have had no snow since May 21, 1931—six snowless years."[15] The dry weather was coupled with some of the hottest summers on record. In Garden City during July 1934, residents suffered from temperatures at or above one hundred degrees for seventeen straight days. When the summer was over, those in the city could count fifty-eight days with temperature readings over one hundred.[16] Dry, hot air was making everyone miserable and destroying the farmers' hopes and fields.

Then the spring winds began to blow the parched earth into towering, rolling clouds of dust. Undoubtedly, Kansans had seen dirt storms before. They had plagued residents from their very first attempts to settle the area. In 1855, the editor of the Lawrence *Kansas Free State* had commented on the spring dust storms visiting the area. The dry and dirty conditions perplexed the former easterner, who was "accustomed to seeing rainy and muddy weather at this season." Residents had made similar comments during every dry spell between 1850 and 1900, as people experienced droughts and attendant dust storms. The gritty clouds seemed to be a predictable component of dry springs, whether an area had been broken to the plow or not. Light, sandy soil, high spring winds, and recurrent drought made periodic dust storms inevitable.[17]

But within recorded history, residents of Kansas had never experienced such severe storms over such an extended period of time. Then again, within local memory, there had never been so dry a spell or so much loose dirt to blow. Historians have characterized the 1920s as the years of the "great plow up" on the southern plains. Between 1910 and 1920, farmers had transformed more than one million unplowed acres into farms. In 1910, 4,634,792 acres of land in southwestern Kansas were in farms; by 1920, farmers worked 6,056,493 acres. Settlers eagerly moved out onto the undeveloped lands during the first twenty years of the century, and the high wheat prices and new technology of the war years greatly accelerated the rate at which farmers turned buffalo grass into cultivated acres.[18]

Farmers had indulged in a second great burst of new cultivation between 1925 and 1930. The amount of land in farms in Morton County, for example, rose by 38 percent, and in Stanton County, directly to the north, by 36 percent. Farmers invested heavily in machinery in order to accomplish this task. In 1930, the average Kansas farmer owned $1,101.50 worth of machinery of all types. In southwestern Kansas, investments of this sort ranged from a low of $1,096.79 in Hamilton County (recently emerged from its grazing era) to a high of $2,793.80 in Ford County. Farmers used this machinery to plow much of their land from fencerow to fencerow, with very little attention to soil-conserving techniques. Because of adequate moisture during the first thirty years of the century, such practices caused few problems. Although farmers resisted the idea, towering clouds of dirt convinced many experts in the USDA, as well as outside observers, that the land had been mismanaged

Dust clouds like this one were a common sight in 1935. (Kansas State Historical Society)

in the golden years before the Great Depression. Indeed, farmers' inattention to conservation during the 1920s came back to haunt them during the "dirty thirties."[19]

Farmers' problems with blowing dirt accelerated rapidly between 1929 and 1935 (and did not abate until 1940). The agricultural agent in Ford County recorded only twenty-four "dusty days" in 1929, and none of those days included "black rollers" of the kind that would visit the area during the thirties. By 1932, residents of Ford County were suffering more than twice as many dirty days—fifty-eight in that year. In 1935, the county agent recorded nearly double the number of storms experienced in 1932. Ford County residents suffered through 102 that year, and more than a few of those were ferocious black-outs.[20] Stanton County farm woman Martha Friesen recorded dust storms from August 1937 until June 1938, which many considered a fairly quiet period during the dirty years. Mrs. Friesen noted ninety days of dirt, ranging from a few minutes of light haze to full blown "dusters" that required the lamps to be lit. The number of dust storms during that period must have been even higher since the

In 1936, high winds piled up dust around this Seward County farmer's barn. (Farm Security Administration photo by Arthur Rothstein; Library of Congress)

Friesens spent parts of March and April (traditionally the dirtiest months) in Oregon, visiting a daughter. Martha Friesen described one of these storms: "Wind is still raging 120 miles an hour. First Mexico rolls by. Then Idaho & then how many more I don't know. And we all Cuddle round in this Dust Bowl."[21]

In 1939 Iman Wiatt rejoiced at seeing March pass without any major dust storms. "This is the first March we have gone through with no black blizzards of dirt since 1933. We have had only one dirt storm this month and it wasn't so very bad. Hope the dust bowl is gone forever." Mr. Wiatt, however, wrote too soon. "The month of April was one of the dirtiest on record. Only .38 of an inch [of rain]." And his troubles carried on into the summer. On August 12, 1939, he recorded that "it was real dirty. I couldn't see in places. Never saw anything like it at this time of year."[22] The decade ended as it had begun, dry and gritty. By the time the 1930s were over, the agricultural agents for Ford County had recorded 724 dirty days—just over two years spent in the dust.

Numbers alone could not explain the awe and fear people experienced as towering, dark dust storms rolled into the area. A contributor to the

A dust storm boils up over Liberal on Black Sunday. (Kansas State Historical Society)

Topeka Journal attempted to describe the intensity of these experiences. "There is no light, no air. My eyes sting and my throat aches. I wonder how long people can live in a cloud of dust. But where would one go? How could one escape? The prairies in all directions must be a seething, swirling world of dust. . . . The darkness and stillness are intense. This is the ultimate darkness, so must come the end of the world."[23] This particular dust storm was a prelude to the infamous "Black Sunday" dust storm of April 14, 1935. The majority of the survivors of that particular afternoon probably still remember where they were and what they were doing when the storm reached them.[24] An enormous dust cloud rolled over the southern plains that afternoon, completely blocking out the sun for several hours. Street lights came on at three in the afternoon, and drivers turned on their headlights. People could not see their hands in front of their faces or the lamps they lit in their homes. Those unfortunate enough to be on the road crept home at a snail's pace, while their passengers leaned out open doors to make sure that the driver did not steer the car into a ditch. One woman remembered a seven-mile drive on Black Sunday which lasted well over an hour. A farmer in Meade County became lost one-eighth of a mile from home, and his family found him behind a hedge, unconscious, just thirty feet from the house. One man crawled home from Meade's downtown area, feeling his way along the gutter. The storm convinced others that the end of the world had come.[25]

While most dust storms caused less panic than Black Sunday, the constant accumulation of grit seriously complicated people's everyday lives. The dust caused them problems in their jobs, whether they were farmers or not. The dust doubled and tripled the daily chores of area homemakers. It could damage people's health, both mental and physical. When people looked back on the thirties, they remembered the many ways in which the drought and accompanying storms altered their daily routines.

Conditions nearly stripped farmers of the ability to produce at all. Crops refused to grow, and the lack of feed forced farmers to slaughter their animals. Farmers who produced $4,000 worth of crops and livestock per year or more before the drought and depression found themselves raising less than $2,000 worth of products a year. The value of farm production in the sixteen southwestern Kansas counties averaged $1,663.68 per farm, per year, from 1933 to 1941.[26] This loss of income was one of the most obvious frustrations that those in agriculture suffered.

Farmers discovered that they had problems they could not have imagined. The static electricity generated by the storms tended to cook wheat on the stalk and blew out any wheat that was not cooked. Animals often fared as badly. A dust storm followed by a light rain blew one woman's chickens into a neighbor's pasture and pasted them to the ground. The woman and her husband gathered the chickens one by one and washed them clean. The little puffs of feathers that dotted the pasture the next morning marked the location of chickens that they, but not the coyotes, had missed. Reflecting upon the experience, she commented: "After it was all over with we laughed, but of course it wasn't funny at all. It was scary because we didn't know how many we could get back and how many we could even find. There were a lot of soapweeds out in the pasture. And we were going to be dependent all year long on the egg production of that little herd of chickens, that little flock of chickens. . . . It seems like a dream that was half nightmare."[27] One farmer discovered that his daughter's saddle horse had been knocked over and strangled by hungry cattle that had broken into the barn in search of feed. A rancher, perplexed by the death of a fine bull, cut him open to see if he could find the cause of death. He found two inches of dirt in the bottom of the bull's stomach, probably deposited there by dirty feed.[28] Incidents such as these added to the headaches and heartaches of already overburdened farming families.

The drought and dust disrupted the plans of farm children involved in 4-H clubs. Uncooperative weather conditions destroyed the boys' crop and animal projects year after discouraging year. In order to keep boys interested in the program, agricultural extension agents tried to involve them in home economics. In 1935, twenty Ford County boys baked, canned, and redecorated their rooms, instead of growing crops or raising animals.[29]

Conditions off the farm created problems as well. Daniel Penner met the challenge of being the janitor for a Mennonite church during the mid-thirties. One Sunday morning he removed thirty-seven gallon containers of dirt from the church before services. "I can't believe those dark suits were 'zestfully clean' after church," he wrote.[30] Teachers had to take special care not to send little children out into approaching dust storms, because "they could get lost before they could get out to the street."[31] Mornings after storms found teachers alone in their schoolrooms, trying to clean the dust off the floor, the desks, and even out of the textbooks. A number of children in area schools had an unexpectedly short spring semester in 1935, since dust conditions forced schools to close two or three weeks early. Some schools even canceled commencement. Dust storms forced the owners of local businesses as well as schoolteachers to close up shop and go home and to suspend operations until the dust cleared. The only winners seemed to be the owners of drug and hardware stores, who managed to deplete their stocks of tools and equipment for coping with dust. The drug stores in Garden City sold their entire supply of goggles and had to wait for more to come on trains delayed by flying dirt. The hardware stores in Bazine did an equally brisk business in brooms.[32]

The business generated by demand for goggles, brooms, and masking tape (used to seal windows) did not, however, compensate for the high cost of cleaning up after the storms. A writer for the *Meade Globe-News* attempted to calculate the losses caused by an April dust storm by surveying merchants, bankers, and homemakers. The writer estimated that the total damage to homes, at $25 per home, would run $7,500. Business owners probably lost $1,000 on items spoiled by the dust and sold at a loss. The average automobile owner expected to spend at least $10 repairing damage to the vehicle. All in all, the investigator estimated that this single storm cost Meade residents $10,800, or $7.20 per capita. In terms of the family budgets of the thirties, this was not an insubstantial sum, since many families subsisted on less than $25 a week.[33] This was also a mere fraction of the ultimate cost of the storms since most families endured several major storms a year, for seven years of the decade.

The storms created an incredible amount of work around the house. The writer who estimated the damage done to the city of Meade informed his readers that he had not calculated the "loss of disposition by the housewives." He further commented that "it would not have been safe to gather the necessary information for this article on some of the windy, dusty days that the people of Meade county have gone through in the last month."[34]

The writings of area women clarified why tempers were so short. One Kansan put her irritation into verse:

> I arise in the morning, greet the world with a grin,
> Ten minutes later, I'm in dirt to my chin;
> I grab up the broom, I grab up the mop,
> I start in cleaning and never stop;
> I don't dare stop, cause if I do,
> Sure as heck, we couldn't wade thru.[35]

Pauline Winkler Grey grimly promised to haunt her husband should she die and be buried in the dusty plains:

> Oh, bury me out on the lone prairie,
> When I'm done with this housekeeping strife
> And I'll come back on a howling wind
> To haunt your second wife. [36]

Many years later, one woman remembered vowing that she would never clean house again, the frustrations of the decade were so great. [37]

The reasons for this frustration were manifestly evident in the daily lives of Dust Bowl women. Digging out following storm after storm required a great deal of perseverance and patience. Even the most tightly made home filled with the fine, powdery dust. One woman likened stepping out of bed the morning after a storm to stepping into a layer of flour or cornstarch. Clearing up this powdery mess was terribly difficult, especially since most families did not own vacuum cleaners. [38]

Watching a dust storm engulf the family home could be devastating. (Kansas State Historical Society)

The storms disrupted women's general cleaning schedules as well. Finding a day to wash at all could be difficult: "Wash days are mighty scarce as the dirt blows so easy."[39] People sacrificed conventions to the needs created by the dirt. Much to her sorrow, circumstances forced Martha Friesen to work on Sunday in order to catch up with her household chores. "The Dust Bowl becomes a determent after all these storms. People work when ever the dust dont blow. Even if they break the Sabath."[40] Women cleaned their kitchens before every meal and cooked in pressure cookers in an attempt to keep the dirt out of the food. Even so, after many a meal, children could draw patterns in the dirt which accumulated on the edge of their plates. Good housekeeping extended to the attic as well. More than a few homeowners were dismayed to find the gritty contents of their attics distributed throughout their houses, as ceilings collapsed under the weight of inches of accumulated dirt.[41]

The writers of an unofficial history of Morton County described the problems of trying to keep a tidy house. "Dust shines against the windows unendingly. Food gets filled with it, clothes weigh heavy and smell shocking, and there is a grittiness about people's skins and hair and mouth that no amount of washing can get rid of."[42] One woman declared: "I think I'm ready to give the country back to the Indians and to give them compensation for ever taking it away from them in the first place."[43] The cost of keeping homes clean, both in time and patience, was incalculable.

The dust also created health problems. A measles epidemic swept southwestern Kansas in 1935, occurring at roughly the same time as the worst of the dust storms. While 8,000 Kansans came down with measles in the first fifteen weeks of 1934, 30,000 suffered with the measles during the same period in 1935. The dirty conditions seemed to induce "dust pneumonia" in those already enduring the measles. In April 1935, 1,500 people in one eastern Colorado and seven western Kansas counties were sick with dust-related illnesses, mostly pneumonia.[44]

Officials of the Federal Emergency Relief Administration, in cooperation with local authorities and area Red Cross chapters, launched community health programs. Red Cross workers set up emergency hospitals in churches and other public buildings, initiated a measles control campaign, and distributed dust masks, while relief workers dust-proofed homes—taping window casings to seal them and closing other cracks with tape and rags as much as possible.[45] Some people died, while many more were either ill or terribly frightened of becoming ill—with good reason. Deaths from pneumonia rose precipitously in most of the dusty counties. In 1935, one-third of the deaths in Ford County resulted from pneumonia. Morton County residents, who normally saw only one or two deaths from pneumonia in a year, buried thirty-one victims in 1935. The populations of only a few southwestern Kansas counties escaped dust pneumonia deaths that year.[46]

County health nurses detected other problems that could have been related either to the depression, the dust, or both. The number of children with physical and mental defects and the number of malnourished and underweight children rose. A full 25 percent of children in the area were at least 10 percent underweight. The infant mortality rate for the state of Kansas climbed in the spring of 1935.[47] Although the acute dust-induced illnesses were probably at their height in 1935 and 1937, the chronic results of drought-induced impoverishment continued.

Edith Stanforth, the public health nurse for Ulysses, wrote sadly about a family with six children, nearly all ailing from the results of hard times. The youngest child suffered from an abscessed ear, caused by a "leaky roof, drafts, dust and not enough fruit juices and fresh vegetables." The oldest child broke his arm in a fall from a tractor. His father had been in the Legion Hospital in Wichita. Two children were on their way to a "preventorium" for a six weeks' stay; their mother consented to the separation, hoping the stay would strengthen them for the next school year. These people, in Edith Stanforth's estimation, were "not poor whites, but poor because of adversity." They were the common people of the county, facing the common results of too much dirt and unrewarded hard work.[48] Although some skeptics doubted the connection between the health problems and the dirt storms and questioned the existence of dust pneumonia itself, most found it hard to believe that the ever-present dust did not threaten the lives of those who were hungry, ailing, very old, or very young.[49]

The storms, too, took a tremendous toll on people's emotional health. In her diary, Martha Friesen noted the sadness brought on by too much wind, dirt, and darkness. The whole family came down with the "blues" when the dirt rolled and tried to find various "blues chasers" to deal with their sorrows. Her husband, George, read his Liberty Magazine to "settle the strain," and her daughter, Margaret, took naps on the couch "to cover Dust blues." Martha herself listened to the phonograph. She would have preferred to listen to the radio, but the static electricity from the dust storms disrupted radio broadcasts. For a farm family, dependent on the radio for much of its entertainment, this was no small sorrow. "Its very

This April 17, 1935, dust storm swept over Garden City at noon. (Kansas Emergency Relief Committee photo; Kansas State Historical Society)

lonesome when we cant have much Radio," she wrote. Even the smallest members of the family suffered. Martha's granddaughter cried in fear during a 1939 dust storm, afraid that her father, who was out in the storm, "would perish." On the other hand, a change in the weather had a rejuvenating effect on the family. A touch of rain in June 1937 made both George and Martha "more Ambitious."[50] Spirits rose and fell with the wind.

These blues seemed to affect entire communities. A. B. Madison, a minister in Meade County, wrote a column for the *Fowler News* in the spring of 1935 in which he claimed that the people in the vicinity of Fowler had "given up trying to be civilized. We are merely trying to exist." As evidence, he cited a general lack of enthusiasm for community functions. People attended school plays and church meetings, but only out of custom and habit. People lost all concern for their clothing. "The Easter parade was a straggling affair for us this season—we could not be bothered." Even bodies sagged. "The typical posture is more nearly that of one who has fallen, headlong in to deep water and has now arisen to stand feet apart, hands hanging a bit away from the body, back slightly bent, clothing dripping and with a facial expression which says, 'Oh, aint this a mess!' The only difference is that the bath is not of water and the dripping is—just dirt."[51] Madison was not the only observer who noticed the general lack of enthusiasm among the people of the Dust Bowl. Warren Zimmerman, editor of the *Liberal News*, wrote to Congressman Clifford Hope that conditions were, simply put, "heart sickening." He felt great concern for his reading public because of the "despair and helplessness that confront so many."[52]

The agricultural extension agents for Ford, Meade, Morton, and Stanton counties all referred to the local malaise in their annual reports. Storms in the spring made people wary of venturing out for any sort of meeting and unwilling to participate in extension activities "because of the danger of being caught out in a severe dust storm." The agent in Meade noted that his clients had become "chronically contentious," due to dirt, drought, and discouragement. The Ford County home demonstration agent (home economist) believed that the spirits of the people had been considerably dampened by years of depression and drought. "There aren't quite so many 'next yearers,'" she wrote. The frustrated agent in Morton County was ready to give up on his discouraged, crushed, and quarreling bunch of farmers.[53]

Surprisingly enough, this contentiousness did not lead couples to dissolve their marriages more frequently. The number of divorces in southwestern Kansas remained relatively stable from 1933 to 1937, the worst of the dirty years. There were less than two divorces per year, per thousand of population, in the five years from 1933 to 1937.[54] Couples may have informally parted, unable to afford formal divorce. People, too, may have been holding on to their families as the only stable elements in their lives, in response to what was happening to their communities, jobs, and homes.

In the midst of all this suffering, people did find a few bright spots. Some credited the storms, which scoured away inches of topsoil, with their improved luck at arrowhead hunting. Clear days found numerous families, picnic basket in hand, out scavenging.[55] Lillian Foster, a young woman who lived in Ness County, kept a scrapbook about the storms, which gave her great pleasure. In the margins of her book, she noted that "the storms at first were fun. Just like 'Old Home Week' with all of us at Abe's usually." The closeness she felt to her friends during that time made the weather more bearable: "Jolly times during the hectic storms, also depressing times—and above all were jolly fine people to spend such times with." People expressed a certain amount of pride in learning to cope with the situation. Foster took great care to record the ways in which she tackled the problems created by the dust and speculated that she would spend time when she was "old and gray . . . looking thru the books and discussing various incidents."[56]

People also vented their frustration in literary efforts. A liberal sprinkling of Dust Bowl poetry and humor peppered area newspapers, balancing the tragedy of the situation against the ability of area residents to endure and laugh at their problems. Dust Bowl poetry rarely approached art, but it did express both the day-to-day and long-term concerns of people living under terrific stress. Although the authors of "Western Kansas Dust" and "Wanted—The Impossible" are unknown, it is highly likely that the rhymers were women, lamenting the ways in which dust storms added to their daily toil. "Western Kansas Dust" captured the spirit of the dejected housewife:

> The dust, the dust, that awful dust
> I think it is worse than rot or rust.
> It grits your teeth, settles in your hair
> That awful dust is everywhere.
> You think it's over, you start to clean
> You think its the worse you have ever seen.
> You get out the broom, also the sweeper
> If you find the rugs you have to dig deeper
> You shake the covers to find the bed
> You won't be buried much more when you're dead.
> It covers the table and every chair
> That awful dust is every where.
> Every curtain and picture has come down.
> Its just that way all over town.
> You clean up the house and think you're in 'clover'
> The very next day its all to do over.
> You clean up till you're too tired to go
> Then discouraged you sit down
> And let her blow.

"P.W.G." expressed the same sentiments and the same discouragement when she prayed: "Let me live in a house where a dust storm can't get."[57]

But for every lamentation, there seemed to be a joke making light of the Dust Bowl's troubles. State representative Joe Benson of Kismet returned to Seward County in April 1933, only to find the dust season in full swing. He told the editor of the *Liberal News*, "I got kind of homesick up at Topeka and wrote down to some of the Kismet folks to save me just one dirt storm. But I didn't aim for it to last a month." Others found humor in the way the dust storms affected their work. The assistant postmaster in Ashland contemplated planting his garden in the post office lobby as he attempted to clean out the dust one April morning. Farmer John Karns of Bucklin discovered "one of his best hens, who had stolen out a nest, hatched, and imagine Mr. Karns' chagrin when he found out of 15 eggs that the hen had hatched he had 12 mud hens and one sandhill crane." One particular tale, a refinement of an old frontier joke, probably stood as the all-time favorite dust story. "A tourist driving through the country and [saw] a Stetson hat out in the field. The tourist went out and picked it up and to his surprise saw there was a man under it. 'Need some help, partner?' inquired the tourist. 'Oh, no, I'm on horseback,' the man is quoted as having replied." Silly as it was, this joke illustrated what Dust Bowlers believed about themselves. They might be buried up to their necks in dirt, but they would manage, and they would find humor in the situation.[58]

Looking back on those years, a number of those who lived through the depression in southwestern Kansas remembered the good times more than they cared to recall the heartbreak. The survivors reminisced about friends, family, and neighbors and, above all, about the sense of fellowship that informed their lives then but seemed to have been lost in the intervening years. People repeatedly commented that this sense of unity was made possible by the fact that the dirt and hard times affected rich and poor alike and that "everyone was in the same boat." They were "as happy as if they had good sense." Perhaps these memories reflected a romanticization of those years over time or the fact that most of these people were fairly young at the onset of the depression. During the thirties, they were children or just starting their adult lives and had little to lose. Although the Dust Bowl might have taken the wind out of their parents' sails, those who still remembered the thirties were, for the most part, young and optimistic during those hard years. Perhaps their good memories most reflected that they had made it through the 1930s intact and were proud of that accomplishment.[59]

For others, family, friends, and good humor was evidently not enough. Thousands of residents of southwestern Kansas, lacking the resources or the stubbornness to endure the depression and dust storms, packed the Model T with all their earthly possessions and drove away. Kansas and other plains states had the dubious distinction of being the only states in the union to lose population during the 1930s. Between 1930 and 1940, Kansas as a whole lost 4.5 percent of its net population, a fairly substantial population loss. But southwestern Kansas lost an even greater percentage of its people: The overall population decline in Dust Bowl counties ranged from a low of 8 percent in Finney County to a high of 47 percent in Morton County, with an average for the area of 24 percent (see Map 2.1).[60] Depopulation was not, however, distributed evenly across the decade. Few residents moved away during the first five years of the decade—depopulation occurred largely from 1935 to 1940.

Between 1930 and 1935, in fact, the farm populations of eight of the sixteen counties actually experienced a small increase, averaging 3.75 percent. The other eight counties lost farmers, but at an average rate of only 3.5 percent. An increase in the total number of farms in twelve of sixteen counties accompanied these small farm population increases. Average farm size also changed little, growing in seven of sixteen counties by 5.7 percent and falling in eight of the sixteen counties by 6.75 percent (one county remained essentially stable). This probably reflected the entry of a number of small farmers, working less than one hundred acres of land, and the subdivision of existing farms within families.[61] The proportion of these small farms, as a percentage of the total number of farms, increased substantially in nearly all counties.[62] That few people moved away between 1930 and 1935 was, perhaps, unsurprising. Farmers still expected to raise a few crops, and the worst of the dust storms did not occur until 1935. Also, times were bad all over and beleaguered farmers had nowhere else to turn.

These changes in farm population paralleled national patterns of population movement. A significant number of Americans took part in a nationwide back-to-the-land movement in the years between 1930 and 1935. In addition, farm youth increasingly remained in rural areas instead of joining the unemployed in the cities. This back-to-the-land movement and forced retention of farm children in rural areas due to high urban unemployment had an effect on the total farm population "so large that had it been the only factor involved, the increase in the total farm population would have been 6.6 percent. Actually the increase was only 4.5 percent." While people moved back to farms, hoping to at least feed themselves and their families, others continued to move to the city. Only in 1932 did the number of people moving to farms outstrip the movement of farmers toward urban areas.[63]

Several factors slowed the movement of Americans from the cities to

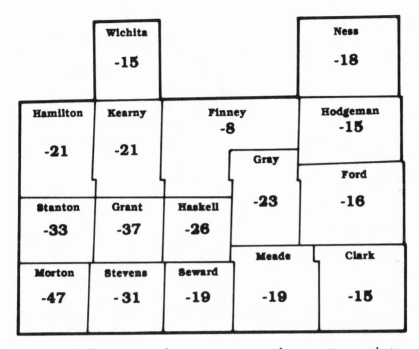

Map 2.1. Study counties, showing percentage decreases in population, 1930–1940. *Source:* U.S. Department of Commerce, Bureau of the Census, Fifteenth and Sixteenth Censuses.

the farms after 1932. Those who had family and friends with whom to take refuge had already done so, and the abandoned farmsteads, shacks, and cabins of rural areas were full to bursting with those fleeing the cities. Additionally, relief officials in cities were doing everything they could to provide facilities to their clients for subsistence gardening. Free seed, fertilizer, equipment, and plots of land were available in parks, vacant lots, and areas adjacent to cities. As adequate urban relief of more substantial varieties became available, the farm-to-city movement resumed.[64]

The pre-1935 stability of the Dust Bowl population vanished in the five years that followed. A drastic decline in population followed the relatively minor changes of 1930 to 1935. The weather worsened, with the "Black Sunday" dust storm making national headlines in April 1935. Farmers' earned incomes, which had fallen below $3,000 per farm, per year, in 1932, remained well below that point until 1941. In no county in southwestern Kansas did the population of farmers grow between 1935 and 1940—the average county lost 30.5 percent of its farm operators, ranging from a low of 18 percent to a high of 53 percent. Fifteen counties showed a decrease in total farms, and farm size grew by 24.4 percent. While the numbers of rural, nonfarm residents and the numbers of "urban" folk living in towns of more than one thousand inhabitants also fell, their numbers did not fall as quickly as those of the farm population. The rural, nonfarm population fell by 7.4 percent across the decade, while the population of towns fell by 8.6 percent. The farm population clearly suffered the most from the adverse environmental and economic conditions of the decade.[65]

Population losses affected the young disproportionately. The farm population fell more quickly than the total number of farms, which suggests that those who left were young people. A look at the age profile of the affected counties shows a "fault line" occurring between the ages of forty and fifty. Above this line, all age groups gained in their proportion of the total population. Below this line, nearly all groups lost as a percentage of total population. The age group from twenty to twenty-four years of age in ten of sixteen cases showed the largest percentage decrease among individuals over the age of ten. The number of children under the age of ten fell consistently, reflecting the outward migration of people of prime childbearing age, as well as apparent fertility restriction on the part of those who remained.[66]

Before the depression, area women were especially prolific. In 1930 the number of children under the age of one for every one thousand women between the ages of twenty and forty-four exceeded the rate in the state of Kansas by a considerable margin. Statewide, there were 97 children under the age of one for every thousand women of childbearing age; in southwestern Kansas, there were 143. The number of infants born in every county exceeded the state rate. By 1940, however, southwestern Kansans were having fewer children. The women of the area still bore children at a greater rate than their counterparts in other parts of Kansas, but the birth rate within the population of women in their childbearing years more closely approximated the state figures. For the state, the number of children under one year of age per one thousand women of childbearing age was 81, compared to 105 for the southwestern corner of the state.[67] The number of births in the Dust Bowl fell almost to the level that Kansas as a whole had experienced in 1930 and showed every sign of falling further and coming into line with statewide trends. Depopulation took more than one form. Families had fewer children, and as economic conditions improved outside of the Dust Bowl, the young people who were most likely to be beginning families chose to make their homes elsewhere.[68]

Mechanization, which many agricultural historians cite as a leading cause of farm depopulation following World War I, probably was not a major factor in this population decline.[69] Farms in southwestern Kansas were already mechanized to a significant degree well before the 1930s. A 1937 USDA report on farm mechanization in Ford County noted that "even in 1919 farmers in Ford County, Kans., were using methods that required little labor in preparing the land and in seeding wheat." Through the 1920s, mechanization continued at a brisk rate, and by 1933 farms were considerably larger and required fewer horses than in 1919. The average farmer owned only two head, instead of eleven.[70]

During the 1930s, however, farmers in western Kansas did little to increase the numbers of machines on their farms. Tractors and combines actually became less prevalent in the Dust Bowl area. Farmers in both eastern and central Kansas purchased combines and tractors at a steady rate during the 1930s, but farmers in western Kansas purchased few new combines, and the number of tractors actually declined.[71] Factors other than the use of new machines were fueling the exodus of western Kansas farmers from their land.[72] The conditions of the 1930s also made it unlikely that farmers would gain much benefit from the equipment they already owned. Many could hardly afford the fuel and the necessary maintenance for their existing tractors and combines, much less purchase new ones. Vehicles and farm equipment developed serious problems because dust crept into engines and into motor oil, wearing away at their parts. One Hugoton resident believed that the "scarcity of money" for repairs had rendered 80 percent of the tractors in Stevens County inoperable.[73] Although mechanization may have displaced farmers in other parts of the country, it was not a significant factor in southwestern Kansas during the thirties.

Even without mechanization displacing farmers, southwestern Kansas lost a large percentage of its population in the 1930s. Kansas as a whole contributed 374,940 people to the stream of migrants on the roads between 1935 and 1940. Forty-three percent of them, or 162,437 people, never left the state. Many moved to an adjacent county or to the next big town, where they perceived opportunities to be better.[74] Others left the state entirely. Between 1935 and 1940, 212,503 persons left Kansas for other areas of the country. By 1940, people who had lived in Kansas in the preceding five years could be found in all forty-eight states of the union. These migrants, however, showed a distinct preference for adjacent and western states. Twenty percent went to California, 17 percent to Missouri, 11 percent to Colorado, 9 percent to Oklahoma, and 7 percent to Washington and Oregon combined. All other states received less than 5 percent of the migratory population.[75] Discontented Kansans were making their homes all across the country, but particularly in states farther to the west.

This migration was a source of considerable irritation and distress to those who stayed behind. Depopulation had a negative impact upon communities, eroding their economic and social fabric. On a very practical level, a declining population wore away at the tax base, leaving communities without adequate resources to maintain roads, build schools, and provide other essential services. People saw their properties decrease in value as unsold homes and businesses sat vacant in the towns and the countryside. Depopulation meant decreased business for owners of businesses, already troubled by the depression. It also created great uncertainty among those left behind, as they watched the dismantling of their neighborhoods, their churches, and their children's schools. The dirt and depression had already discouraged many residents of southwestern Kansas; the depopulation of their communities compounded the hurt.

Newspaper editors, inveterate community boosters, tried to convince their readers that no exodus was under way. In 1934, the editor of the *Garden City Daily Telegram* was willing to bet that mass migration out of southwest Kansas was not going to occur. "So if Kansas can speak for the entire drought area, the answer is 'No, there is no general exodus from the middle Western agricultural area. You folks in the East may frequently hear stories about our leaving the West and going east to live on our relatives, but don't you believe it until you see our tent pitched in the back yard.'"[76] Within a year, the editor was proven wrong by scores of people on the move. Even so, writers tried to preserve the illusion that nothing was wrong. In 1935, a writer for the *Bucklin Banner* reported that "no one here that we know of is figuring on moving." In 1936, the *Garden City Daily Telegram* reported that neither the county superintendent of instruction, the Farm Bureau officials, nor the head of the circulation department of the paper had noticed any outward movement. "A few families had their subscriptions transferred to points outside the so-called 'dust bowl' temporarily last spring and later returned. But even this trend has not been noticeable this spring."[77] All concerned were trying their hardest to maintain the illusion that nothing was wrong.

Nevertheless, the population problem intruded into the rest of the newspaper. Writers noted the dreary results of the yearly agricultural census as they became available and documented the departures of friends, neighbors, and acquaintances. The pastor of the Church of God in Grant County moved in August 1936, and the newspaper reported the pastor's comment that "we are not leaving because of any grievance in the church . . . but we feel it is advisable to get out of this dust bowl for our health's sake." The writers at the *Elkhart Tri-State News* paid a good-bye tribute to six families in one week in 1937, even though they were "inclined to feel that they are leaving at the wrong time. The darkest hours of night are just before dawn." The owners of the *Grant County Republican* moved away in 1937 and informed their readers that "we feel it our duty to take our children some place where the scourge of dust will not endanger their future health. We would have liked to have stayed and done our bit in holding Grant County on an even keel until Nature smiles on us again, and brings out the wonderful crops that we have seen grown in the past, but our circumstances will not permit." Anybody who could read the paper was faced with incontrovertible evidence that dirt and hard times were forcing their neighbors to make difficult choices for the sake of their health, the health of their children, and their emotional and financial well-being.[78]

For those who stayed behind, it was a decade of challenges. For people who depended upon agriculture for a living, the price crash in 1931 was disaster enough. The farmers of southwestern Kansas, like those throughout the country, could not cover the cost of production with the prices paid for agricultural commodities in 1931, 1932, and 1933. Unfortunately for the farmers of the Great Plains, their problems had only begun with rock-bottom prices, for wheat, sorghum, and other crops would not even grow with only ten to fifteen inches of moisture a year.[79] The suffering extended beyond the agricultural community, since the area's manufacturers and service industries depended upon the farmers for their livelihood. Ugly dirt storms further complicated an already impossible situation. No one escaped the choking, all-pervasive clouds of dirt. Given these conditions, staying was not simply a matter of inertia, but an act of will.

3. A COW IN EVERY YARD

The failure of farming families in southwestern Kansas to make a living on the land also meant disaster in the towns, ranging from minuscule Richfield to respectably sized Dodge City. From the smallest, most isolated general store to the Garden City Company's sugar plant, all of the businesses and industries of southwestern Kansas had farming at their roots.[1] The crisis in the countryside made its presence known in slower business, growing unemployment, and county services strained to their limits by desperate citizens. Owners of local businesses tried their best to attract trade and make opportunities out of hardship. Members of charitable organizations threw themselves into drives to improve the quality of life for the "deserving" poor in their communities. On discovering their cupboards bare, families developed their own piecemeal solutions to poverty. Unfortunately, these expenditures of time and effort were inadequate for the overwhelming problems facing southwestern Kansans.

The glow of the 1920s began to fade soon after the stock market crash. It was not long before the banks in the region were in trouble. The Grant County State Bank closed on November 13, 1930, as a result of "the damnable effects of rumors which it is now learned were started some time ago." Although the bank reopened a month and a half later, under new management, its failure badly shook the community. Most of the area's banks did not suffer the same fate, and some, in fact, were in fine shape. The Southwestern Banker's Association protested the bank holiday of 1933, claiming that the region's banks did not need a "holiday" to put their business in order. While this may have been true for some banks, it was not true of all of them; southwestern Kansas would see its share of bank failures throughout the thirties. The Englewood Bank in Clark County failed early in 1933, as did the First National Bank at Fowler, in

A dust storm engulfs a southwestern Kansas town. (Kansas State Historical Society)

Meade County. As late as 1937, the First National Bank in Hugoton closed its doors; it had been in business since 1907.[2] The closings reflected a generally slow business climate and the effects of the drought, which left the area's farmers without adequate income for nearly a decade. For example, in 1937 and 1938, the First State Bank in Ness City carried nearly $200,000 in chattel mortgages alone, many of which show no sign of ever having been paid.[3] Most outstanding loans, either mortgages or chattel mortgages, were balanced against farm incomes, one way or another, and farmers had little success in meeting their debts during the 1930s.

Business closings and reductions in services reflected the hard times facing owners of area stores. As in the case of area banks, individuals in arrears on payments were often the culprits. Residents took out chattel mortgages with a number of businesses, and often these debts went unpaid. In 1937 and 1938, the Ness City Lumber Company held $13,322.89 in such mortgages, the A. A. Doerr Mercantile Company, $13,109.39, and the Bauer Store and Garage, $12,179.78. Many of these debts remained on the books for years, and many were never paid at all.[4] Business closings often resulted. For example, the citizens of Johnson lost their dry goods store, the J. C. Penney Company in Elkhart closed its doors after twelve years in business, and the Home Cafe in Ulysses went out of business, the proprietors recouping only a small portion of their loss. The cafe's owners began with an investment of more than $4,000, but the auction of the fixtures and furniture brought a return of only $700.[5]

Owners of local businesses cut their commitments to the community in their struggles to make ends meet. After years of supporting the local chautauqua, the business people of Johnson refused to guarantee it in 1932 because they saw too little benefit to themselves in relation to the cost. The four grocery stores and meat markets in Bucklin, which traditionally supplied credit lines to their customers, went on a cash basis in 1933 in an attempt to limit losses from unpaid debts. The members of the Liberal Chamber of Commerce voted to cut their budget by 20 percent, while at the same time exhorting people not to "lay down" and to continue to push "civic and commercial development."[6] Funds could only be stretched so far, and merchants sometimes cut services to the community in order to survive.

Times were even rougher for providers of nonessential services that could be eliminated from family budgets or whose offices could be avoided when bills came due. The Patton family, a father and two daughters, lived on the daughters' earnings throughout the depression. Lois and Fern Patton were a teacher and welfare worker, respectively, and their father sold insurance. Mr. Patton earned little or no money because people allowed their insurance to lapse in an attempt to pay for more immediate needs, such as food and clothing. Doctors, dentists, and funeral directors experienced the same difficulties. People took advantage of their services and then avoided paying the bills. The phone company might shut off service, as would the gas or electric company, but the doctor could not repossess a baby or put back a ruptured appendix. In 1934, the *Bazine Advocate* reported that a local doctor, C. C. Bennett, had committed suicide. The writer blamed Bennett's act on economic conditions. "He told us just a few days ago that money was an impossibility now, and the letters indicate that financial troubles are the cause of his act."[7] Although doctors and other professionals were eligible to compete for county contracts to care for the poor, there was not enough money or enough business for all.

Hard times required inventive solutions, and many area businesspeople were able to retain enough of their customers to get by. One way in which area business owners sought to maintain their trade and build good will with their customers was in accepting farm commodities in lieu of cash for purchases. Newspapers often did the same. During the wheat price crisis of 1931, the *Johnson Pioneer* allowed farmers to exchange three bushels of wheat, at market price, for a year's subscription to the paper. The *Grant County Republican* made the same offer and promised to keep the wheat off the market until the first of December. In 1937, the Hugoton paper accepted chickens in trade and pledged to "allow you a good price on them." It was a clever way to encourage people to continue to purchase a "luxury" item, their weekly newspaper. [8]

Other businesses accepted farm produce in lieu of cash as well. The W. W. Beard Grocery and D. M. Walker Clothing, both in Fowler, offered farmers five and six cents per bushel above the local market price for their wheat and applied this to outstanding bills or toward goods in their stores. Customers could even use the wheat to set up credit accounts for future purchases. The management of the DeLuxe Theatre in Bucklin offered to accept eggs in trade for show tickets at one cent each, roughly the market price for eggs. [9] Taking goods in trade might not have been as lucrative as selling to cash-paying customers, but it did keep some business coming in to local merchants.

While some stores and businesses advertised these special arrangements, others must have made them quietly, on a daily basis, simply to keep bankruptcy at bay. One family financed the burial of their three-year-old daughter with hams delivered to the owner of the funeral home over a period of several years. They finished paying the debt when they sold out and left farming in 1942. A Garden City family kept a cow in a vacant lot one summer and supplied six quarts of milk per day at five cents a quart to pay a debt to a drugstore downtown that had a soda fountain and used the milk for shakes. A farmer living outside of Garden City remembered going to town for groceries one day, without money and without any prospect of earning any, unsure of how he would pay the bill. His wife spotted some onions lying in a ditch, lost from a passing truck. They gathered the onions, about half a bushel, and traded them in town for $3 worth of groceries. The grocer told the couple that he needed to buy his onions from someone, and it might as well be them. [10] Again, the payments were not in the most acceptable form, cash, but the merchant could sell goods traded to him or use them to feed his family.

Professionals had options unavailable to most merchants. Receiving and maintaining contracts with the county to perform necessary services was a guaranteed source of a small, steady income. Newspapers competed for county printing work, doctors vied for the chance to treat the county's poor cases, and even funeral directors benefited from the relative bounty of local government contracts. The county usually paid cash in full—which regular patients and customers rarely did—even if the payments were sometimes a little late. When the Seward County commissioners opened bids for the burial of the poor, E. H. McFall and Son, undertakers, submitted the following proposal to the county:

> ADULT CASES—6 ft., 3 in., Casket cloth covered, suitably lined, three pair metal handles, outside box and metal grave marker. We pay the sextant charge for opening and closing grave. We furnish Funeral coach and where necessary one passenger car for the conveyance of family or pall bearers. We offer this complete funeral service and merchandise as outlined for $29.85.

In addition to this package, McFall and Son offered to bury indigent children for $14.75. Contracts such as this became very important to struggling individuals in the service sector. Because of this, many a county administrator decided to divide the patronage between several doctors, competing funeral homes, and more than one local newspaper. Keeping as many businesses as possible afloat by patronizing multiple firms limited the number of unemployed whom the county would have to support.[11]

Groups of merchants within towns came together to sponsor auctions, sale days, and other "good will" events that brought shoppers in from the countryside and, hopefully, the "trade territories" of neighboring towns. The merchants of Grant County sponsored a farmers-merchants supper to bring farmers to town to capture their business. Two hundred and fifty people attended the event and discussed the wheat crop, a uniform wage scale, and ways to find a veterinarian for the county. Theirs was an indirect approach to building community support for hometown businesses; other attempts were much more direct.[12]

Merchants regularly sponsored special events on weekends to attract business from the country and surrounding towns and cities. The businesses of Ashland organized a barbecue, inviting people from throughout the area, and sponsored the same day a "trade merit" sale, where merchants sold "at great sacrifice a large variety of good, seasonable merchandise in all lines." Two thousand people turned out, from five counties in Kansas and Oklahoma. Businesses in both Ulysses and Johnson issued

coupons for every dollar of purchases made in their stores and held Saturday auctions, accepting only those coupons as payment for auction goods.
The merchants of Liberal developed perhaps the most blatant scheme for
nonresident business. They prepared a series of Saturday programs of
entertainment and prizes for customers and promised a special prize of $75
to one visitor from outside Liberal. Merchants quite literally paid shoppers to patronize the stores in their communities.[13]

When these schemes bore fruit, it was cause for celebration. In 1938,
the *Hugoton Hermes* reported that many residents of Morton County had
been trading in Hugoton, presumably because of business closings due to
the even harder times and worse drought conditions in the Elkhart area.
"Many from that county have registered in our Merchants Trades Day
Program. We extend a cordial welcome to these good people." What the
struggling merchants of Elkhart thought of this, the *Hermes* did not
report.[14]

While businessmen brought in new customers, they also cooperated
with the newspapers in a campaign to shame old customers into remaining faithful. Given the availability of mail order catalogs and the hundreds of itinerant salespeople on the road during the 1930s, newspaper
editors, on behalf of local business, attempted to convince their readers
that they had a vested interest in patronizing the stores in their home-

*The first of three photographs showing a dust storm approaching Elkhart in May 1937.
(Library of Congress)*

The storm comes closer to Elkhart in May 1937. (Library of Congress)

The storm arrives in Elkhart in May 1937. (Library of Congress)

towns. One notice urged the sensible shopper to avoid using mail order at Christmastime. The local merchant "carried" local shoppers when times were hard, but "the mail order houses demand cash for your purchases." According to the papers, local residents were equally obligated to steer clear of peddlers and traveling salesmen. Hometown businessmen served the customer more cheaply, provided service after the purchase, "and they also pay taxes." In cooperation with the Boy Scouts, the Liberal Chamber of Commerce delivered "no peddler" cards throughout the city. They carried the information that homeowners displaying the cards "believed in patronizing Liberal merchants and do not buy from itinerant merchants or salesmen."[15] Community solidarity began with loyalty to locally owned stores.

Although traveling salesmen and catalog sales lured away some bargain-hunting customers, the stores in the next town down the road were even more threatening. The advent of inexpensive automobiles and greater mobility in the years following the First World War made it more difficult for small-town merchants to maintain their customers' loyalty. The possibility of greater savings in larger towns, in addition to the excitement of visiting the "big city," sent farm families and residents of smaller towns farther and farther afield on their shopping expeditions. For merchants struggling with the economic troubles of the 1930s, the prospect of losing their customers to the next larger town down the highway was almost unbearable. Town boosters made "trade at home" their slogan, particularly during the shopping season before Christmas. The *Grant County Republican* extolled the virtues of a "hundred per cent trade at home Christmas" on the front page of the paper in 1932. "See just how much better you will feel over the knowledge that your purchases are instrumental in keeping someone employed who might otherwise be forced to accept relief from the county. This reward in itself is worth a whole lot to the conscience of a loyalty booster." Writers issued these appeals most frequently during the Christmas season, but also year round. Shopping at home was loyal and patriotic and ensured that "happy days will be here again."[16]

Local shopping expeditions also meant that dollars spent by the community would be reinvested there, according to the editor of the *Elkhart Tri-State News*. "Business people, sales people, trades people of various kinds and teachers derive their income directly from the community and it is only fair that whenever possible they put back into the community what they take out of it. Otherwise they become dangerously near to becoming parasites." Whether the tactic worked or not, printers churned out page after page of similar material for local businessmen, in the hope that shame and a sense of responsibility would keep residents at home when they made their purchases.[17]

Jobless and underemployed people lacked the funds to purchase goods and services, and businesspeople who were unable to sell their products laid off their workers. The editor of the *Liberal News* commented in his column that the depression had slipped up on "a lot of us who have been coasting along these days faring fairly well in spite of the general collapse of affairs." He turned away from one to three applicants for printing jobs nearly every day. He noted that "many of the applicants are not of the bum variety either."[18]

Although there was no general "census" of the unemployed until 1937, they were a tangible presence in each of the Dust Bowl counties. Worries over the "unemployment situation" kept the Ford County Board of Commissioners in session between January 16 and 19, 1933, far longer than the usual board meeting.[19] In 1933, when Stevens County registered those out of work for re-employment, 763 jobless people came to the office; the county could provide work for only half of them.[20] Even in 1937, with federal employment programs well under way, the number of unemployed persons in southwestern Kansas counties (which did not include those on federal or county work relief) ranged from a high of 547 in Ford County to a low of 29 in Grant County.[21] The situation led the editor of the *Liberal News* to issue a warning to those fortunate enough to have jobs. "Just watch what you are doing and pay a little closer attention to it than you have for some time . . . all business is affected mightily these days and many an employer is going to have to do things in the next year that he never thought possible in 1929."[22] This none-too-subtle hint accurately reflected the employment situation in southwestern Kansas, as well as most of the rest of the country. There were too few positions for the working population and little chance that private sector employers would be able to create more opportunities.

Transients in towns throughout the area also provided visual evidence that hard times had arrived. The residents of Liberal coped with the ever growing number of migrants with a locally run work program that allowed the visitors, who were almost always looking for employment, to receive one meal of coffee and hot cakes or stew in return for a day's work. In 1934, the overwhelming volume of transients forced the Kansas Emergency Relief Committee to establish a camp in Liberal to care for them. On average, 120 migrants stopped in town each day during the second week of June 1934, and they continued to come throughout the decade.[23]

The constant presence of unemployed laborers willing to work for pennies and meals caused considerable concern to resident workers. When railroad construction began in the Liberal area in 1938, hundreds of men from Texas, Missouri, Oklahoma, and Arkansas flooded into the city clerk's office looking for work. The city clerk, J. N. Evans, responded by telling the workers that the contractor had agreed to hire local laborers before hiring outsiders for unskilled work. Everyone except the transient unemployed seemed to agree that it was only fair to hire residents before visitors since it would lower the relief burden and keep as much money as possible within the community.[24]

Unemployment, underemployment, and the threat of poverty forced people all across southwestern Kansas to adapt their home lives to fit their reduced circumstances. Although drought conditions limited their chances of success, many people gardened in order to feed their families. Through various relief programs, cities and counties provided plots and seeds to those who needed them. In fact, more people wanted to garden than cities could supply with land. In Gray County, any gardener who did not properly cultivate his or her garden lost it to another relief client. In Stanton County, those receiving relief tried to find farms to rent or positions on farms "in order that they may provide for themselves more satisfactorily than they do at the present time on the relief rolls." Given the dryness of those years, it is highly unlikely that without irrigation a larger garden or a farm plot would have made a significant impact on the family budget, but people still associated growing their own food with an increased standard of living. For people with wells, irrigation systems, and protected garden sites, gardening or keeping a cow in the backyard made a great deal of sense. As one woman explained, "That's why we had food at our house."[25]

Women turned to the newspapers to find ways to make their food budgets stretch when family incomes fell. One article explained how to make sandwiches from leftover beans, stuffed peppers from the odds and ends of a ham, and pudding from stale bread and old jelly, suggestions characteristic of those published each week in area newspapers. The recipes used common, inexpensive food items and suggested new ways to use ingredients that were becoming monotonous to the family.[26]

Women worked out their own solutions as well. Macaroni, canned tomatoes, and spinach were inexpensive and nourishing, as were eggs and potatoes. Cornmeal mush could be eaten for dinner, then fried for breakfast the next morning. Hamburger and oatmeal could be cooked in many different ways. If the children tired of them, mothers could serve the same old food in different plates and bowls. Families went in groups to the sand hills along the river in Stevens County to pick the plums that grew wild there and thrived in hot weather. Innovations such as these kept families fed and satisfied when there was little money in the house.[27]

Agricultural extension agents and workers from other agencies answered questions about good nutrition on a restricted budget, and families accepted that help far more readily than in the past. Although money for memberships was hard to come by, more women than ever joined extension homemakers' units throughout southwestern Kansas. In 1933, the home demonstration agent for Ford County commented that "canning, storing or preserving in any manner is quite out of the normal life for Ford County families. It is something they have not wanted to do, until the present conditions came to hand. Now they all want to do it." In Dodge City, "men, women, boys and girls all worked" in the community garden, and with the help of the home demonstration agent, they canned 2,180 quarts of vegetables, made 52 gallon barrels of pickled corn, and one sugar sack filled with dried corn that year. The agent judged the program a success.[28]

In Liberal, Connie Foote, a traveling home economist from Kansas State Agricultural College (now Kansas State University), taught classes in menu planning. Although she designed the classes for mothers of families on relief, they were open to all and showed women how to purchase and prepare foods for a balanced diet on a limited income. Foote also provided a week's worth of low-budget menus to area newspapers, which women could clip and save. The ingredients in the menus corresponded very closely with the lists of commodities distributed by aid organizations to relief families.[29] Again, the idea was to provide healthy and inexpensive, yet tempting, meals. People who had largely ignored extension services because of their residence in town welcomed their help for the duration of hard times.

Nationwide, the Great Depression found more women than ever working for wages outside of the home. The same was true of Dust Bowl women. Many who might not have worked outside of the home in better times did what they could to supplement the inadequate wages of husbands and fathers or replace the wages of unemployed men. Some women found employment through relief agencies, although the number of jobs available was quite limited. Government policy generally prohibited the hiring of both husband and wife, in the belief that married men with children deserved work more than women who presumably had husbands

Home economists, like this one in Grant County giving a dried skim milk demonstration, provided enormously valuable information to families in distress. (Kansas Emergency Relief Committee photo; Kansas State Historical Society)

to support them. Nevertheless, women worked for relief agencies, and sometimes they were married. Most worked in sewing rooms or in school lunch programs; a few had prized clerical jobs. Often, the presence of women in clerical positions indicated the lack of men with the necessary training, as Rep. Clifford Hope explained to an irate male constituent.[30]

Most women working in nonrelief positions had poorly paid, traditionally female occupations. Many unmarried women taught school and suffered drastic pay reductions early in the decade. In order to keep their jobs, some concealed marriages from parents, friends, and the school board. Other women worked in laundries for ten cents an hour or cleaned homes for a dollar a day. Taking in boarders allowed one grandmother to remain independent. The J. C. Penney store in Liberal paid twenty-five cents an hour to its female help for long days with only an hour's break at noon.[31] Most "women's work" consisted of long hours at low wages in jobs that many men, even in hard times, would have disdained.

It was easier for women to find employment outside the home if they had no children or their children were old enough to care for themselves. Social conventions discouraged women with small children from seeking wage work. As one woman wrote, "Mothers were frowned on then if their children were put with baby sitters so I simply did what I had to do after my children came"—she left the workplace to care for her children. And because baby-sitters and clothing suitable for work were expensive, others who would have gladly worked could not afford to do so. Commented one woman, "By the time I would have extra clothes . . . and hiring a baby sitter, I'd be working for nothing. We felt like it would be to our advantage, to the children's advantage, for me to stay at home and patch and sew."[32] These women focused greater attention on tasks they could accomplish from inside their homes, such as cooking, sewing, and gardening.

Although the New Deal attempted to discourage child labor in industry, federal officials realized that many children needed to work to provide for themselves and their families. Many found jobs through a New Deal jobs program for high school and college students, the National Youth Administration (NYA). Like jobs for women, these positions were usually menial, but they provided young people whose families were on relief a way to help. The jobs were generally "work-study" positions, providing supplemental funds to students. Orphaned in 1935, Opal Musselman lived with a series of friends and relatives while she finished high school in Ness City. Her job with the NYA, washing blackboards and helping a teacher grade homework, allowed her to save money for business college. She had no other options; "nobody baby sat then. There wasn't anybody going anywhere."[33] Federal work programs offered her the only hope of an education beyond high school.

Some children, like Carl Clare of Dodge City, simply raised a little money to provide for their own entertainment. Very few parents could afford to purchase "fun" for their children. Carl and his friends gathered bottles, cleaned, and sold them. This included whiskey bottles, which they marketed to Dodge City bootleggers. The whiskey bottles had to be cleaned very carefully, because even a trace of alcohol could get a person in trouble with the law if caught with the bottle. He and a cousin made money from bootlegging in other ways as well. "We used to find the bootleg whiskey. Our house, where it sit we could watch at night and we'd see the cars go up the road and stop. . . . we'd go up there the next morning and we'd look around that telephone pole, we'd come up with a bottle of whiskey or a jug of whiskey, and then call the chief of police up here. He'd go with us to go out and pick it up, and he'd pay us fifty cents for turning it in." After three summers, they "outgrew" this activity. As Mr. Clare noted, they were fortunate; the bootleggers might have shot them for their troubles. Children's work spanned the whole spectrum, from providing for their own very basic needs, to doing occasional work, just for fun.[34]

When all else failed, families attempted to create their own opportunities until "real" jobs came along. Probably the best example of this was the experience of Lois Stringfield Harmon and her husband of Garden City. Mr. Harmon lost his job in 1931 and was out of work until the late spring of 1933 when he went to work as an assistant city clerk. Mrs. Harmon became the private secretary to the president of the Fidelity Bank of Garden City. The Harmons put together a tremendous array of innovations that kept them fed and clothed between 1931 and 1933. They obtained permission from a neighbor to use a block-long vacant lot for a garden. They planted "every vegetable known to man" and even managed to revive some apparently dead apple trees on the lot. Additionally, they borrowed a cow from a friend who had an extra and kept her in a barn on the lot. Thus, they had their own cream, milk, butter, fresh produce, and three hundred jars of jellies, butters, and jams. Although they only had permission to use the vacant lot for one year, it was a significant help during that time.

This, however, was not enough to keep the family going. Mrs. Harmon borrowed an old counter from a store and received permission from the manager of the Windsor Hotel to set it up in the lobby. She used the counter to display serialized stories gleaned from old magazines in the basements of friends and jigsaw puzzles provided by a sister living in New York. She allowed people to check out stories and puzzles for a few cents a night and managed to make a little money that way. "Believe it or not, we made money on those jigsaw puzzles." The next summer, she and her husband borrowed money from an aunt to purchase a root beer barrel that a bank had repossessed. They then built a root beer stand, made root beer, and managed to get by a little while longer. Again, they provided inexpensive entertainment to people. Parents purchased their mugs of root beer at full price—a few cents—and children received a small mug free. It was an evening's adventure for very little money, and enough people patronized their establishment to provide a slim living.

When her husband wanted to innovate a little further and move the family into a freight car, Mrs. Harmon balked. She arranged to defer payments on the private loan on their home, but her husband was unhappy with this. He wanted to buy a freight car for ten dollars, clean it up, and live in it at the edge of town. She told her husband, "When things begin to open up, and jobs become available, don't think for a minute that whoever has a job to offer is going to go out and get a guy who is living in an old freight car out on the edge of town. They want somebody who's kept their self-respect." She added, "I never heard any more about that freight car again." Maybe it was wise that the innovating stopped short of changing the family's living arrangements. Very shortly, both of the Harmons had jobs, and the truly hard years of the depression were over for them. With imagination and a good deal of help from willing friends and relatives they managed to keep themselves afloat.[35]

Fontell Littrell's parents, who lived in Hugoton, chose to innovate in other ways. While her mother worked in a cleaning shop, her grandmother took in boarders, and the children worked at various jobs, including those provided by the Civilian Conservation Corps. Her father bootlegged and ran a poker game. Although he was in and out of jail regularly, he managed to support a substantial extended family of at least ten people. One of the people was his mother, a very religious Latter-Day Saint. She took the bootlegging in stride, commenting that "the Lord works in mysterious ways, his miracles to perform."[36]

But these attempts to ameliorate poverty in the garden or the kitchen or through the efforts of the entire family were often inadequate. With so many local people jobless or underemployed and so many transients in the area, devising some means of relief became absolutely imperative. Before 1933, when federal money became available on a large scale, relief was local in origin, and a major component of that was provided by private charity. Members of fraternal organizations, schoolchildren, and businesspeople all chipped in to help feed and clothe the needy within Dust Bowl communities. Unfortunately, sponsors of local charities made their efforts sporadically, focusing their attentions on Thanksgiving and Christmas when they truly believed that they could not let their less fortunate neighbors go hungry. Even so, in the grim years before federal relief, voluntarism and community-wide cooperation was an important element in the fight against the effects of the depression.

Members of organizations such as the American Legion and its auxiliary, the Elks, the Lions, and Rotary clubs provided significant support to charity. In Liberal, the American Legion was the most active promoter of relief activities. The local post organized a drive to find employment for Liberal's jobless. They registered 117 workers to do odd jobs around the homes of employed residents. The women of the auxiliary created a school lunch program that fed between one hundred and four hundred students a day during the spring of 1933, financing the lunches through donations. The men and women of the post and auxiliary later formed a Community Welfare Club, which sponsored a number of welfare programs, such as providing needy children with school clothes and glasses, purchasing milk for a family of six, and serving hot Christmas dinners to "the aged and crippled needy of Liberal."[37]

Other fraternal organizations throughout the area regularly organized drives to distribute Thanksgiving dinners, as well as Christmas gifts and dinners for some of the most impoverished families in the area. In 1935, the Lions Club of Garden City delivered thirty-seven Christmas boxes containing potatoes, rice, flour, sugar, raisins, canned vegetables, and beans; those recipients with children received Christmas candy as well. When appealing for donations, newspaper editors and other leaders knew to direct their attention to the clubs. For instance, when a blind resident of Clark County needed a radio, the notice in the *Clark County Clipper* read: "Perhaps your club or lodge would like to help a little. Let's 'chip in' and provide some happy hours for this unfortunate man."[38]

Schoolchildren also did their share of work to make Christmas and Thanksgiving more joyous for the poor in their communities. Boy Scouts were particularly active in this effort, repairing cast-off toys for distribution and delivering food baskets contributed by other charitable organizations. Teachers also involved their classes in similar projects. First grade students in Liberal made "kitten dolls" from stockings and delivered them to the Red Cross for distribution, and high school students provided "mystery families" with baskets of food over the holidays.[39]

Recipients of Christmas food baskets did not always welcome the attention this gesture brought to them. When newspapers throughout the area asked for Christmas donations from schools, organizations, churches, and individuals, the appeals usually included descriptions of the families to be aided. Writers used no names, but in small communities the identity of a widowed mother of eight or a family of six with a blind father was readily apparent. Only in one year did a newspaper attempt to limit the potential hurt caused by such advertisements. In 1939, the Southwest Daily Times declined to publish a "needy family list," even though the paper continued its usual Christmas campaign. Additionally, the coordinator of the charity drive decided not to print a list of donors. "This does not mean that there are no needy families in Liberal and this county, but publication of description has, in past years, led to some embarrassment. Anyone really interested in helping less fortunate persons this Christmas may do so, without embarrassment or publicity." Even with such precautions, poverty and visibility tended to go hand in hand in small communities.[40]

The owners of area businesses, either through the actions of the Chamber of Commerce or personal efforts, also played an important role in the campaign against hard times. In Garden City, Dodge City, and Liberal, the Chambers of Commerce organized drives to locate work for the jobless. Volunteers registered the unemployed and potential employers. In Liberal, they located short-term jobs for two hundred men, paying $1.50 to $2.50 per day.[41] The owners of local newspapers also dedicated columns to the needs of the community. In both Grant County and Finney County, the primary newspaper allowed the unemployed to place free classified advertisements in the "situations wanted" columns. The Elkhart Tri-State News offered a similar service to Morton County farmers, allowing them to use a "swap column" to advertise anything but land. But the paper warned that "this service is free only to dirt farmers and not for the use of canvassers or others selling articles for profit."[42] Four dentists and three doctors in Liberal provided dental and eye examinations free of charge to area schoolchildren before classes began in the fall of 1934.[43] None of these efforts was particularly costly; for the most part, people donated their time and took advantage of unused space in their newspapers. But in making contributions such as these, businesspeople did some good for their communities and probably for themselves as well. The depression and drought could not last indefinitely, and people would remember who had been helpful and who had failed the community, even after times improved.

Newspaper editors, too, tried to create a consensus within their readership that aid was necessary and that local citizens had a duty to provide for their own. The suicide of a thirteen-year-old Dodge City boy, worried that his parents could not afford to buy schoolbooks for him, prompted one writer to ask if it was not time to remake the community to provide security for all. Christmas of 1935 and the realization that many local children might go without presents prompted another writer to ask the people of the community, "Just how would you feel," under the same circumstances? His answer was that "you would feel there was little to live for. You would feel that everything just wasn't right." The answer, according to the writer, was participation in the county relief administration's drive for Christmas toys, clothes, and shoes for area children. And, as was the case with "shopping at home," writers asked that residents give at home and refuse to make donations to organizations that did not spend their money within the community.[44] Newspaper editors discovered that one of their main occupations throughout the decade was drumming up support for relief.

Clearly, as sincere as these efforts were, they were not adequate for the deepening economic and environmental crisis facing the people of southwestern Kansas. One organization, which hovered somewhere between private charity and public relief, filled a few of the gaps. Nearly every county in southwestern Kansas sponsored a chapter of the American Red Cross, and county commissioners were in the habit of consulting this organization when unexpected problems arose. The Finney County commissioners asked the advice of members of the local chapter when they were considering hiring a social worker for the county. When a devastating tornado hit Liberal in 1933 and an unexpected cold snap increased the demand for relief in Clark County in 1936, the Red Cross coordinated the emergency effort.[45] The organization had the funds as well as the fund-raising machinery to meet crisis situations when county governments could not.

During the 1930s, the Seward County chapter of the American Red Cross regularly reported its activities to the local paper. Those reports illustrated the degree to which the county's poor relied upon the organization. In 1930, local organizers for the Red Cross decided to coordinate all the charity efforts of clubs, churches, and other county organizations in an attempt to eliminate duplicated efforts (one family had received four

The Red Cross provided aid when a tornado devastated Liberal in 1933. (Photo by James Harvey Riney; by permission of Elsie Riney)

different Thanksgiving baskets). The Red Cross Welfare Committee, as the organization christened itself, assumed responsibility for a soup kitchen and storehouse for relief supplies. From then on, the Red Cross provided regular aid to needy people who came to their office. They distributed mounds of clothing, innumerable sacks of groceries, much bedding, heating fuel, and gasoline, and even provided the money for occasional car repairs. Red Cross volunteers sometimes gave families funds for nursing care when it was needed.

In January 1931, thirty-one Seward County families received aid from the Red Cross, and their numbers rose precipitously as the months and years passed. The organization often aided more than fifty cases a month, or more than two hundred individuals. To support these efforts, Red Cross volunteers solicited one dollar donations, cast-off clothing, garden vegetables, and any other useful items that people might be willing to offer. Sometimes they made appeals to meet special needs, such as a call for a pair of size ten work shoes needed by a "very deserving" aged man who was attempting to support himself and his wife with odd jobs. In the fall of 1940, on the Welfare Committee's tenth birthday, the committee congratulated itself for a job well done and reported that their burden was still heavy; they had assisted 301 people during the preceding month, and there was no end in sight.[46]

Although churches have traditionally filled a charitable role within their communities, they were conspicuously absent from the lists of primary aid-giving institutions and organizations in southwestern Kansas during this period. The churches continued to offer their members emotional strength and social contacts, but they had little else to offer. Congregations did attempt to join other local organizations in relief drives but did so less consistently than the American Legion or the Elks, for example. Members made voluntary contributions that supported the church, but the funds raised were too meager to allow for any contributions by congregations to community purposes. This was particularly true of small churches or of churches in areas worst damaged by the drought.

Comments in the Bucklin Banner's church notes suggested that poverty discouraged people from even going to services. They lacked the proper attire and were too embarrassed to arrive in their worn clothing. The notice encouraged them with the words, "Thank God for the Pleasant Valley folks who are worth more than the clothes they wear, who come to church to worship and not to show themselves." Tattered clothing was not the only concern keeping people at home. Terrible weather compounded other concerns, reducing attendance even further. Spring dust storms forced churches to cancel meetings, and fear of storms kept people at home even on clear days.[47]

The churches themselves struggled. People had little money to support their families, let alone funds to contribute to the support of ministers and church facilities. Financial ruin faced many a church and minister. Methodist churches in the small communities of Ulysses, Satanta, Syracuse, and Bucklin all skirted bankruptcy during the 1930s, as did the Presbyterian church in Syracuse.[48]

The experience of the congregation of the Epworth Memorial (Methodist) Church in Elkhart illustrates the troubles of churches in counties particularly hard hit by the drought. By 1935, the church was in serious financial trouble due to declining membership and the poverty of remaining members. The minister sent a notice to congregants in 1936 reporting that "one-half the families in the church have not paid anything to the support of the church this year." In 1937, financial pressures left the janitor unpaid and various other bills neglected. The minister explained, "Under present conditions the Church can hardly be expected to meet all of its obligations in full." The budget was $930 short of the church's needs for the year. The church's greatest problem was simply attrition. Ninety-three members of a congregation that numbered only a few hundred moved to other parts of Kansas or out of the state between 1930 and 1936. With its membership and consequently its financial assets dwindling, the church barely survived the decade.[49]

The same problems plagued smaller congregations that were more accustomed to operating on limited budgets. Mennonites throughout the Dust Bowl supported ministers on minimal salaries that were often inadequate to their needs. In his correspondence with the Home Mission Committee, Rev. A. L. Jantzen marveled that his congregation at Ransom managed to raise $40 a month for his salary and noted that the contributions strained people to their financial limits. Jantzen and his family managed to scrape by only because they had the use of a house, as well as a garden, a cow, and fifteen acres of pasture. A. S. Bechtel, minister to the Hanston congregation, wrote that he and his family managed to make do because "most ministers wives are experts in that line [economizing] so far as providing meals is concerned and in dressing too."[50]

For some Mennonite ministers, continuing to work for their church required tremendous sacrifices. Rev. Abe Schmidt of Montezuma pleaded with the Home Mission Committee for aid; he earned less than $40 a month from his church. "We can not stay the way it is. No work here. We pay rent and by coal for heating stove and gas for cooking and we dont keep anything for living. I have bin buying on time to keep goin. I am sorry that I ask for more. . . . We may haf to leave and go were we can make a living . . . so when ever you hear we are not here any more dont let that surprise you." The Home Mission Committee referred his case to the Relief Committee because they could not "let him and his family suffer." Schmidt, however, left his congregation, hoping to find a job that would allow him to support his family.[51] For the Schmidts, serving the church entailed sacrifices too great for their health and well-being.

Even larger congregations in the region's principal towns fought for survival. Correspondence between Jess Denious, Kansas state senator and Dodge City resident, and members of the First Presbyterian Church of Dodge City demonstrated the lengths to which congregations went to raise money. Robert Thomas, the minister, organized a pledge drive and asked a group of influential men, Denious included, to commit $5 a week to the church. In the 1930s, this was a princely sum, and the minister hoped that such a large commitment on the part of a few would encourage others to give. Additionally, he read a telegram from Denious from the pulpit in order to encourage even more subscriptions. Thomas then organized a house-to-house canvas of church members to raise money. The canvassers added one final element to their plan. "If these people fail to make their payments they will soon find a couple of canvassers sitting on their front steps. It will be a 'sit down strike' until they pay up." Extraordinary measures such as these illustrated the difficulties churches and their members faced.[52] They barely continued to function, let alone provide any meaningful amount of charity to the community.

Nevertheless, the churches did provide badly needed emotional support to desperate people. Making the sacrifices necessary to paint their church and varnish the woodwork and pews created pride and a sense of achievement for the members of the Mennonite congregation at Kismet. Simply going to church gave the congregants of the Pleasant Valley church "courage and hope." As they wrote, their church activities "point us to a source of strength that nothing else can supply." Conditions made courage, hope, and pride sorely needed commodities, and what churches could not offer in the way of financial support, they attempted to provide in emotional strength.[53]

Private efforts by churches and other organizations were largely inadequate to the task of providing food, shelter, and clothing to the needy of the Dust Bowl. The amount of private aid varied from county to county, and its total impact was relatively small, overshadowed by the efforts of public institutions, on both a local and national scale. The number of dollars contributed to and spent by charities rose in many cases between 1930 and 1933, but the level of need rose even more rapidly.[54]

Private organizations could only afford to spend pennies per person, when they desperately needed dollars to purchase food, medical supplies, and shelter for growing numbers of desperate, jobless people. As this impoverished population grew, the amount of available charity, relative to the needy population, fell. As in the case of families attempting to pull themselves up by the bootstraps, the effort was valiant and the results were sometimes remarkable, but in the long run the effort was unsustainable.

In the towns of southwestern Kansas, homegrown solutions to the twin troubles of drought and depression had only limited effectiveness. Businesses could not rely upon their customers to pay their bills, and individuals could not count on their employers to continue to provide work for them. Families tried to solve their own problems, and communities attempted to take care of their own, but the environmental and economic problems ran too deep. People increasingly turned to government—local and national—for solutions to the decades' troubles.

4. "EVERYTHING COMES FROM WASHINGTON"

Hundreds of thousands of dollars of aid—local, state, and federal—kept the people of southwestern Kansas fed, clothed, and sheltered through a decade of hard times. Public relief for the townspeople came in several different forms: direct and work relief from the counties, federal aid administered through the state, and federal work relief provided directly to clients through the Works Progress Administration (WPA), National Youth Administration (NYA), and other "alphabet soup" agencies. Between 1930 and 1933, most aid derived from local sources and generally failed to meet the needs of the community. Local administrators heaved a sigh of relief when the federal government took over responsibility for poor relief after Franklin Roosevelt's inauguration in March 1933. Federal money made life itself possible for thousands of southwestern Kansans who might otherwise have starved or been forced to move and remained an absolute necessity well into 1940. Even so, acceptance of either local or federal aid did not come easily—it challenged people's perceptions of themselves as independent, self-supporting inheritors of a pioneer tradition.

Between 1930 and early 1933, most of the welfare burden fell upon the unprepared shoulders of local government officials. By early 1931, it was clear that many of the people of southwestern Kansas could not survive without liberal amounts of relief. The wheat price crash had devastated the local economy, and the drought was already under way.

But officials of local governments were entirely unprepared to administer relief on a large scale. No formal welfare structures existed, and county commissioners traditionally provided the little aid that they normally allotted on a haphazard, case-by-case basis. In January 1930, the Haskell County commissioners presided over a welfare program that consisted of only a few dollars expended for rent on one woman's home. By July 1931, their disbursals had risen to only $3.57, allocated for supplies for the poor. Not until December 1931 did the commissioners create a poor fund, allocating $23.97 for two cases.[1]

Even as commissioners recognized the need for welfare programs and created poor funds, they still remained unsure of how to handle the day-to-day business of providing relief. Only after local grocers began handling relief cases did the Stevens County commissioners decide that they had to limit food aid to a few staple goods. Instead of allowing clients to purchase anything, the board limited them to basic items such as flour, salt meat, beans, rice, coffee, lard, sugar, and potatoes. In Stanton County, officials found it impossible to keep up with the cost of grocery orders and instead created a storeroom in the basement of the courthouse, hoping to reduce costs through bulk buying. While they experimented with ways of providing necessities to their constituents, most counties still relied on a cumbersome investigation procedure that required the commissioners, meeting in full session, to vote on each case. They had yet to discover the virtues of, or feel the necessity for, full-time caseworkers.[2]

Most of these counties lacked even the traditional means of caring for indigent citizens—the county poor farm. A survey by the Kansas Emergency Relief Committee (KERC) revealed that only three of the sixteen Dust Bowl counties operated poor farms. Wichita County housed less than ten people, Ford County between ten and twenty, and Finney County fewer than thirty. Finney County's commissioners lamented these inadequate facilities, because the situation forced the county to pay more than $125 a month in rent for families unable to afford their own lodging. The commissioners made plans, never carried out, to build barracks and cabin camps to house their relief families. Only the advent of federally funded housing programs forestalled disaster.[3]

Inexperience, the growing number of jobless workers, and the high cost of providing relief soon bankrupted most county governments. By mid-1932 and early 1933, county commissioners presided over empty poor funds. Hamilton County's Board of Commissioners issued the following statement, effectively abandoning its relief program: "Whereas the Poor Fund of Hamilton County has long since been exhausted, further pauper aid must of necessity be discontinued from and after this date." This situation still existed in the summer of 1933, when the board informed the township trustees that it would endorse orders against the poor fund "only in extreme emergency."[4]

Empty coffers were common to most county governments throughout southwestern Kansas. In 1933 Haskell County was on the verge of bankruptcy and owed large amounts of money to its creditors. The county had $12,000 in the bank, but this money could not be diverted from the road fund. Even when federal loan money became available and county commissioners were free to apply for their share of three billion dollars in public works funds, some were unsure how to go about securing the money. Stanton County officials registered their unemployed and then failed to take the necessary steps to obtain the funds for their "re-employment" program. A writer for the *Johnson Pioneer* commented that "someone should volunteer to get behind the matter and push it to the utmost." Lack of money and lack of initiative left some county governments and the individuals dependent upon them stranded.[5]

Given situations such as these, township trustees and county commissioners attempted to meet the needs of their poor partially through publicly orchestrated voluntarism. Mrs. Fred Maxwell, poor commissioner for Grant County, contended that the local government was doing all that it could, but that it would be impossible for the county to aid all its needy without the concerted effort of everyone.[6] Maxwell, and others like her, appealed to those with resources beyond their needs to donate outgrown clothing, shoes, bedding, canning jars, mattresses, canned goods, and numerous other basic items.

The case of Finney County provides a particularly clear example of the inadequacy of county-based efforts to meet the challenge of providing consistent and adequate relief to impoverished residents.[7] Finney County's struggles with problems of relief administration were a larger, and perhaps more confused, version of the problems that plagued county commissioners all across the region. Over ten thousand people lived in Finney County in 1930—more than six thousand in Garden City. In the area only Dodge City and Ford County exceeded these population totals.

Finney County began the 1930s with a minimal, rudimentary relief system, the county commissioners distributing aid on an individual basis. They provided mother's pensions to a few widows and old age pensions to a few of their indigent elderly, but they operated no formal welfare system.[8] In 1930, members of the Provident Association, a private organization coordinating all of the charitable associations in the county, worked with the county to supply food and clothing to the needy, operating out of a room at the old courthouse. The local government was equipped to meet the most basic needs of only a small number of destitute people. In the early 1930s, the "city fathers" of Garden City still hoped that charity could begin and end at home and believed that they could meet the needs of the poor through community action. Large advertisements in the local newspaper, placed by Arthur Woods, chairman of President Hoover's Emergency Committee for Employment, encouraged the employed of Garden City to care for the less fortunate. The ads exhorted those with jobs to look around their homes and find work for their neighbors. "There are plenty of ways, right in your own home, of *investing* your money in labor and materials, putting in needed improvements, repairs, additions. . . . You are not wasting a penny. You are putting idle money to work profitably, productively, and patriotically, *if it is promptly done.*"9 The advertiser then provided a list of one hundred possible jobs, ranging from painting the house to disinfecting the cellar to caring for children. This advertisement reflected the hope of solving the growing local and national unemployment problem privately and with minimal public expenditures for relief.

By early spring 1931, it was becoming quite evident that these tactics were inadequate to the dimensions of the situation. The county commissioners were spending more than $2,000 per month on poor relief, excluding the aid provided by the Provident Association, and their funds were running low. In June, the Provident Association relinquished its responsibility for local relief to a national organization, the Volunteers of America. With a regional office in Denver, the Volunteers operated much like the Salvation Army, offering the needy shelter as well as guidance based on Christian principles. Workers drew no salary from the organization, but lived on donations. The Volunteers were to cooperate with the Red Cross and Salvation Army, as well as the county commissioners.10 Even given this new arrangement, the members of the Finney County Board of Commissioners were none too sure of their ability to care for the poor. They had more than exhausted the allowable levy for the poor fund, and there were still more demands to meet.

The commissioners tended to blame their predicament on the families of county prisoners and the Mexican population. They even began to wonder if they should stop enforcing liquor laws in the county. The people of Finney County approved of prohibition, but "what the commission would like is for Mr. Volstead [to] arrange to take care of the families while the violator is serving his sentence." The Mexican population of Finney County, drawn to the area by jobs with the railroads and in the sugar beet fields, drew a good deal of criticism as well. "They cannot be deported, it is said, and the only thing for the county to do is support them or let them starve." Whatever the degree of justice in these accusations, the commissioners saw a large part of their problem stemming from the needs of these marginalized members of the community, and they were at a loss for solutions. The board meeting of July 7, 1931, went on for more than a day and ended without the commissioners formulating any new plans. 11

Nevertheless, the relief administered through the combined efforts of private agencies and the county allowed the people of Finney County to limp along for the next eleven months. The Volunteers of America took over an increasing share of welfare work in the county, with the funding coming from the local government and donations. Between July and October of 1931, the Volunteers provided 2,864 free meals and 444 nights lodging, aided nearly four hundred families with grocery purchases, gave out seven hundred pieces of clothing, and found jobs for nearly four hundred people, both men and women. When hungry people came begging for food at homes and businesses, the Volunteers asked that they not be fed but sent to their headquarters. 12 Other local organizations pitched in with relief as well. Members of the Finney County Junior Red Cross collected empty jars, cans, fruit, and vegetables for a canning project, and girls in the public school home economics classes did the work. Through this joint effort they donated ninety quarts of food to the local relief committee. Boy Scouts and Girl Scouts sold tickets for a movie showing at the State Theater to benefit the Volunteers. The Elks cooperated with the Volunteers in distributing Christmas baskets to the needy. 13

County efforts, however, garnered less praise and seemed to work less smoothly. In June 1932, more than one hundred residents came to a meeting concerning poor relief at the county courthouse. They expressed criticism of the way the commission was handling poor relief and even suggested "that the county officers contribute ten per cent of their monthly wages to the county poor fund." The final outcome of the meeting was an attempt to move relief even further into the private sector by forming a committee of church and civic leaders to raise funds for relief. 14 County officials were increasingly unsure of their ability to continue providing publicly funded aid to the poor.

Four days later, the county commissioners gave up. During their meeting of June 7 and 8, 1932, they conceded the bankruptcy of the poor relief fund and resolved to let the community deal with the situation. "Ways and means were discussed as to the handling of the poor situation, and it was decided that the county could not support the poor any longer as the funds were far overdrawn, and that it would be compelled to let the community handle the poor for the balance of the current year."15 The county poor fund had accumulated an overdraft of more than $9,000, and the Board of County Commissioners was no longer willing to release funds when the situation seemed so hopeless. Thus, Garden City and Finney County were entirely without a public relief program. 16

In response, a group of civic-minded individuals created a new relief agency, christened the Emergency Relief Committee, to work under the board of directors of the old Provident Association. The members of this committee planned to carry on relief work in the county, in conjunction with the Volunteers of America. The Volunteers were to provide aid to families facing emergencies and transients, while the committee undertook the distribution of general relief. 17

The largest problem facing the Emergency Relief Committee was fund raising. Its members called for all salaried workers in Garden City to contribute 3 percent of their incomes to the relief fund and for professionals to contribute 3 percent of their earnings as well. They asked retired farmers and businessmen to contribute a lump sum. In order to stretch these funds further and build public confidence, the committee pledged to distribute its money only to "bona fide relief organizations" and to require those organizations to screen applicants very carefully. "The applicant must sign that he fully acknowledges his obligation both moral and financial and agrees to tender a first lien on any and all property owned by himself, as security for the payment of the funds expended on his behalf. He further pledges that he is willing to perform such labor as the committee may prescribe at such rates of pay as prescribed by them."18 The Volunteers also established more stringent rules for aid recipients. Captain Boone, head of Garden City operations, explained that the Volunteers would require transients who were physically able to work two hours for supper, lodging, and breakfast, and to work eight hours in order to receive a second day's aid. To encourage contributions, the committee promised that "there will be no aid for the drone or the family which is not worthy" and that the committee, composed of "eleven Garden City business men," would keep a close eye on the funds and the storeroom from which supplies would be issued. 19 Under these rules, the Emergency Relief Committee began operations in the summer of 1932.

The committee's members carried out the relief obligations of Finney County on a small scale through the summer and fall of 1932. By August, they had collected more than $400 and out of that provided $150 to the Volunteers. An agreement with area grocery stores allowed the Emergency Relief Committee to purchase food at reduced prices, which stretched charity dollars further. In September, the committee aided thirty-three families (eighty-six individuals). In October, the committee reported that it had received enough contributions for the time being but that the funds on hand would probably be inadequate for the winter months. Whether aid came through private or public organizations, the cold winter months posed special problems in relief distribution.[20]

In the fall of 1932, city and county government officials, as well as members of the local relief committee, began to explore the possibility of the county obtaining federal relief funds. In July, President Hoover had signed into law the Relief and Construction Act, which allowed the Reconstruction Finance Corporation (RFC) to loan money to states for public works projects. The state of Kansas secured $2,750,000 in RFC funds, and local government officials, including Fred Evans and Emergency Relief Committee chairman R. N. Downie, immediately went to work to secure for the unemployed of Finney County their fair share. In anticipation of the plan's approval, the city clerk began registering the unemployed for relief work. Rejoicing followed when the state awarded Finney County $3,456. According to plan, county officials used the funds to widen a storm sewer in a Garden City park, eventually hiring about sixty men to work on the project. This money, however, was only a drop in the bucket; nearly two hundred men applied for the jobs.[21] Finney County, along with the rest of the country, faced a grim season.

Either through apathy or hopelessness, it appeared that the people of Finney County were willing to let the Emergency Relief Committee die in the winter of 1932. Following a "poorly attended and disapproving meeting" in early December, R. N. Downie, chairman of the committee, announced that it would be suspending operations. "It appeared that people were not interested enough to attend the meeting to express a willingness that the organization continue with its work or even ask it to cease, and that the committee was not going to force itself upon the people unless it was really desired."[22] The announcement precipitated an appeal from the editor of the Garden City Daily Telegram. He placed no blame for the collapse of the program with the Emergency Relief Committee but instead with the people of Garden City and Finney County. The county government was still very low on funds, and the best way to continue to provide relief to the needy was through private, community wide effort. "The time for action has arrived."[23] They had little option but to push for the continuation of privately sponsored relief; the county poor fund was overdrawn by more than $10,000.[24]

By the beginning of January, the Emergency Relief Committee was back in business but still operating on the most minimal of funding. The *Garden City Daily Telegram* published a subscription pledge form in the paper so that "everyone [would] have a chance to aid in furnishing funds to take care of the needy." The committee had already mailed the forms to some local firms and individuals and was desperate for funds. Although the RFC loan still provided workers with jobs, there were more unemployed than jobs, and cold weather hampered relief work. The county commissioners responded by cutting relief wages from twenty-five cents an hour to fifteen cents an hour in order to employ more men, and the Emergency Relief Committee contemplated a house-to-house canvas for subscriptions. The committee, with only the few dollars collected early in its existence, could not bear the weight of a growing number of very poor people.[25]

The committee also voted to create a subcommittee to present the names of nonresident families that had applied for relief in Finney County to the county attorney, requesting that these newcomers "be sent back where they came from according to state law." Neither the members of the Emergency Relief Committee nor the members of the county government wanted to be responsible for incoming, indigent outsiders. To further discourage this migration, they voted to reduce the rations for the transients at the Volunteers' mission to mulligan stew and coffee.[26]

By the winter of 1933, the situation in Finney County and across the entire nation was indeed grim. The level of funding provided under the RFC was relatively low, the state had scanty provisions for the poor, the county budget was clearly inadequate, and the Emergency Relief Committee could do very little, relying only on voluntary contributions in a time of great scarcity. One indicator of the severity of the situation was that the commissioners were even disallowing mothers' pensions, or as they put it, "Mothers Aid." In March, they tabled two requests for mothers' pensions, "due to the fact that the poor fund was far overdrawn, but suggested that if necessary, help in the way of food and clothing would be provided."[27]

Fortunately for the people of Garden City and Finney County, lawmakers in Washington, D.C., were beginning a massive response to the problems of unemployment and poverty in the spring of 1933. When federal relief funds became available in the summer and fall of 1933, the members of the committee breathed a sigh of relief and ceased operations.[28] As the drought worsened in 1934 and 1935, the needs of the county increased, and the county's dependence upon federal relief increased likewise. By the summer of 1934, ten people per day were making applications for funding through the county. Many of these people received relief only because the federal government had largely taken over the burden of funding welfare. In September, officials in Finney County distributed $14,252.44 in aid, of which $12,143.48 was federal money, allocated by the Kansas Emergency Relief Committee (KERC).[29] Many of the residents of Finney County, like the residents of all of the southwestern Kansas counties, came to rely on the federal government for the maintenance of their families, homes, and communities. It was a reliance that showed no sign of diminishing well into 1940. County officials allocated more money for relief in that year than they had in any year previously.

What happened to the people of Finney County was repeated all across the southwestern corner of the state. The evidence of an area-wide failure to recover from the early shocks of the depression was in repeated budget slashing by county officials, continual inability of the county to collect more than a small portion of outstanding taxes, and persistent attempts to secure permission from the state tax commission to issue more poor relief bonds. Most budget cuts came early in the decade and resulted in significantly lower wages for all county employees, from laborers on the road crew, to teachers, to the county engineer. Schools often absorbed the brunt of budget cuts, suffering enormous reductions in funding. In 1932, the school budget in Hugoton fell from $28,000 a year to $16,000. In 1933, the grade school in Ulysses received only $9,200, half its allowed appropriation. Teachers took home "no-fund" warrants instead of cash, and districts eliminated programs, such as kindergarten, music lessons, physical education, advanced home economics, and drama.[30]

Budget cuts, however, had only a limited impact on the financial crisis because county officials had little or no ability to pay bills, even at reduced rates. Citizens left their taxes unpaid for years at a time, and property assessments for tax purposes fell precipitously. Between 1933 and 1938, county officials took little action to recover lost revenue, knowing that few locals had the money to pay. Confiscating homes, land, and businesses for back taxes would have been futile as well, since real estate was virtually worthless due to drought conditions and depopulation. Only in 1938 and 1939 did county officers begin to enforce the tax laws again.[31]

In a desperate effort to stay afloat, county officials repeatedly appealed to the Kansas State Tax Commission for permission to increase the levy for the poor fund and to issue emergency warrants and additional bonds for poor relief. During 1939, Morton County's commissioners even asked that the state of Kansas pay 30 percent of the approved social welfare budget of the county. The drought had produced particularly devastating effects in that county, driving away almost 50 percent of the population and leaving the county's major town, Elkhart, a ghost of its former self.[32] Although Morton County's case was extreme, similar problems on a lesser scale plagued the entire area. Budgets created for 1940 included significant increases in funding for social welfare, in anticipation of another year of disaster for the people of southwestern Kansas.[33]

Much of the relief federal officials distributed to Kansans in 1933 and 1934 came from funds provided by the Federal Emergency Relief Administration (FERA). FERA, a precursor to job programs administered directly by the federal government, provided federal funds to states. The states were then responsible for screening applications and funding relief programs created by the state and county governments. In Kansas, FERA funds were administered by the Kansas Emergency Relief Committee (KERC). The state of Kansas provided very little of the relief money allocated within its borders. Nearly three quarters of all relief money originated with the federal government, just over a quarter of the money came from local governments, and the state provided less than 1 percent of relief dollars spent.[34]

Using this federal money, the KERC implemented a number of programs. It sponsored work relief projects in all of the counties, much like those begun with RFC funds. At the same time, administrators designed a number of practical programs to allow people to become as self-sufficient as possible. The KERC's organizers encouraged citywide participation in gardening and canning projects and provided facilities to process surplus commodities for distribution. Most of these programs required minimal funding, supervision, and technical expertise. Unfortunately, given the worsening drought conditions, they did not always have the desired effect of making their participants self-supporting.

At the most basic level, the KERC funneled federal funds into a number of unsophisticated, easily accomplished work programs. Relief clients dug wells, overflow dams, and garden ponds. They made furniture for county offices, cleaned up cemeteries, and sewed mattresses and garments for themselves and other relief clients. Some recipients of KERC funds taught helpful classes in their communities. One woman "work[ed] out her budget deficit" teaching canning to other women, while a male relief client taught a "fix it" class through the Leisure Time Activities Program.[35] Many of these programs, such as school lunchrooms, playground projects, and sewing rooms, provided supplemental income to women whose families depended upon relief.

Additionally, the KERC required that all of its relief clients plant gardens and encouraged city and county governments to provide the necessary land to those without suitable plots. The gardens served multiple purposes, according to administrators. Primarily, they hoped that gardening would reduce the relief load, since families with successful plots would require less food aid from their offices. Administrators also believed that gardening produced potentially significant moral benefits. They stressed that gardening, even on a small scale, imparted important rural values to relief clients. Work in a garden, they argued, encouraged thrift and hard work and provided "families with a new heritage of modern methods in gardening and dependability in rural occupations." Relief agents in Seward County were convinced that gardening had a positive

The Dunn family of Haskell County produced this subirrigated garden under the KERC's garden program. (Kansas Emergency Relief Committee photo; Kansas State Historical Society)

impact on families. "The clients that have gardens are by all means making a better showing than those that have no gardens. They need less for subsistence and will be the first to become self-supporting."[36] This praise of hard work and industry, as well as rural values, harked back to the traditional pioneer spirit of southwestern Kansas. The federal government, too, promoted agrarian values. Many New Dealers and many New Deal programs touted the idea of "Jeffersonian simplicity." Americans could regain their pride, their heritage, and their standard of living by returning to an earlier day when they worked with their hands on the land.[37]

The Dunns of Haskell County, a family of nine, illustrated what could be accomplished through relief gardening and canning of commodities purchased in bulk with the aid of the KERC. A partial inventory of Mrs. Dunn's efforts included

155 half gallon jars of peaches
69 half gallon jars of beans
42 half gallon jars of peas
20 half gallon jars of beets
82 half gallon jars of grapes
20 half gallon jars of cherries
75 gallons of cucumbers
2 quarts of dried peas

Although the family purchased the peaches, grapes, and cherries, the beans, peas, beets, and cucumbers all came from Mrs. Dunn's relief garden. Her success, however, was unusual. Drought conditions destroyed most of the gardeners' efforts. Only in Grant County, where the city provided free water, did the program have much success. All other county administrators judged the condition of their clients' plots from fair to complete failures, due to heat and dust.[38]

On the other hand, drought conditions made one program possible. The state sponsored a leather and wool processing program, which made use of the products of animals purchased and slaughtered because of feed shortages. In June 1935, 566 women throughout southwestern Kansas sewed, knitted, and crafted various items out of leather and wool, and the KERC distributed the fruits of their labor to relief programs throughout the area. Organizers of work programs for women, such as the leather and wool project, hired women for jobs that most already knew, requiring only basic sewing, knitting, and handicraft skills. Jobs for men under the program were usually more complicated. They learned to make harnesses and shoes, most likely in the hope that they would acquire skills which would allow them to secure private employment in the future.[39]

Purchases of drought-ravaged herds also made it possible for the state to provide canned and fresh beef to relief clients. In 1934 and 1935, state inspectors purchased more than eighty thousand cattle from farmers and ranchers in southwestern Kansas. Those that were fit, the state sold; the rest became canned or fresh beef on the dinner tables of hungry families. In Finney County alone, relief workers distributed 26,241 pounds of beef, giving 194 pounds to each client. Additionally, the slaughtering and canning provided work to people in the vicinity of processing plants.[40] Through this and similar projects requiring a minimum of supplies and technical expertise, the KERC managed the greater part of relief administration throughout southwestern Kansas in 1933 and 1934.

In 1935, however, Congress created the Works Progress Administration (WPA), and it assumed responsibility for most of the work relief received by the needy in the towns of the Dust Bowl, providing billions of dollars in aid to the unemployed through various work programs. The KERC transferred its work relief clients to the WPA, leaving the county governments responsible only for individuals in need of direct relief, generally meaning women with small children, as well as those who were physically unable to work.[41] The WPA cooperated with local governments, providing the bulk of the funding needed for building projects both large and small, if the local community would contribute a percentage of the money. Although children joked that the initials WPA stood for "we're probably asleep," the program provided small but livable wages for thousands who could find no other work and visibly improved the physical surroundings in many a community.

The WPA hired its workers for a wide array of jobs, many fairly simple and unsophisticated and similar to KERC work relief. Men commonly worked on roads, dug sewer extensions, improved county fairgrounds, and built simple sanitary outhouses. The jobs required little capital investment and took a great deal of time when done by hand, a prerequisite of many WPA projects. The administrators' major concern was not to finish projects quickly, with a minimum of effort, but to provide as much work as possible for as many men as possible, as long as the funding lasted.[42]

The WPA created jobs for women as well, nearly always capitalizing on skills women already possessed, instead of developing new ones. Most commonly, women worked in WPA sewing rooms, making clothing for themselves and other relief clients. The WPA usually provided only a few sewing machines, so women spent their time doing handwork on shirts, dresses, layettes, sheets, and pillow slips, which stocked commodity distribution centers. Women provided the labor for another service as well, the school hot lunch program. Seward County also provided some women with jobs as emergency helpers—cooking, sewing, cleaning, canning, and doing anything necessary for families strained by illness and other troubles.[43] Relief employment for men and women alike accomplished two things: It gave people work in exchange for aid and kept them off county direct relief rolls.

The WPA also invested in large-scale building projects throughout southwestern Kansas. A review of improvements made in six counties during 1937 revealed that, aside from investments made by oil and gas companies, most building projects originated from work relief money. In 1937 alone, the WPA helped finance and build swimming pools in Hugoton, Fowler, and Sublette, stadiums in Liberal and Meade, a public library in Hugoton, and a new adobe city hall in Elkhart. Highway construction programs in Grant, Stevens, Seward, Haskell, Meade, and Morton counties all used federal money.[44]

Although the WPA was certainly the most important program directly affecting the towns, a number of young people participated in other programs, such as the Civilian Conservation Corps (CCC). Young men whose families relied upon relief were eligible to join the CCC, which employed them in conservation projects in various locations throughout the region. They earned a small amount of money for themselves, and $25 a month was sent to their parents. In southwestern Kansas, most of the members of the CCC helped build state lakes, which became recreation areas for the surrounding counties.[45]

The National Youth Administration (NYA) employed both women and men in high school and college in a variety of jobs. Among other projects, the youth collected and repaired toys for needy children at Christmas, worked in clerical and manual jobs around high schools and colleges, and helped plan, arrange, and supervise playgrounds. The NYA even recruited secondary school teachers to provide college-level instruction at the local high schools for young people unable to afford further education. The students could transfer the credits to state schools when they saved enough money to go to college.[46] Like the aid that went to their parents, aid for young people kept them busy, fed, and out of unemployment lines.

Reshaping local institutions in the wake of the distress caused by the drought and depression and accepting federal aid required adaptation, innovation, and compromise on the part of area residents. To many, taking aid meant losing independence, and once a person lost his or her independence, "you are a human derelict on the wide ocean of indifference."[47] Critics of federal aid believed that government money eroded the recipient's morale and caused people to lose confidence in their own abilities. And "easy" government money, accepted when people forgot how to help themselves, fell outside the traditions of southwestern Kansas.[48]

> Those sturdy old pioneers who settled this country were not "leaners." They knew how to help themselves. In their day there were no roads, modern houses or barns; no fast transportation; money was very scarce. When they needed water to make crops grow they dug irrigation ditches and built their own dams. They didn't wait for the government to do it for them. As a result many of us now are enjoying blessings that came through the ability of those pioneers to help themselves.[49]

Believing in these settlement myths, latter-day southwestern Kansans naturally felt uncomfortable with the idea of relief.

But they and their neighbors were hungry, and the itinerant poor were flooding their towns. The lean years before the advent of federal relief forced people to temper their value of self-reliance with compassion and to develop community-based programs to aid the needy. Later, as federal aid became available, county officials had to learn to petition for funds, and residents had to accept help when it was needed. The decade and the depression ended before most people had become comfortable with either the concept or the reality of welfare. Predictably, these attempts to support the needy created conflict, as commissioners tried to identify the "deserving poor" and determine how aid could be provided to them without offending their more prosperous constituents.

Taxpayer anger with seemingly high levies during years of scarcity complicated the work of county commissioners considerably. Residents regularly let their commissioners know that they expected economizing at the courthouse. In 1930, voters in Grant County turned down a bond issue supporting a new school, even though population growth during the last decade made larger facilities necessary. Prospects for the wheat crop looked poor, and most believed this was not "the proper time to erect a new building." In 1931, a delegation of taxpayers in Hamilton County appeared before the board of commissioners to protest construction of a new courthouse, again, because the "times" did not warrant expenditures of that size.[50] Even when the WPA approved projects and funded a large percentage of their cost people had to be persuaded to take advantage of the situation. Political advertisements showing the black and clawed hand of federal spending snatching sleeping toddlers from their beds illustrated people's fears of dependence on the government.[51]

Defeats of single projects, such as the construction of a new school or courthouse, went hand in hand with more pointed protests about waste in particular county programs. The residents of Ford County were especially active in their attempts to make their Board of Commissioners responsive to voters' needs. A taxpayer-appointed committee presented its version of the "fourteen points" to the commissioners, outlining "a plan for the reduction of a proposed budget for the year 1932." The suggested revisions to the budget included reducing salaries for deputies and assistants by one-third, eliminating new road construction, and discontinuing county appropriations for the Farm Bureau. The taxpayers believed it would be a good idea to take up the budget item "Miscellaneous Expense" with the commissioners as well.[52]

The agitation by Ford County's taxpayers continued in later years with demands that the county director of poor funds and the commodity distribution clerk be removed, presumably for inappropriate use of funds. The commissioners hoped to cool the protest with a meeting to explain in detail the social welfare program and its functions. In 1939, taxpayers brought pressure on the board to begin collection of back taxes, which the county eventually did.[53] People had little sympathy for what they perceived to be runaway budgets and increased county expenditures when their own spending was seriously limited. Like the people of Hamilton County, most urged their officials to practice "the general trend of economy that is necessary under present conditions" at the courthouse, just as it was being practiced in local "business[es] and in the homes of [the] County."[54]

Condemnation of excess county spending inevitably led to condemnation of the most obvious reason for increased spending, the relief clients. Not all relief clients, however, were equally culpable in the eyes of

BECAUSE
"WE PLANNED IT
THAT WAY"

PARENTS ---- Wake Up!

Do Not Be
LULLED TO SLEEP
By Self Praise

This 1936 ad from the Clark County Clipper *illustrated people's worst fears about federal aid.* (Clark County Clipper)

the general public. Transients, who paid no taxes and who many believed had come only to take aid and jobs from worthy locals, received some of the harshest criticism. People also targeted prisoners whose families relied upon relief. Others receiving welfare were less offensive to most observers, but both officials and others insisted that their lives and purchases be fairly heavily regulated to prevent waste of taxpayers' money.

People's attitudes about relief expenditures varied with their economic status. Most people who were neither transients nor prisoners probably disapproved of county spending on their behalf, although many would have been reluctant to let anyone starve, particularly women and children. Criticism of work and direct relief clients may have come largely from those who continued to pay their taxes through the 1930s, although that group probably never included more than 50 percent of the property owners in any Dust Bowl county in the thirties. Those who were not actively critical, silenced by their own needs, most likely regretted the necessity of welfare and their own dependence. One woman, reflecting on her own experience with relief, commented, "We despised the position we were in. Most of us tried to get out of it as quickly as possible."[55]

Commentary in the area's newspapers suggested that locals generally resented the transients who presented themselves at the county courthouse or at their back doors. In the eyes of town residents, they were "moochers," "bums," and practitioners of a "'sympathy' racket." Mostly, they were guilty of being outsiders in need of help, when there were "home men" and "home people" competing with them for a limited supply of aid and jobs. In the same way that the newspapers encouraged people to shop at home, they encouraged people to give at home and to refuse food and money to the person on the back porch and send him or her to the city clerk instead. The clerk could then investigate and decide if the person was deserving of any help or not. Those in Garden City who gave aid to "back door knockers" instead of sending them to the city offices could be fined up to $100 for that act.[56]

A good number of the transients who showed up in the towns of southwestern Kansas looking for work or aid found themselves on their way back home again. State and county governments throughout the nation had policies that required the return of nonresidents to their former homes. Although it was against federal law for officials to give transients a bus ticket or just enough gas to drive across county lines, this was common practice during the 1930s. Residents of other counties who

asked for relief or were "likely to become a public charge" earned themselves a seat on a bus or train or just enough money for gasoline to get
home again. The rules might be bent for a person too ill or too old to
travel, but generally, no person was "entitled to more than temporary
assistance unless they [were] legally settled in the County, as provided by
Statute."[57]

The county commissioners were equally unhappy at the prospect of
providing for prisoners in the county jail and their families. The City of
Elkhart announced that it refused to aid the families of prisoners. "The
city never has nor never will provide for the families of prisoners. Under
the present state law it is unlawful for the city to provide for the poor. So if
your old man gets in jail, don't expect the city to provide your grub and
fuel. The City of Elkhart."[58] But when the city would not provide,
county officials found themselves in charge. One way to lighten both the
relief load and the cost of providing for prisoners at the county jail was to
release them when the costs grew too great. County commissioners fairly
regularly released prisoners convicted of misdemeanors and violations of
prohibition if their families became wards of the county. Most of these
men had served most or all of their sentences but were unable to pay their
fines. The counties waived the fines, balancing the slim possibility of
repayment against the sure cost of caring for the prisoner's indigent
family.[59]

When officials approved requests for federal and local aid, they carefully
specified who would receive it and why particular people were eligible.
Administrators primarily asked that relief clients be "worthy." They mea-
sured worthiness in a number of ways. A man with a family was more
worthy than a single man or woman and received first consideration for
work relief jobs. Additionally, the size of the family involved affected the
total number of work relief hours the county allotted, with large families
receiving preference. No able-bodied man was eligible for direct relief,
since he could work for the county in partial payment of his obligations.
Widowed women generally received direct relief instead of work relief,
much as they had before the depression when some had received mother's
pensions.[60]

Being worthy also required that the relief client have the correct attitude. Marian Thompson, case supervisor for Ness County, made this
patently clear in a notice published in the Bazine Advocate. "If you are laid
off through any fault of your own such as slack work, laziness or slowness,

there will be little consideration shown to you from this office."[61] The same conditions applied to those already on relief. In both Gray and Stanton counties, for example, any worker showing dissatisfaction with his or her assignment could be removed from the relief rolls and replaced with someone on the waiting list. Commissioner H. L. Tucker of Stanton County announced through the local paper that "any one found kicking on the relief plan or trying to stir up trouble among the workers will be taken off the list and will not receive any further aid." Furthermore, in most counties, if a relief client received a job offer of any sort, even at wages below relief rates, that person was obligated to accept the job.[62]

In order to keep members of the general public satisfied and, again, to reduce costs, officials also strictly regulated the ways in which relief clients were allowed to spend county and federal money. Several counties required relief clients who lived in town to relinquish titles and license plates for any automobiles they owned and allowed no expenditures for gasoline. Others provided their clients with grocery orders and specified only certain items for purchase. They limited electricity charges and asked that radios not be used.[63] Stanton County provided relief clients with a fairly comprehensive list of items that could and could not be paid for with public assistance funds: "They shall not be permitted to attend picture shows, dance halls, play pool, or any other luxuries purchased through soft drink parlors, such as beer, malted milk, ice cream, and soft drinks, from money which is obtained from tax payers and self-supporting people. Such funds must be used for rent, food, clothing, medical care and necessities of the household."[64] Poor Commissioner Belle Watson's meaning was clear. Aid clients might spend the government's money on essential items but had no right to squander the hard-earned dollars of those who continued to pay their taxes.

Perhaps as an incentive to keep less needy individuals off the rolls or to allow more careful policing of those who used welfare money, many county boards published their monthly expenditures, welfare included, with names attached. On October 15, 1937, a reader of the *Elkhart Tri-State News* would have seen that thirty-two of his neighbors received public assistance that month and that their grants ranged from $6.50 to $55.00. Being an aid client was public business; neighbors might know the size of a person's allotment and how he or she had a right to spend that money. Sometimes, people were invited to police their neighbors' expenditures. When the Liberal Chamber of Commerce protested high relief payments in 1938, John C. King, director of social welfare for Seward County, invited anyone knowing about welfare "chiselers" to come to his office and inspect the welfare rolls. Presumably, since public money supported welfare recipients, the public had a duty to aid welfare officials in determining the worthiness of recipients.[65]

Criticism of the welfare system usually did not include aid provided to area farmers. In commissioners' journals and local newspapers criticism of farmers was virtually absent. Both recipients and observers saw aid to agriculture in a different light than other types of relief, perhaps because the devastation of area farms was so visible and so total and appeared to be an "act of God," rather than the product of sloth or other character flaws. Elfreda Penner Fast, whose parents accepted farm aid during the depression, commented, "Well, we didn't consider it relief. We just considered it the government subsidy, or government program, and we felt that the government was really on the ball to provide this sort of a thing because it did help the farmers to get on their feet."[66] Many within both the agricultural and urban communities saw farm aid as absolutely essential, and, in a sense, a subsidy that the government owed to beleaguered farmers.

Those southwestern Kansans who found their names on welfare lists could take some comfort in the knowledge that a large percentage of their friends, acquaintances, and neighbors had been in a similar situation during part or all of the decade. As much as people complained about expenditures for aid, both federal and local, that influx of aid money most likely kept either them or a friend fed or indirectly provided the money that kept their businesses afloat. This knowledge sometimes bred sympathy for the recipients of aid. Fifty years later, sisters Elsie Swafford Riney and Leota Swafford Lambert explained their response to the subject of relief. On the one hand, "everyone that could get on" was on relief and generally glad to have it. On the other hand, it was difficult to accept charity. Families "didn't like to take it, and yet, what could you do?"[67]

The fortunes of individuals, cities, and counties rose and fell with the creation of new federal programs and their continued funding. The difficult transition from the KERC to the WPA in 1935 caused a great deal of alarm, as did any delay in the arrival of relief checks or threatened cutbacks in programs. The payment of the federal wheat bonus in 1933 brought tolerable times to both the country and the towns, and the Supreme Court's finding the Agricultural Adjustment Act unconstitutional in 1935 caused as much panic in the banks and general stores as on the farm.[68] Aid of one sort or another continued to sustain people in the area's towns well into 1940. As one Wichita County poet wrote in 1936:

> But as it is
> It's lots of fun—
> Everything comes
> From Washington.[69]

5. THE HARDEST OF TIMES

The troubles of the 1930s struck the hardest at the farmers who attempted to wrestle a living from the hard, dry, and drifting soil. While all Dust Bowl Kansans suffered from the unpleasant effects of dirt and the economic depression, farming families suffered the most. Of all groups (urban, rural nonfarm, and farm), the farm population had the lowest persistence rate for the decade. Their numbers declined absolutely and as a percentage of the total population. First, the price paid for wheat failed to meet operating costs in 1931, and then the weather proved disastrous for farmers throughout the rest of the decade. Dirt storms and dry conditions eroded the farmers' topsoil and scattered their efforts to the wind.

Americans, with their nostalgia for the rural past, have often argued that farms are the safest places to take shelter during economic downturns; ideally, farm families can grow a garden, raise cows, pigs, and chickens, and eat what they cannot sell. They do not starve.[1] For thousands of Dust Bowl families, however, this generalization proved untrue. Raising a garden required expenditures for irrigation, and raising animals for subsistence required feed crops, often destroyed by drought. Dust Bowl farms were hardly comfortable places on which to ride out the depression. Between 1931 and 1940, farming yielded only the most minimal of incomes.

Prior to the 1930s, most of the farming population of southwestern Kansas had not been particularly disadvantaged. According to the USDA's Bureau of Agricultural Economics, farmers throughout the area enjoyed a fairly high standard of living, compared to other rural communities. The bureau defined disadvantage as a combination of high levels of hired labor, tenancy, outward migration, and relief (1935), and a low standard of living based upon an index combining electricity, telephones, radios,

This farm in the vicinity of Liberal was nearly swallowed up by drifting dirt. (Farm Security Administration photo by Arthur Rothstein; Library of Congress)

automobiles, and piped water. Most of the Dust Bowl region showed little or moderate disadvantage. (The most serious pockets of rural poverty were in the south-central and southeastern United States, as well as in a few areas in the southwest.) Economic conditions in southwestern Kansas approximated those in the relatively prosperous Midwest.[2] In the ten years prior to the Dust Bowl, the area was not known for its poverty, but for moderately well-off farmers, tending their large, mechanized wheat farms.

Within this stereotype of the southern plains wheat farmer was considerable diversity. Although wheat farming surpassed cattle raising as the area's primary agricultural pursuit during and after the First World War, cattle remained important in several counties—Clark, Hamilton, and Ness, particularly. In April 1931, Hamilton County became the last county in Kansas to adopt herd laws requiring that animals be fenced and not allowed to roam free. Additionally, many farmers along the western border of Kansas planted large acreages of sorghum and plots of broom-corn, an especially drought resistant crop. In the low-lying areas along the Arkansas River, some farmers irrigated alfalfa, sugar beets, and grain sorghums or raised truck gardens. The farmers on irrigated plots tended to plant more diversified crops than those on nonirrigated farms. Families often raised a few chickens and pigs for home consumption and kept a milk cow or two, but in many homes this was not a priority. The Clark County agricultural extension agent noted in his report for 1930 that "many farmers keep little or no livestock." Farm homes in newer areas tended to be a little primitive, but those in more established areas were generally "modern and comfortable."[3]

From roughly the turn of the century until 1931, farming in south-western Kansas paid, and paid well. In 1929, 28 percent of all farm families in the United States reported that the value of the products that they sold, used, or traded, amounted to less than $600 a year. In fourteen of sixteen southwestern Kansas counties, fewer than 10 percent of farm families lived on incomes that meager. In 1929 the mean value of prod-ucts produced by a family on a southwestern Kansas farm was $5,476.94, largely derived from the winter wheat crop.[4] Those evaluating the wealth of southwestern Kansas, unmindful of the disaster to come, laid prosperity at the door of the area's farmers. Wrote one columnist, "Agriculture is not only fundamentally the basic industry but is actually the foundation on which all worldly possessions rest." Another claimed that "what wheat has done . . . to other counties, it has done more lavishly in this county," bringing hotels overburdened in the harvest season, land buyers, and a booming population. Agriculture was the "good news of 1930" and much of the previous decade.[5]

The agricultural reports for the 1930s, on the other hand, were con-sistently poor. Although most southwestern Kansas farmers did not feel the drought until the months following the harvest of 1931, some saw a change for the worse in 1930. Wheat production in Gray County fell from eighteen bushels per acre to thirteen, and farmers in Meade and Clark counties also suffered from a lack of moisture. In 1930, the extension agent in Meade County foresaw disaster. The "whole county had gone wheat mad," and because of the drought the crop would not "furnish adequate returns." He predicted serious difficulties for many of his county's farmers because "many wheat growers will be ruined before they will milk a cow or feed a hog intelligently."[6]

Following the harvest of 1931, the agricultural depression became general. The price per bushel of wheat at local elevators fell from approximately seventy-five cents to thirty-five cents or less, while farmers harvested a record crop, leaving them unable to pay the costs of production. This, in turn, hurt the thousands of harvest hands who migrated yearly to Kansas, hoping to make some money from the wheat crop. Although there was plenty of wheat, there was little work. As one columnist wrote, "The present discouraging wheat market makes it imperative that wheat be harvest at lowest expense if growers are to break even, and labor . . . will be curtailed as much as possible."[7] Even economizing at the expense of hired labor left bills unpaid after harvest time.

Unfortunately, neither farmers nor laborers were able to recoup their losses in 1932. Although New Year's predictions called for rising wheat and cattle prices, a positive local balance of trade, and "rational prosperity," worsening economic and drought conditions wrecked everyone's hopes.[8] On extension agent referred to the drought and price crash as "the Chastisement of 1932."[9] The experience of Grant County's farmers was typical. The wheat crop in 1932 averaged only six to seven bushels an acre for those acres actually harvested. Late rains encouraged weeds and forced the farmers to abandon thousands of acres, thinly covered with wheat, but more thickly covered with other worthless greenery. As their agricultural agent commented, crop failure in combination with low prices "worked a hardship upon farmers and business men who were in debt and in this area it is the largest percent."[10] Of course, no one knew that the drought would be a long-term problem, and farmers hoped that the next year would bring rain, better crops, and higher prices for agricultural products.

But weather conditions and farm incomes continued their unchecked downhill slide. On June 16, 1933, a group of concerned farmers met in Guymon, Oklahoma. The minutes of their meeting revealed the degree of devastation throughout the southern plains. Mr. E. B. Edson of Rolla reported that "practically the entire county has suffered from the sandstorms and there is not enough living vegetation in the entire county [Morton] to keep any livestock." With rather remarkable foresight, he predicted that Morton County would certainly lose half of its population if rain did not come and come soon. I. H. Cook of Haskell County was equally pessimistic about his county's prospects. He told the assembled farmers that "most of the land has been planted and blowed under or has got so dry it won't come up or is dying. I don't see how Haskell County is going to get through without some aid from somewhere. We haven't laid down, they don't want to lay down, but the funds have given out and they are up against it." Almost without exception, the assembled farmers had no hope for a return to prosperity in 1933.[11] Unfortunately, their pessimism was well founded.

The drought continued unabated throughout 1934 and into 1935. The editor of the *Johnson Pioneer* attempted to comfort his readers by pointing out that Stanton County did indeed raise a wheat crop in 1935, just under 8,000 bushels.[12] This information was small comfort indeed. In 1930, farmers there had raised close to 700,000 bushels of wheat on 83,102 acres of land. In 1935, only 4,000 acres could be farmed and yielded just over two bushels per acre.[13] If the wheat harvest was not a complete failure, it came close. People could only hope that "the trials we have all endured during the past three years will soon be forgotten"—and that the rains would come and return life to normal.[14]

Through 1934 and 1935, farmers were unable to raise enough forage

This Ford County field had little to offer to hungry livestock. (Farm Security Administration photo by Arthur Rothstein; Library of Congress)

crops to feed their animals. A few farmers and ranchers with greater financial resources were able to ship their cattle temporarily to pastures in Arizona and Oklahoma.[15] Others watched in despair as their grasslands dried up and their cattle starved. When the federal government initiated programs to buy out cattle herds, farmers were quick to take advantage of the offer. Beginning January 15, 1935, the government made emergency cattle purchases in all sixteen Dust Bowl counties. As of May 1, 1935, federal agents had purchased 83,699 cattle from beleaguered farmers. Cattle in the worst shape were immediately killed and buried, while others were shipped to packing plants to be slaughtered and canned as relief rations or sold to farmers in less droughty regions.[16]

The buying program was a great boon to many farmers. As the county agent in Stanton County commented, "The government cattle buying program was a God-send to many farmers, as they could not afford to keep their cattle, and the government paid a better price than they could obtain in local markets."[17] The government also bought up swine and killed them and later paid farmers for every pig they did not raise.[18] One man who grew up in Meade County claimed that the five dollars per pig that the government paid allowed his father's farm to continue operating. The program, he said, "was a life saver." The government stock buying program offered beleaguered ranchers and farmers the opportunity to avoid a total loss.[19]

The increasing seriousness of the drought in 1934 and 1935 compounded farmers' problems by sending clouds of dust to choke their crops or scour their fields bare. In his 1936 annual report, the Morton County agricultural agent described the impact of dust storms on local farms. "Since the soil is very susceptible to blowing and there has been no vegetation on the soil the past three years, the farmers have seen their hopes of crops fade. The wheat was either blown out or covered up with sifting silt from neighboring farms. Row crops died from lack of moisture, and much of the livestock has been shipped due to lack of feed."[20] Similar conditions continued into 1937, with yields per acre of winter wheat running from three to five bushels in Seward, Stevens, and Meade counties. Grasshopper infestation reduced yields even further. The Meade County agricultural agent wrote that the outlook for the year was "none too promising."[21]

Even those who persisted through the 1930s doubted themselves in 1937. They had believed that drought conditions could get no worse than those of 1935, and yet 1937 was nearly as dirty and as disappointing as that terrible year. A Clark County man commented, "This country needs help if it ever needed it."[22] Martha and George Friesen, suffering through the Dust Bowl on their Hamilton County farm, considered abandoning their land in 1937. On May 19, George came into the house and said, "Lets go and get clear out of the County. Moving . . . some where [along] the River isn't far enough." Although they did not leave the farm then, they continued to talk about it through the long, hot summer. "We two where reading and disguessing this Dust bowl. And how things would be, when we pulled ourselves up, by the Roots, and planted them on some different place. George told about Oren Jourey's Machinery, was all by its only self all blowed full of Dust. And he says that's the way ours il be when we're gone." Martha and George could hardly bear the thought of leaving, but they, like their neighbors, knew that they could not survive many more seasons of drought and discouragement. Instead of abandoning their farm entirely, the Friesens made a trip to visit their eldest daughter in "the Garden of Eden"—Oregon. [23]

In 1938 and 1939, farmers vacillated between hope and despair. The spring rains of 1938 promised fair crops to farm operators in some counties, while others faced the disappointment of yet another year of bad luck. The adequate crops in some locales, such as Seward, Ness, and Grant counties, encouraged farmers to invest money in much needed repairs for the first time in years. But when farmers lost most of their 1939 wheat crop due to drought, they were unable to meet their obligations.[24] Iman Wiatt, a Kearny County farmer, made his final pronouncement about the year on December 31, 1939: "And so ends a year that promised so much and produced little except drought and war."[25] Farmers had endured eight years of dry, dirty weather, with little reason to hope that conditions would improve soon. From the perspective of January 1, 1940, it looked as if the next decade could be as difficult as the last.

The 1930s challenged farmers in every way imaginable. They were unable to raise cash crops, and many were also unable to maintain the animals and gardens that might have made it possible for them to limit costs by feeding their families from the products of their land. Immediately following the price crash and before the drought deepened, extension directors in several counties had argued that the time had come for farming families throughout the area to begin "live at home" programs— to provide all of the needs of the family on the farm. The agents encouraged operators to broaden their horizons, to move away from their reliance on cash crops and toward "a better understanding of the home as a place for the solution of economic problems." This meant greater emphasis on the production of animals for home use and sale and more gardening.[26]

Unfortunately, the drought largely precluded families from implementing subsistence programs on their farms. In some counties, it was entirely unlikely that farmers would turn to cows to solve their economic troubles; they had no history of doing so in the past. As the agent in Grant County explained, most farmers in his jurisdiction owned no pasture and kept no cattle. The agent in Stanton County made more pointed comments. Of the farmers he served, he wrote, "They cannot conceive the idea of milking cows or feeding grain and forage to livestock instead of selling it for cash." In other places, the drought forced farmers to abandon what animal production they normally practiced. So many farmers in Meade County gave up their dairy cattle that townspeople were threatened with a milk shortage. Feed was both too scarce and too costly for many farmers to maintain any type of livestock, especially when the market prices for cattle, hogs, and dairy products would not pay the cost of their production. The Gray County agricultural agent noted that the drought had "temporarily wrecked the hog business" in his county. Farmers sold and slaughtered animals, rather than watch them starve.[27]

Flocks of chickens faced the same fate. The scarcity and price of feed, in addition to hot, dusty conditions that smothered chicks, forced farmers to cut back on poultry production, even though it had traditionally provided farm families with a small income during hard times. One agent commented that "the cost of feed has been out of proportion to the price received for eggs. Although the production was satisfactory the income was small or negligible." An article in the *Johnson Pioneer* recommended that the "cheapest way to keep chickens this year is in jars." Thus, butter and egg money did not provide farm families quite the hedge against poverty that it had given them in other difficult, but greener, times.[28]

Gardening, another hedge against starvation, often went the way of cream and egg production. Although farm families showed increased enthusiasm for extension gardening programs in response to their greater needs, weather conditions discouraged their efforts. Hot, dry winds and dusty days buried gardens in layers of dirt, scorched them, or sandblasted the leaves right off the plants. As one farmer put it, vegetables "get up an inch out of the ground and a sand storm comes through and cuts them off like a razor." The Stanton County extension agent estimated that the drought and dust storms had reduced the output of vegetables in 1935 on county farms to 10 percent of the normal yield.[29] The desire to garden and provide for a family was often thwarted by nature.

Some farm women faced the problem in other ways. The accounts of the Friesen family of Hamilton County, largely unable to garden during the 1930s, show that in the summer of 1935, at the height of the growing season, the family's grocery purchases included tomatoes, lettuce, carrots, peas, peaches, strawberries, string beans, potatoes, cantaloupe, cabbage, and bananas. The grocers could purchase fresh produce from irrigated lands along the Arkansas River in Kansas and Colorado or from growers on the western slopes of the Rocky Mountains in Colorado. The family also purchased large amounts of inexpensive produce intended for canning. For example, between August and November of 1937, Martha Friesen preserved nearly forty gallon-jars of fruit, pickles, butters, and jams, as well as ninety-three smaller jars of the same.[30] This approach was not as economical as raising one's own produce for canning but was less expensive than purchasing the same products from the grocery store throughout the year.

Long-established farm families, such as the Friesens, were sometimes able to continue chicken and egg production as well, which often contributed significant sums to the family income. Martha Friesen's poultry flock was essential to the family's survival. In 1935 her eggs brought in $221.85, and chicken sales added an additional $42.15. Because she had to purchase chicken feed, her profit was only $181.91. Most of the receipts were applied to the family's grocery bill, which amounted to $264.28 that year.[31] The receipts from George's enterprises help to put the importance of Martha's contribution in perspective. In 1935, George sold two loads of wheat for $134. He also sold livestock worth $141, while purchasing a bull for $50. The expenses involved in maintaining George's side of the farming operation were also substantial, $390.60, the largest cost being $274.07 expended upon the upkeep and fuel for the family's tractor. The result was that the expense of maintaining the crop and livestock operations of the farm was greater than the income produced. Like most of his neighbors, George Friesen's operating expenditures exceeded his profits, and the Friesen farm survived only because of an adequate combination of the husband's and wife's efforts, plus a generous dollop of federal aid.[32]

Otto Feldman, a Meade County farmer, wrote to Kansas Republican senator Arthur Capper that "if it wasent for my milk cows I would have to give up." Because he kept milk cows and his wife kept chickens, he explained that they had "ten cents to the good last week." It was the most minimal of profits, but a profit nonetheless.[33] If a family had access to irrigation equipment, gardening became a possibility. In 1938, the McKee family of Stanton County produced $114 worth of vegetables on an irrigated half-acre plot, significantly decreasing their living costs. Both of these examples, however, illustrate that a farmer needed financial resources to practice subsistence agriculture. The feed for Mr. Feldman's cows cost $2.40 per hundredweight, and the investment in irrigation pipe and windmill on the McKee family's farm probably dated to the years prior to the drought and depression.[34] Because of the costs involved, gardening and keeping livestock were out of reach of those most in need of the income and sustenance from these economic sidelines.

The seriousness of the farm crisis was evident in the numbers of farmers who decided that they would leave southwestern Kansas and make their living elsewhere.[35] There were large absolute declines in the number of people in all groups of southwestern Kansans (urban, rural nonfarm,

The Wiebe family of Meade County showed off their garden, irrigated by a windmill constructed from old automobile frames at a cost of two dollars. (Kansas Emergency Relief Committee photo; Kansas State Historical Society)

and rural farm), but the rural farm population experienced the most serious decline in numbers. All towns over one thousand inhabitants, save Garden City, experienced declines in total population between 1 and 37 percent. The rural nonfarm population declined in total numbers as well. However, both of these groups gained as a percentage of the total population (see Tables A.3 and A.4). The farm population followed a different trend, declining more drastically than any other group not only in absolute numbers but also relative to the urban and rural nonfarm populations (see Table A.5). The farm population fell more quickly than the total number of farms, which reinforce other evidence suggesting that most of those who left were young people. Single men and women and young married couples left the area, while their parents continued to operate the family farm.

The drought struck at the very roots of southwestern Kansas' rural communities, most evident in the loss of the rural schools. The schools were multipurpose meeting places and provided a common cause and unity to all the families in a district. The 1930s drained rural neighborhoods of their populations, and rural districts could not afford to maintain facilities and teachers for only two or three children. Before closing the schools, school boards cut budgets to the bone, forcing rural teachers to make do with starvation wages. In 1935 in Finney County, many country schoolteachers earned only $40 a month and the mean salary for rural schoolteachers in the county was $65 a month. Country schoolteachers earned $20 to $35 a month less than their colleagues in town. They, like the families and communities they served, were barely holding body and soul together.[36]

Faced with conditions that would not even provide their teachers a meager living, country school board members voted to close their neighborhood schools and send children to the next largest district or to town. Morton County residents lost eleven of their seventeen rural schools between 1937 and 1940, including those in Wilburton and Richfield (then the county seat). Although the situation in Morton County was the most extreme, all Dust Bowl counties experienced similar losses. With the schools, parents and children lost the single neighborhood institution that concerned them all, unlike churches, which potentially divided neighbor from neighbor. The population shifted toward town and took the community's most central institution with it.[37]

The farming family, as an institution, suffered as well. Many young people left their parents' farms, a painful necessity during such difficult times. Martha and George Friesen of Hamilton County watched their family scatter to the winds. Each of their three children spent large portions of the second half of the decade looking for their fortunes beyond the family farm and Hamilton County. Two children went to Oregon, and a third sought employment in other parts of western and central Kansas. Their parents' farm, which suffered persistent crop failures during those years, could not support an extended family.

Few hands made heavy work for Martha and George Friesen. Martha's work consisted of a heavy schedule of milking, caring for poultry, preserving food, sewing, cooking, and cleaning. The absence of her daughters made these tasks all the more difficult to accomplish. Dirt storms additionally complicated her work schedule, making it necessary to repeat chores she had hoped were completed. On one March day in 1937, she contemplated the effects of dust storms upon her laundry. "Today we're drying the ramains of our clothes in the house & some of them ought to be washed over & will have to be." Dirt storms had a similar effect upon other household tasks. "Dust blowed hard after midnight when we got up this morning house was all sifted full of dust. Couldn't see that Mo had it all cleaned up yesterday."[38] George faced his own problems and also suffered from his son's absence. These burdens occasionally forced him to hire extra help, adding to the cost of the farming operation.[39]

The departure of a child was an occasion for mourning. Her son's departure for work on a Civilian Conservation Corps project left Martha "very broken hearted . . . tears came in her eyes o she was so lonesome." A daughter's departure for a job in Hutchinson elicited the same response. The elder Friesens "both where very lonesome" in the days that followed.[40] Their loneliness must have been compounded by the depopulation of their township as well. By 1940, more than 40 percent of the inhabitants of Lamont Township had departed, leaving that corner of Hamilton County very empty. The pain of those who had to tear up their roots and leave has often been described, but as the Friesens' example shows, it was also acutely felt by those who remained behind, watching their families and their neighborhoods disintegrate around them.[41]

The end of the country school and the disintegration of many farm families were indicative of the losses that the people of farm communities experienced during the decade. Besides losing the ability to support themselves, they saw essential community institutions and services and their young people absorbed by the cities and towns of the area. The region had been known for its thriving, growing country neighborhoods. The depres-

An abandoned farm near Syracuse, Kansas, in 1939. (Farm Security Administration photo by Russell Lee; Library of Congress)

sion and Dust Bowl put an end to the primacy of rural institutions and focused the attentions of even the rural communities more firmly upon the towns.

As grim as the situation was, it could have been significantly worse. Undoubtedly, federal support payments to farmers through the Agricultural Adjustment Act and Soil Conservation Service restrained outward migration.[42] Although government officials claimed to support the reduction of human pressure on the land through migration out of the Great Plains, federal policy often worked against rural depopulation. Aid dollars provided by the Agricultural Adjustment Administration and Soil Conservation Service allowed farmers to struggle on, despite cropless years. Granted, officials did not always administer the farm program flawlessly, and they did not meet all of their clients' needs all of the time. Nevertheless, farming families found that they could rely upon the government to meet their basic needs most of the time and that when more help was needed, political pressure judiciously applied usually produced results. The farmers themselves found that they could alter the course of the farm program when needed. Indeed, as is seen in Chapter 6, farmers were able to defeat a land retirement program they believed to be unfair. On the whole, both the farmers and the agricultural extension agents who served them approved of the federal farm program and believed that it was instrumental in providing Dust Bowl farmers what little security they had.

Comparison of the decade from 1890 to 1900 with the decade from 1930 to 1940 helps to show the impact of federal programs on population migration. In both cases depressions diminished farm incomes and environmental conditions threatened crop production. And yet the results in terms of outward migration were far less dramatic in the 1930s. Those fourteen counties that lost population in both periods generally lost significantly greater proportions of their population during the 1890s. Losses in the 1890s were nearly double those of the 1930s.

In some ways, the greater losses of the 1890s were to be expected. Farming families had only recently settled southwestern Kansas, and it is reasonable to expect that newcomers would be less committed to the success of their farms and communities than longer-term residents. Nevertheless, what happened in the 1890s could have recurred in the 1930s. The Dust Bowl's communities had aged somewhat and the people had become more rooted, but the environmental and economic problems that plagued the residents during the thirties were far deeper and longer lasting than those of the 1890s. What farmers confronted in the 1930s was disastrous depression of agricultural prices concurrent with a nine-year drought. Without aid, only the smallest number of the Dust Bowlers could have remained.

Comparisons between aid available in the 1890s and federal aid in the 1930s help to explain greater persistence during the 1930s. Volunteers donated ninety-nine carloads of provisions and $3,154.59 in cash for stranded western Kansas farmers in 1895, and the Kansas legislature allotted $100,000 for seed grain, which local authorities distributed as loans, not gifts.[43] This barely scratched the surface, compared to federal relief activities in the 1930s. Benefit payments to farmers provided a large proportion of farm income for southwestern Kansas farmers in the 1930s. In these sixteen counties the average value of crops per farm, per year, from 1933 to 1940, was $1,663.68. The average federal benefit payment per farm, per year, was $674.32.[44] A Farm Security Administration (FSA) study of farm poverty found that southwestern Kansas was not a particularly disadvantaged rural area of the United States, and yet its farmers received one of the highest levels of aid in the country. The report concluded, "Relief has been considerably more of an emergency measure than some people have been led to believe. It was not given in great quantities in low-income areas except in cases where economic or physical catastrophes had struck."[45] High levels of aid went to chronically poor areas only when disasters, such as floods, accompanied their poverty.

By some standards, these southwestern Kansas farm incomes, even before federal aid, might have looked downright luxurious. However, they represented a substantial decline in the incomes of local farmers and certainly did not meet the operating costs of the farms, let alone the subsistence needs of the families. For example, during any given year during the thirties, the average landowner in Medway Township, Hamilton County, owed $4,600.02 on the land on his farm, as well as $765.16 in chattel mortgages.[46] This was due to the extremely high cost of doing business in this environment. Most farmers in the area worked in excess of 400 acres and needed both tractors and combines to manage that much land. The dry conditions of the decade compounded farmers' costs, since local ordinances required that blowing and drifting soil on the land be controlled. That might cost a farm owner fifty cents to a dollar per acre, per storm.

Case files from the FSA's Rural Rehabilitation Loan program provide abundant evidence that the apparently high farm incomes in southwestern Kansas in fact were not. In 1939, a Ness County farmer submitted his yearly budget to the agency. In it, he estimated that his income would amount to $1,095, deriving from crop and livestock sales, Agricultural Adjustment Administration (AAA) payments, and other miscellaneous sources. Unfortunately, his estimate fell short of his projected family expenses, which amounted to $1,210. Part of the reason for this budget shortfall was the family's inability to produce much of its own food. Drought conditions had made gardening impossible, so more than $200 had to be allotted for grocery purchases. By the end of the year, the farmer and his family were even further in debt than they had planned. The 40 acres of wheat they had planted "was entirely destroyed by rabbits" in the spring. His income evaporated before he could meet the cost of maintaining his family and his farm.[47]

Many farming families would have faced utter devastation in the absence of federal farm assistance. An FSA study of Haskell County supported the assertion that federal farm programs allowed people to remain on the land. Although income from agriculture declined steeply in the early 1930s, the benefit payments, which began in 1933, helped to control losses of farm population. Government checks allowed farmers to continue planting despite crop failures and families to stem the decline in their standard of living. The report concluded that "as compared with normal family budgets, expenditures for living during 1936 were only moderately reduced, the greatest curtailment of expenditures being made for clothing, advancement [education, reading materials], entertainment, and food." Federal payments mitigated actual distress, and "most residents have been able to remain there without suffering greatly from a lack of food and clothing." The people of Haskell County were sure that federal assistance had slowed outward migration. "Local residents estimate that the net loss of population, if they had not received Federal aid, would probably have run from 50 to 90 percent." In the end, only 26 percent of the total population of Haskell County and 43 percent of its farmers left.[48]

Federal aid, which encouraged farmers to stay on their farms, came despite government pronouncements about the necessity of migration. Policymakers generally agreed that the population of the Great Plains greatly exceeded the number of farmers that the land could support successfully without grave environmental damage. The USDA suggested that "the problem is nothing less than the total adjustment of our population to the available resources and economic opportunities." Officials of the Bureau of Agricultural Economics envisioned a program of "rural-slum clearance," "promoting proper use of soils in problem areas."[49] Continued migration out of the Great Plains was the key to this adjustment of natural to human resources. As Frances Perkins, Secretary of Labor, commented: "Even the drought refugees who have failed to settle permanently in any other new location are probably in better circumstances, both temporarily and permanently, than they would be in their former homes on the Great Plains. The best information now available indicates that large-scale interstate emigration from the Great Plains is still necessary to correct the previous oversettlement of this area."[50] Nevertheless, federal policy and federal aid continued to hold people to the land.

As much as federal officials would have liked to restructure landholding and farm size in the Great Plains and as much as it might have alleviated stress on the land, the circumstances of the thirties prevented agencies from acting. H. R. Tolley, chief of the USDA's Bureau of Agricultural Economics, stated, "We cannot afford to lose from the farms anything like half of the people now located there, even if for no other reason than the absence of a better place for them to go." The federal farm program allowed families to continue living where they were and avoided even greater overburdening of social services in areas already strained by migrating farmers—California, Oregon, and Washington.[51]

Franklin Roosevelt signed the Agricultural Adjustment Act, which created the Agricultural Adjustment Administration (AAA), on May 12, 1933. This New Deal program, financed by taxes on food processors, provided subsidies to farmers who volunteered to reduce their production. The program took months to get running because it required local committees to determine production quotas. For the farmers of southwestern Kansas, the act provided welcome relief. By the time policymakers initiated the AAA late in 1933, people were becoming desperate. By Christmas 1933 farmers were "living in hopes" that their government checks would come through. On December 2, Iman Wiatt wrote in his diary, "Everybody broke and hoping for the wheat bonus." Based on the five-year average wheat acreage planted for harvest from 1928 to 1932, farmers signed contracts to reduce their planting to 60 percent of the average production in that period. They received benefits of approximately thirty cents a bushel for the land they did not plant, again based on averaged 1928 to 1932 production. The plan also provided for allotments on corn and hogs, but most Dust Bowl farmers participated most heavily in the wheat allotment program.[52]

Government failure to deliver benefit checks immediately after the program's initiation in 1933 created some resentment among area farmers, but when they arrived before Christmas, everyone rejoiced, and area merchants noticed the first increase in sales in two years.[53] The government also aided farmers with deliveries of gasoline, kerosene, and oil to be used to fuel their tractors while working on conservation tilling. One county agent termed the plan a "God send to this county. Many of the farms would have been abandoned had the farmers not received some allotment to take care of them during the drought."[54] Dust Bowl farmers continued to benefit from the AAA until the Supreme Court declared its commodity provisions unconstitutional in 1936,[55] but while the AAA lasted, farm operators found the program indispensable.

Congress attempted to patch the holes left by the defunct AAA with the Soil Conservation and Domestic Allotment Act of 1936, which paid farmers to follow improved practices on their farms. The Soil Conservation Service (SCS) provided payments to farmers for listing their land against wind erosion, terracing, planting ground cover, and taking other conservation measures. Money received under the auspices of the

A farmer signs a wind-erosion agreement. He will receive twenty cents an acre for listing his land. (Farm Security Administration photo by Arthur Rothstein; Library of Congress)

SCS became one of the primary sources of income for the rural residents of southwestern Kansas, much as the allotment payments had been before. In 1937, the agent in Morton County claimed that federal support payments were the only source of income in his area and that compliance was nearly 100 percent. His report for 1939 showed that 98 percent of the farmers were dependent on the SCS. While other areas were not as severely depressed as Morton County, their agricultural agents credited government farm programs with saving the rural population from starvation and keeping them on the land.[56]

The hardest-pressed farmers had access to the Resettlement Administration. The RA was created to move farmers on submarginal lands off their farms and onto new farms in more suitable areas. They would be provided new houses in model communities. The Farm Security Administration largely replaced the RA, providing loans and other assistance to tenant farmers and very poor landowners. In southwestern Kansas, the FSA largely functioned as a lending agency, and administrators attempted to restructure individual farms toward greater self-sufficiency. Clients received loans, usually amounting to $12 to $15 a month. In return the agency required farmers to improve their farms through more accurate record keeping, diversified cropping, keeping livestock, and participating in subsistence activities, such as gardening and keeping chickens. Children of clients received grants to participate in 4-H programs. In Finney, Haskell, Morton, and Stanton counties, clients engaged in cooperative buying programs, and those in Finney County participated in a cooperative medical insurance plan. Under FSA medical insurance, clients paid a flat rate each year for any necessary emergency medical treatment or hospitalization. Physicians in Finney County were willing to accept this plan, in "preference to the uncertainty of payment which always exists when low-income families neglect to budget for this unexpected and inevitable expense." Through insurance and planning, FSA officials hoped to eliminate suffering and uncertainty in the lives of low-income farm families.[57]

While some aspects of the FSA program were a success, clients encountered the usual Dust Bowl troubles with subsistence gardening. The Ben F. German family of Seward County provides an example of what the "live at home" program was intended to accomplish. This family did produce enough meat, vegetables, and fruit on its farm and in its irrigated, protected garden for Mrs. German to can between five and six hundred quarts of food. They also brought enough fish home from a three-day fishing trip in Two Buttes, Colorado, to can forty quarts of fish. The food would provide the German family an adequate diet throughout the winter and early spring months when food production on the farm was at its lowest. That was what the program's clients were supposed to do: Raise and preserve enough food to meet the majority of their family's needs between harvests.[58]

But the weather did not always cooperate. In many cases, farm families working with the FSA arranged instead to purchase fruit and vegetables from truck farmers in Colorado because they were unable to raise enough to preserve. Out of eighty-six farming families on the program in Ness County in 1937, only five raised enough garden produce to meet their needs. Most ended up eating their chickens instead of keeping them for eggs, because of the lack of feed. One FSA supervisor's report about a client underscored this reality. "Their standards of living have not improved. They have tried to have a garden and increase the use of fruits and vegetables. They have not been able to raise vegetables for canning and the income from their chickens does not enable them to buy fruit."⁵⁹ Because of these realities, most FSA clients could not achieve the self-sufficiency desired by the agency.

For recipients of FSA help, participation in the program did not come without a dose of humiliation. The administration's agents collected reams of information about each client family, including yearly and quarterly budgets, accounting for their income down to the last penny. In addition to the budgeting, officials visited FSA homes regularly to ensure that the family was using the agency's funds as allowed. With the inspections came instructions on how families were to live their lives and spend their money, sometimes in excruciating detail. Helen J. Greene, a home management supervisor for Ness County, instructed one of her clients, a mother of ten children, on how she should spend their July FSA grant. "Your July Grant also includes $15.00 for clothing for the school children. We want you to buy first of all overalls for the boys and material for the girls' dresses. Buy a pretty good grade of print so that you will get a return for your labor and sewing." A mother with so much experience probably did not need these FSA instructions. Another supervisor in Ness County, unsympathetic to the dietary preferences of a family of German descent, commented, "We are planning more fruit and vegetables and less sugar next winter. As usual, it was very hard to show these people the harm in using too much sugar and carbohydrate foods."⁶⁰ These aid recipients, like those on direct relief in town, faced a choice: Endure the inconvenience and embarrassment involved in relief programs, or face the possibility of starvation.

One problem that persistently caused headaches for farmers and relief administrators alike lay in the definition of unemployment. Farmers participating in the AAA, RA, FSA, or SCS programs were periodically declared ineligible for work relief in their counties, although many found the money necessary. According to relief agencies, farmers could not be unemployed because they continued to work on their farms in spite of the drought. Therefore, they were not generally eligible for work relief. From the perspective of the farmers, however, they might as well have been unemployed, because they gained no income from their labors. After the payment of the wheat bonus in 1933, the Seward County commissioners examined their books and asked a number of farmers who received the bonus to resign from relief jobs. In 1935, the commissioners required all farmers to resign from work relief jobs and enter the homestead rehabilitation program of the RA. In 1937, the WPA notified case supervisors in all

A farmer attempts to repair his wind-blown fields. (Kansas State Cooperative Extension Service photo; Kansas State Historical Society)

counties to remove farmers from their rolls and to see that they applied to a farm program. Additionally, many counties excluded farmers from their own direct relief programs, "except in case of extreme emergency." During times of extreme hardship, or transition from one farm program to another, farming families sometimes found themselves unable to feed their families or pay their bills.[61]

The farmers' representatives protested to Washington, venting their frustration and anger with the failure of federal relief to cover all the needs of their constituents. During the transition from the AAA to the SCS in the spring of 1936, the Resettlement Supervisor in Gray County advised the county commissioners that subsistence grants for families not yet on a standard RA plan would be discontinued. The commissioners then discovered that the RA would accept no more applications for initial loans on standard yearly plans. The commissioners urged Harry Hopkins, head of the WPA, that "subsistence grants be continued in Gray County for another 60 days" and that the administration give farmers whatever assistance they needed to save the soil and become self-supporting in the future. It is unclear what immediate aid the farmers in Gray County received. However, in December 1936, an administrator for the WPA assured Sen. George McGill of Kansas that any "drought sufferers" dropped from WPA rolls would be accepted without investigation by the RA and would receive their first months' grant. Only after the agency

A 1939 scene from an abandoned farm near Syracuse. (Farm Security Administration photo by Russell Lee; Library of Congress)

provided for pressing needs would families be reviewed and accepted or rejected as continuing clients.[62]

In 1938, farmers and their representatives were again in an uproar about restrictions on direct and work relief to those covered by the agricultural program. A group of senators and representatives from the Dust Bowl states pleaded for exceptions to WPA rules in drought-stricken counties. The congressmen asked that the WPA make allowances for the "emergency situation" existing in the affected areas and to provide work to farmers that would feed their families and help to conserve a "national resource, namely our soil." A memo from within the WPA suggested that farmers could indeed be employed to list their own land to prevent blowing and recommended that the program be implemented in twenty counties, including Stevens, Seward, Grant, Kearny, Haskell, Hamilton, and Stanton counties in Kansas.[63] Listing consisted of plowing deep furrows in a field, at right angles to the prevailing winds. The wind would move the dirt into the furrows, instead of blowing it away completely. Once the furrows filled with dirt, the farmer would have to list his land again. An unfortunate side effect of listing was that the soil eventually became pulverized and blew even more easily. Farmers did eventually receive federal money, at approximately fifty cents an acre, to list their lands.

Struggles with the federal bureaucracy were for most Dust Bowl farmers, however, the acceptable and necessary cost of remaining on their land. Given the choice between starvation, relocation, or government aid, most chose the latter, exchanging the uncertainties of independence for the relative security of a government check, although the money often came with strings attached. The outcome of federal farm programs within the Dust Bowl was a rural population that was far more stable than could have been expected otherwise. The 1890s and that decade's massive exodus provide a point of comparison, although the circumstances of the two depressions are not exactly comparable. The farmers of the 1930s entered the Great Depression with heavier investments in land and equipment than their forebears, and the extent of this depression offered them little chance to move and succeed in farming elsewhere. Thus, the economic and environmental troubles that area residents faced in the 1930s were deeper and longer lasting than those of earlier decades. That so many stayed through the 1930s was, in part, a testament to the successes of the federal farm program.

6. DOWN BUT NOT OUT

Although persistent crop failures rendered farmers throughout Dust Bowl Kansas highly dependent upon relief throughout the 1930s, they did not accept their poverty passively, and they did not stop searching for ways out of their environmental and economic dilemma. Throughout the decade, the farmers of southwestern Kansas developed alternative sources of income, demanded attention from Washington, and sought increasingly to adapt their agriculture to the plains, or the plains to their conception of agriculture. Whether farm families were finding new ways to market their products or discussing the possibilities of irrigation, they were attempting to alter their farming operations to meet the demands of nature. Although innovation could not end the drought and did not allow most farmers to free themselves from dependence upon government programs, these efforts reflected the commitment of the persisting population to the future of their region.[1]

Hanging on for year after disappointing year required a stubbornness and determination that not everyone could muster. Lawrence Svobida's autobiographical account of farming in Meade County, entitled *Empire of Dust* (reissued as *Farming the Dust Bowl*), described the tenacity required of Dust Bowl farmers and the ways in which that tenacity could be eroded by too many years of bad luck. Svobida moved from Nebraska to Meade County, Kansas, in 1929. His timing was poor. In the first year, he lost most of his wheat crop to hail, although enough survived for him to judge the year a success. His 1931 crop, like those all over Kansas, was record-setting, but because of the price crash he earned barely enough to cover his expenses. As he remarked, he "still had to make good as a wheat farmer." Instead, he lost nearly every crop until 1939, when he gave up his farm to "drift with the tide."[2]

In the years before disaster overcame Svobida, however, he showed the persistence and dedication that allowed people all over the Dust Bowl to continue farming. In 1932, he sowed his wheat in dry soil, hoping that the necessary moisture would come. When it looked as if his wheat would fail, he planted barley. Both crops blew out in terrific spring gales. Svobida continued to hope for a crop, listed his land to prevent blowing, and planted maize (sorghum). Unfortunately, he lost his maize as well. The next year, he planted wheat and maize again, only to lose two more crops. What followed was a succession of plantings and losses, typical of the experience of farmers throughout the area. Through heroic efforts, Svobida harvested a small crop of wheat in 1938, only to experience a total loss in 1939. Although his attempt to farm the Dust Bowl failed, there was little to criticize in the degree of effort he poured into his farm. He, like thousands of others across southwestern Kansas, planted their crops, replanted them when they blew out, and tended their fields to prevent their destruction and the destruction of neighboring lands. As in Svobida's case, the attempts were often futile, but they represented the best that the farmers could do for their families and for themselves.

Most farming families followed the same path as Svobida, planting and replanting fields and hoping that the effort would bear fruit. They knew, though, that they were unlikely to earn a living for themselves and their families through their usual farming activities. As a result, many families ventured into agricultural and household experimentation. They improvised and adapted their farming enterprises in order to earn what little they could. One Seward County farmer found that the surest way to earn an income from his hogs was to sell them outside the usual channels. Instead of taking the animals to market, where he received pitifully low prices, he butchered the hogs and took the meat to Liberal. There he sold it door-to-door to the employees of Panhandle Eastern Pipeline Company, who received better incomes than most of their neighbors. As his son later commented, the meat "sold good to people who could afford it." The Scheer family of Finney County operated on the same principle, selling homemade butter, cottage cheese, and fresh eggs to regular clients in Garden City. Through this strategy and great frugality, the widowed Mrs. Scheer fed her family and aided her brothers through the depression.[3]

A group of ten Mennonite farmers in Gray County decided to diversify their holdings by raising leghorn chickens in large, adobe barns. The Penner family joined this community effort and constructed a twenty-by-forty-foot chicken house for their flocks, as well as several other struc-

Mrs. Penner with her chicken house, made from adobe bricks manufactured by the Mennonite community. (By permission of Daniel Penner and Elfreda Penner Fast)

Daniel Penner (in the suit) with friends, showing his sheep and adobe sheep pen. (By permission of Daniel Penner)

tures. The barn kept the chickens cool, healthy, and dust free. A son, Daniel, succeeded in making good quality feed for the chickens, at low cost. He built a cooker from a fifteen-gallon barrel and in it boiled down rabbits brought home from rabbit drives. He claimed that the "high protein diet really caused the chickens to lay eggs."[4]

Those who had horses and could grow the forage crops necessary to feed them reverted to horse power. Horses worked without benefit of costly oil, gasoline, and parts. Many a farmer, short on feed, cut the Russian thistles from his fields and fed them to his cattle. As long as the farmer cut them while they were green and not yet dried to their hard, spiny, tumbleweed form, cattle generally ate them. Farmers sometimes cured the thistles with salt to improve their flavor.[5]

In 1934, the women of the Ford County Farm Bureau organized a farmers' market in Dodge City. They sold cakes, bread, other baked goods, dressed chickens, fresh meat, cheese, noodles, and other home and farm products. The market was still in operation five years later, and several women reported that the proceeds had helped them put their children through school.[6]

There was plenty of opportunity for economizing around farm homes as well. If oleomargarine could be purchased for six cents a pound and cream could be sold for fifteen cents a pound, then women served their families oleomargarine instead of butter. The foam from the top of skim milk gave the illusion of marshmallows when a family could not afford to buy them for their cocoa. People reverted to the humblest of fuels, cow "chips," to heat their homes. The Scheer family made do with half a load of coal each winter and only burned it in the parlor stove when company came. Otherwise, they burned cow chips for heat, used corn cobs for baking, and largely confined themselves to the kitchen. One man, with more inge-nuity than scruples, waited until his neighbors were away and then cut down their fence posts for fuel. Families did their own sewing and canning when possible.[7] Money saved could be applied to rent, taxes, fuel bills, and the other unavoidable costs of living.

Family cooperation, important to people in town, was just as important in the country. Adult children with jobs in cities sent money home to their parents, and parents sometimes sent their children to town. A farm girl in Seward County moved to Liberal with her mother, brother, and sister at the height of the dust storms. Forced to leave school two years earlier because of the depression, she worked at the five-and-dime store and helped to support her sister who was attending high school. Of the seven dollars she earned every week, three went to her mother.[8] Other children contributed to the family income or reduced their parents' financial burdens by taking jobs off of the farm. Children of high school age whose parents were on relief were eligible for jobs with the NYA.[9] Older children often ventured farther afield to work in agricultural communities that actually needed harvest hands. One young man from a strict Mennonite community scandalized the neighbors by going away to work during the harvest in Corn, Oklahoma. He earned between $2.50 and $3.00 a day.[10] Martha Friesen's son, Will, traveled throughout the southwestern United States picking cotton and later went to California and Oregon. He, like thousands of other farm children, was earning his own living, relieving pressure on his parents' slender resources.[11]

Kin connections tied many country dwellers to townspeople, and these relationships were sometimes a great benefit to both groups. The grown children of farming families sometimes made their way into town, and their incomes often helped to sustain their parents through these difficult years. In 1933, the Swafford family moved from a farm near Pratt to a farm in Seward County. A couple of their children who lived in Liberal contributed part of their income to this endeavor.[12] Well-established rural parents might also contribute to their urban children's well-being. Pauline Renick Owens remembered the ways in which her grandparents, living on a Seward County farm, helped to maintain her parents' household. Her father, known locally as "Andy the Iceman," saw his income fall by half in the early years of the depression. In spite of this, the family "always ate well," a fact she at least partially attributed to her grandparents' additions of meat and eggs to their diet. They also moved in with her grandparents temporarily, trying to live rent free while growing vegetables and raising chickens. Although this effort ultimately failed, it is a good illustration of the interdependence between the rural and urban communities.[13]

Extra income was squeezed out of what little time farm women could spare above and beyond their normal work routines. Hazel Shriver of Kearny County worked as a substitute teacher when she could, as did Louise Schroeder of Jetmore. When Mrs. Schroeder's husband found work with the highway crew in town, she carried on with the farm work, because she "could run a tractor the same as he could." More members of the family in the work force meant a better chance of holding the farm for another year.[14]

The goal of all this effort was not necessarily to make a profit, but to find a way to hang on until "next year." This year's wind blew crops from the ground, and this year's rain refused to fall, but next year would surely bring better times. A writer for the *Elkhart Tri-State News* expressed this attitude, writing that "with one good crop year this section will be on its feet and if the weather man will just give us a break (or even a cloud burst), next spring will put us right. Here's hopin'."[15] An exchange between a father and daughter was equally illustrative of the "next year" spirit. When the father talked about his plans for the ranch "when it rained," the daughter, "with the arrogance of a teenager," said, "Don't you mean if it rains?" "He said, 'Oh no, it will rain, it always has.'"[16] Although historian Donald Worster declared this attitude a form of "lunacy," it was, as he admitted, a result of living and farming in this particular environment.[17] Farmers expected to have a crop failure once every five years and moderate to overwhelming success in the intervening years. But nothing had prepared them for a bumper crop followed by eight years of total or near crop failure. It was not lunacy but their recent experience on the Great Plains that sustained Dust Bowl farmers. The promise of better times and the memory of the fruits of 1931 kept families going when the skies were their blackest. Those who maintained their stubbornness and faith in the slow-coming rain into the forties ultimately received the rewards of their tenacity.

Resident farmers also poured their energies into efforts to obtain political solutions to their troubles. Voting by Dust Bowl residents reflected a desire to search outside the usual channels for aid. In this traditionally Republican corner of a Republican state, people voted for Franklin D. Roosevelt, the Democratic presidential candidate, when he seemed to be their best hope. They "became Democrats" for "the only time in our lives" during the presidential elections of 1932 and 1936, as one woman confessed.[18] It was indeed noteworthy when southwestern Kansas voted with the nation in 1932 in electing Roosevelt. In 1936, the area's people again voted Democratic, with farmers particularly supporting Roosevelt. A straw poll of rural voters in Finney County showed them to be casting their ballots for the president by a margin of almost two to one.[19] As the *Garden City Daily Telegram* reported: "Regardless of what one thinks of the new deal in general and irrespective of political affiliations, it should be reassuring to know that there is at least one class of people in the country [the farmers] which appreciates the help it has received and which is willing to show its gratitude in the face of growing opposition to the president."[20] By 1940, however, the farmers' brief foray into Democratic presidential politics was over. Although Clark County voters supported Roosevelt by a narrow eleven votes, Wendell Willkie carried the rest of the Kansas Dust Bowl. By that point, their need of the New Deal farm program was waning, and they preferred to return to their traditional support for Republican presidential candidates.[21]

Farmers also approached their problems through protest actions directed at the perceived sources of their trouble. During the wheat strike of 1931, farmers sought to raise the price of wheat to a dollar a bushel. Although this attempt failed, protests against other perceived injustices followed. In an isolated incident in 1933, Meade County farmers banded together to prevent foreclosure on a farmer's land. Three years later, approximately 250 residents of Stevens and Seward counties petitioned the secretary of agriculture, Henry Wallace, the Emergency Drought Relief Committee, and several other officials and agencies to undertake a study to "determine the actual cost and advisability of irrigation in this area." In the same year, three hundred farmers protested possible bias in the distribution of the crop allotments in Morton County. The county's farm operators, believing that the committee had apportioned the lion's share of the allowable acres to the large farmers at the expense of the small, forced the committee in charge to reappraise their lands.[22]

The best known of the farm organizations to arise out of the Dust Bowl was the Southwest Agricultural Association, which attracted farmers from the five affected southwestern plains states—Kansas, Oklahoma, Texas, Colorado, and New Mexico. In April 1937, its Farm Practice and Legislative Committee met to discuss what action the association should support. Committee members endorsed four courses of action: First, that the compliance date for wind erosion control measures be extended by a month; second, that farmers be paid more than seventy-five cents an acre for conservation work; third, that all farmers be required to leave fourteen inches of stubble on harvested land; and finally, that cover crops be established not only on land under cultivation, but on abandoned land as well. The committee suggested that this could best be accomplished by "an authority set up within the confines of the Dust Bowl."[23]

What followed was a drive to organize members of the association for a regional meeting to be held in May 1937. Leaders within the organization sent a telegram to President Roosevelt explaining the action they believed necessary to halt large-scale devastation:

Drouth conditions in the Dust Bowl have reached emergency state requiring drastic action. We appeal to the federal government for the preservation of life and property in the Dust Bowl. . . . Work must be done under federal supervision working the soil with an army of trac-tors and listers planting seed with the first operation and covering the area systematically under orders beginning at the south and west sides of the Dust Bowl leaving no cultivated land untouched and proceed until the entire area is covered.[24]

The organization also requested that the government declare an emer-gency and "place martial law in effect throughout the Dust Bowl" in order to forestall the "utter destruction of our soil." They followed this telegram with a flood of communications to area governors, including Walter Hux-man of Kansas. In a letter to Huxman, H. A. Kinney, the secretary of the Chamber of Commerce in Liberal, wrote that the destruction of land throughout the area was serious and becoming worse. Careless farmers let their fields drift onto their neighbors' lands, and financial woes kept even good farmers from adequately meeting the dust menace. Kinney wrote that "the problem in the 'dust bowl' is entirely too large for the remaining good farmers to even make a start to cope with. They must have help and it's imperative they have help now."[25] Although Governor Huxman was unwilling to declare martial law, he was ready to "do anything I can and take all proper steps to be of assistance to the effected [sic] area." He promised to send his representative to an upcoming association meeting.[26]

These efforts culminated in a meeting at Boise City, Oklahoma, on May 12, 1937. Six hundred and fifty farmers and the representatives of four governors attended and issued a call for the creation of a "Dust Bowl Authority," "a little TVA for the Dust Bowl region," to combat the problems generated by the drought. The assembled farmers discussed and passed a five-part resolution requesting a coordinated, comprehensive response to the drought, including increased efforts in the areas of water conservation, flood control, and retirement of nonproductive lands.[27]

Although government officials initially appeared to greet the program favorably, Secretary of Agriculture Henry Wallace announced within the week that he saw no reason for a special authority, outside the operating farm program.[28] Ray Jackson, chairman of the board of directors of the association, alleged that Wallace's objections stemmed from his fear that a Dust Bowl authority, purchasing land at low government rates, would depress land values throughout the region. Jackson thought that this was nonsense. "If he would come out here he would find we have no land values in the dust bowl to be hurt, and the only way land values can ever be restored will be through a government program that will really do work."29 Wallace was unswayed, but despite the rejection, the members of the association continued to agitate for agricultural reform along the lines suggested in the original resolution. Even though support for the group was by no means unanimous (a group of twenty-six Morton County farmers announced their disapproval in the local paper), the Southwest Agricultural Association was the largest and most vocal of all protest groups in the Dust Bowl region and could claim much of the responsibility for keeping the problems of Dust Bowl farmers in the minds of lawmakers in both Kansas and Washington, D.C.30

Farmers in southwestern Kansas were trying to discover a way to stay on the land and make their agricultural operations profitable again—a goal that seemed as elusive in 1939 as it had in 1935. Suggestions for reform ranged from greater diversification to an assortment of conservation measures to irrigation. All of these proposals received at least a limited trial during the 1930s.

The agricultural agents of the extension service talked about diversification mostly as a means of stabilizing farm incomes. Their calls for "live at home" programs at the decade's outset were essentially pleas for greater diversity in the farm enterprise. They hoped that chickens, pigs, and less reliance upon wheat as a primary crop would foster a more stable, prosperous farming community. Indeed, this focus upon self-sufficiency was also a central concern of early New Deal planners, who hoped to return Americans to an earlier era of Jeffersonian competency.31 Despite the challenges that the 1930s presented to this program, it remained a recurring theme in the advice to farmers.

In 1940, the Ford County agricultural agent outlined his plan for prosperity in a feature story entitled "Let's Look at the Facts." He wrote that wheat had "made this country rich," but that it was also the crop that had reduced the area to its current wind-blown, poverty-stricken condition. Thus, the area had become a magnet for federal money, but he asked, "What good has that money done?" Although it had fed thousands of farm households and had kept families on the land and off the WPA, these people would be left desolate if the farm program ceased to exist.

Instead, he proposed a diversified farm program, which he called a "sound farm program," to improve the prospects of farmers throughout the region. "Row crop on summerfallow land for feed and grain. A dozen cows on every 640 acres of land, one half dozen brood sows, a couple of hundred good laying hens and 100 turkeys. That will make them a living, pay taxes, interest, and then if you, Mr. Farmer, must gambel [sic], put the rest of your ground to wheat." He acknowledged that this plan would force farmers to work harder, but he noted that the farmer planting 800 acres of wheat only worked 411 hours during the year, and "no man ever was truly successful who loafed ¾ of the time."[32]

Diversification was a compelling idea but one that was not always practical at the height of the drought. C. C. Isely, a Ford County businessman, cherished the same idea of self-sufficiency and attempted to implement it through a housing and subsistence farming project funded by the Reconstruction Finance Corporation. He located his project near Dodge City along the Arkansas River and named it Wilroads Gardens. Isely believed that small irrigated farms would allow the poor a chance to pull their own weight. He called his settlement a "self-help project" and planned a community of approximately one thousand "neat, attractive and sanitary" homes. The project began in 1933, but by 1935, the residents of Wilroads Gardens were in "a most tragic situation," unable even to raise chickens, despite their access to river water. T. L. Ferratt, an RFC official who visited the project in April 1939, wondered how the residents were able to survive.[33] The residents of Wilroads Gardens endured the depression and drought but never managed to establish a successful subsistence project because so many arrived with few resources. The settlement functioned more as a housing project than as a community of small, self-sufficient farmers.[34]

In the midst of the Dust Bowl, conservation seemed to farmers to be a more likely means than diversification by which to gain some control over their fields and futures. Farmers experimented with new farming tools and methods. One such method was listing. Farmers used listers to plow especially deep furrows, hoping that the prevailing winds would blow loose dirt into the furrows instead of their neighbors' fields. Duckfoot cultivators killed weeds, but left the debris on the surface of the field, protecting it against wind erosion. Contour plowing and terracing helped to protect the soil and capture what little moisture was available. Informed farmers could take advantage of these methods or others to try to preserve the fertility of their lands.[35] Unfortunately, their use was not universal, and many a farmer, Svobida included, saw their efforts ruined by the inactivity of their neighbors. A single blowing field could ruin the prospects of a whole community of farmers by smothering seedlings or cutting them off at ground level.

Mindful of this fact, Kansas law allowed county commissioners to enact "soil drifting" resolutions. A typical county resolution, adopted in Ness County, read as follows: "Under authority of Sec. 19-2611 of the revised statutes of 1923, the Board of County Commissioners will cause all lands in Ness county subject to excessive soil drifting which have not been cultivated by the owner to keep from drifting on adjoining lands to be strip listed and a reasonable charge be levied against said land."[36] In most counties, the commissioners worked out cooperative plans with the extension and farmers to survey lands periodically for soil blowing hazards or asked farmers to report problems in their neighbor's fields. Although disgruntled farmers, who were often nonresidents, periodically challenged this authority in court, soil drifting laws remained in force in one form or another throughout the 1930s.[37] The district court in Haskell County even upheld the right of a farmer to enter a neighbor's field and cultivate it to prevent soil from blowing onto his property.[38]

Based upon their concerns about erosion control, farmers throughout the region protested government attempts to decrease conservation payments through restrictions on the number of eligible acres on individual farms. Most Dust Bowl farmers worked large farms, and many had assumed the task of caring for abandoned lands. A member of the Grant County conservation committee protested limitations to Sen. George McGill. "The Dust Bowl would be in lots worse shape than at present if some of the operators had not the Guts to take over the deserted farms and tried to prevent the soil from all blowing away. They were able to do this only by means of ACP [Agricultural Conservation Program] payments." The SCS made ACP payments to farmers to encourage and assist them in carrying out conservation practices such as improving soil fertility, minimizing erosion, and conserving resources. In their successful fight against acreage restrictions on conservation payments, farmers maintained the funding (fifty to seventy-five cents an acre) that made it possible for them to comply with local soil blowing ordinances.[39]

Beyond these simple measures farmers were not always willing to proceed. Although they petitioned the government for a massive, federally sponsored erosion control program in 1937, they were less enthused about federally initiated programs, such as the organization of conservation

A farmer listing his fields to fight wind erosion. (Farm Security Administration photo by Arthur Rothstein; Library of Congress)

Terrace construction on a Seward County farm in 1937. (Soil Conservation Service photo; Library of Congress)

districts, which administrators began to try to organize in that same year, and a land acquisition program, which began in earnest in 1938. Perhaps this lack of enthusiasm on the part of the region's farmers stemmed from confusion about the programs, lack of local control over federal policies, or anger at having their own suggestions ignored. Ray Jackson, a spokesman for the Southwest Agricultural Association, suggested that this last was indeed the case.

One of Jackson's strongest criticisms of the government, when protesting Secretary of Agriculture Wallace's failure to endorse a "Dust Bowl authority," was that the government was rejecting a farmer-developed solution. He argued that "if we are going to have cooperation, it should begin with the making of the program; the farmer should have a voice in it—something they have never had yet." He linked farmer cooperation with farmer participation in the policy development process and further urged that policymakers be required to come to the Dust Bowl "and STAY until the program is written and approved," in order to guarantee its success. Because federal solutions were not their own, many farmers questioned their efficacy in fighting the drought.[40]

Under the Soil Conservation Service, organized in 1935, farmers were allowed to form soil conservation districts. Although a majority usually cast their ballots in favor of organizing these districts, farmers regularly failed to give them the three-quarters vote necessary for approval. In some counties farmers voted every six months, as allowed by law, and rejected the districts just as regularly. Observers blamed the stalemate on a lack of understanding about the districts and fear of the compulsory aspects of the program. If the program passed, the district members would have wide powers to impose conservation measures following a vote by those occupying the land and would have police powers with which to compel farmers to obey ordinances. Officials at the USDA admitted that some conservation measures imposed by members of the districts might be unprofitable to the individual operator. Many farmers feared that required conservation measures might well restrict profits during periods of abundant moisture.[41]

Area residents were even less enthusiastic about government plans to buy up hundreds of thousands of acres of dry and unproductive land in southwestern Kansas. This displeasure, however, was not immediately apparent when government officials broached the subject in 1935. Although they thought $2.75 an acre was too little, many Stevens County farmers appeared indifferent to the plan on first hearing. An editorial in the *Johnson Pioneer* seemed to support the government. The editor did not want to see farmers moved by force but reasoned that not "even the wildest booster" could claim that "not an acre of this section is submarginal." Some land was too poor to farm, and farmers could eke out only a meager existence if they insisted on farming it. The editor of the *Garden City Daily Telegram* was equally accepting of federal land purchases, provided that the government directed its efforts against farmers who failed to follow conservation practices. There were "'sub-marginal' land users who must be driven out" to make way for "conscientious, cooperating" farmers. This seeming assent to government plans to control and manage hundreds of thousands of acres of land coincided with the worst dust storms of the entire decade.[42]

Given the severity of conditions in 1937, the members of the Farm Practice Committee of the Southwest Agricultural Association endorsed land retirement. Although they gave up the idea of a Dust Bowl authority after Secretary of Agriculture Wallace's rejection, they continued to demand that the government take an active role in solving the area's problems, even to the extent of encouraging increased government land ownership. In resolutions published June 25, 1937, they outlined their plans for government action: "Submarginal land should be returned to grass. Either by government purchase and control or through paying a reasonable benefit to the owner who will put the land under control and protect it against grazing or erosion until such time as it has a productive value for grazing purposes."[43] Again, these plans coincided with a time of great environmental stress. For the region's farmers, 1937 was nearly as bad a year as 1935, and people were increasingly pessimistic about the chances for a quick end to the drought.

When the Farm Security Administration began its land buying program in Morton County, however, the affected farmers reacted with greater resistance.[44] Although farmers in the Wilburton area voted to accept land sales, they objected to being resettled by the FSA and to the large-scale land purchases, without regard to the virtues of the individual farm. After considering the program, the editor of the local newspaper commented that the idea of reseeding the area to grass was a bit dubious, "but commendable." Farmers and local observers at first tended to accept federal intervention as long as it seemed to be the only option.[45]

However, within a year, farmers in Morton County were petitioning Washington to discontinue the land purchases. Federal agents had acquired 55,000 acres and appeared to be emptying entire townships. The two townships where most of the government acquisitions occurred, Jones and Cimarron, lost the majority of their farmers. Jones Township was home to forty-one farming families in 1930. In 1940, ten families resided there, and another five farmers owned land as absentees. Cimarron Township began the decade with forty-eight families and ended it with seventeen and one absentee. Federally sponsored depopulation disturbed and angered many residents.[46]

Protesters criticized government officials and their administration of the program on a number of grounds. The residents alleged that FSA officers were purchasing good land, as well as bad, and "soliciting business" even from farmers who were doing comparatively well. Those farmers who sold their land found themselves "forced on to the W.P.A." Additionally, they worried that the tax base would be damaged beyond redemption should more land pass into government hands. Congressman Clifford Hope joined in the protest, commenting that "too much government owned land means too few farmers to make business."[47] Z. W. Johnson, the county agricultural extension agent, protested too. In a letter to the area's elected officials, he outlined his objections. The government was "buying the best land and refusing the poor, . . . forcing the tenants into town and upon relief rolls." According to Johnson, the county would have been better off had the residents remained and "aided in controlling our wind erosion problem. So many people leaving has thrown a double load upon the few who have remained." The federal land buy-out seemed to be working counter to the original proposal and against the best interests of the people of Morton County.[48]

The protests against federal purchases of land in Morton County eventually succeeded. In 1938, under the provisions of the Bankhead-Jones Farm Tenant Act, the Soil Conservation Service took control of the federally owned lands in Morton County. In the spring of 1939, the government buyers suspended their activities in the county and confined themselves to the administration and rehabilitation of the land they had purchased.[49] Between 1938 and 1954, the SCS worked to reseed and improve the (approximately) 107,000 acres of land in Morton County under its supervision. Since 1954, the Forest Service has overseen this project, now called the Cimarron National Grassland.[50]

In retrospect, the weather may have been the biggest consideration in determining the farmers' willingness to cooperate with federal farm programs such as land retirement. The most comprehensive of the land preservation schemes from Washington, D.C., came in the years from 1937 to 1939. Although 1937 was the second driest year of the decade, 1938 provided a slight reprieve, and some farmers harvested a small crop. So just as the government was initiating its land retirement program and other more comprehensive land-use planning, farmers were beginning to see the waning of hard times. It was difficult for them to accept government propositions that they found meddlesome when it appeared they might be able to make a living in the near future without federal intervention.

Area farmers found commitment to long-term conservation plans or acceptance of radical changes in land management less attractive than the idea of irrigation. Many residents of the Dust Bowl believed that use of underground water resources provided the best opportunity on a long-term basis to avoid the hazards of the semiarid environment. Farmers along the Arkansas River already irrigated some of their fields, and the drought encouraged others to explore the possibilities of abundant groundwater. Because of the Ogallala Aquifer underlying most of southwestern Kansas, farmers generally could pump enough water for their cattle, even if they did not have enough for forage crops. They reasoned that the same water could be used to protect their fields from drought.[51]

Although large-scale irrigation did not become a reality until the 1950s, Dust Bowl farmers experimented with a few projects during the 1930s. Talk in the early years of the decade led to demonstration projects in its middle years to a few wells by the end of the decade. Newspapers were liberally sprinkled with stories of farmers putting in pumping equipment and their neighbors coming over to inspect and observe. In 1937, the people of the Liberal area were so excited by the drilling of the first deep well in their vicinity that they held a celebration. "A parade was held in Liberal this afternoon at 1:30 o'clock, showing the practical visions of the various merchants or just what irrigation in this region would mean. The parade then wound its way to the well, where hundreds of people and cars gathered to watch the spudding ceremony."[52]

Although there were a few dissenting voices, many farmers believed in the power of irrigation to retrieve their shattered fortunes. Federal money made it a possibility even in hard times; farmers in Kearny, Gray, Ford, and Finney counties became eligible for grants to install pump irrigation on their farms, in return for implementing sound land management practices.[53] Irrigation provided the one thing they did not have—water— although at a cost. But the water came without the extra hours and seeming coercion of conservation districts or the community outrage generated by land retirement programs.

Irrigation affirmed the possibilities inherent in their land instead of emphasizing its faults, an appealing concept to people who were tired of hearing their land classed as "submarginal." Instead of discussing limitations, irrigation's proponents emphasized the seemingly boundless availability of underground water resources. And, in the 1930s, there was little concern about the long-term environmental implications of large-scale irrigation that surfaced in later years.[54] To desperate farmers, it seemed like the ideal solution. Although the return of the rains in 1940 postponed large-scale ventures into irrigated agriculture, the idea remained and took root, for use in later decades.

In making these plans, the people of southwestern Kansas were not acting out of any perverse compulsion to ruin the land, as some environmental historians have suggested. They were ordinary people, trying to support their families under extraordinarily bad circumstances. The decisions that farming families made about land use were shaped by the problems that they faced in the here and now. They made short-term decisions based on a desire to put food on their tables and keep roofs over their heads. Hanging on to their farms for another year was uppermost in their concerns. They made long-term decisions without any knowledge that federal farm programs would be a staple of life in years to come and with the fresh memory of ten years of Dust Bowl conditions. They sought to capitalize upon the known strengths of their region and to act upon their immediate need to see the fruits of their labors. Plans made under these conditions were unlikely to bear the stamp of the long-range environmental concerns of the latter half of the twentieth century.

7. FACING A CRISIS
OF CONFIDENCE

If the problem of day-to-day survival could be put aside, the greatest challenge facing southwestern Kansans was the re-creation of the area's image, essential to the continuing viability of their communities. The state had traditionally received little national attention, except for "Bleeding Kansas" and the troubles of the Civil War. The natural disasters of the 1930s thrust southwestern Kansas into the spotlight, and, as in the case of the Morton County land buy-out, much of the attention was unwanted and unflattering. Although the area's residents needed government aid to survive the drought and dust, successful appeals brought more scrutiny. Government officials descended upon the area in droves, and soon they were issuing bleak reports about a ruined land and incompetent farming. They suggested also that local farmers were unfit to manage the land and that they would be wise to move on to greener pastures. The national press echoed much of this criticism. Writer upon writer blamed farmers for their own plight and publicized the terrors of life in the Dust Bowl. The problems of people of the Dust Bowl became public property.

The editors of southwestern Kansas newspapers believed themselves duty-bound to fight back. Adverse publicity from the government and the press threatened the area's sense of identity and its people's ability to maintain viable communities and farms. If so negative a description of the area remained unchallenged, the residents of the towns and counties of the Dust Bowl could hardly expect to attract tourists or trade or to see migrants return from their wanderings. Few local boosters could hope that their messages would travel far, but self-respect demanded a response.[1] The nation might be down on Kansas, but in the 1930s southwestern Kansans, despite adversity, were decidedly "up."

Many of the first reports of Dust Bowl conditions provided to the general public came from the federal government. After several years of drought, depression, and searching for solutions, Congress authorized the Great Plains Committee to study the problems of the Dust Bowl and to suggest strategies to fight the effects of drought and depression throughout the Great Plains. One of the committee's 1936 reports described the area as a devastated, denuded landscape. "Today we see foothills shorn of timber, deeply gullied, useless or rapidly losing their fertile soil under unwise cultivation; the fertile earth itself drifts with the wind in sand hills and dust clouds." The devastation affected more than the land. "Men struggle vainly for a living on too few acres . . . communities, for all the courage of their people, fall into decay, with poor schools, shabby houses, the sad cycle of tax sales, relief, aimless migrations."[2] The situation, the author concluded, was hopeless.

Other government studies came to the same conclusion and placed much of the blame for this state of affairs on the area's residents. Although a measure of the blame was attributed to the difficult climate and past federal policies that failed to take it adequately into account, the critics stressed inept farming and ranching methods. Writers in government publications were careful to avoid personal attacks, but the farmer was obviously the villain. Who else could be responsible for "extreme" levels of "soil misuse?"[3] The writers traced the problem to "destruction of millions of acres of . . . natural cover," caused "partly by over-grazing, partly by excessive plowing." "The settlers lacked both the knowledge and the incentive necessary to avoid these mistakes." Hugh Bennett and Frederick Fowler, the report's authors, painted a picture of inept, profit-chasing farmers being led astray by an equally inept government.[4] To the accused farmers, this was a harsh assessment.

Carried to their logical conclusion, such criticisms implied that the people of the plains were unfit to manage their own land and that the federal government should become the chief agricultural planner for the area. Indeed, the federal government both advocated and carried out management programs throughout the plains. Those in favor of government management argued that a fragile environment had already been ruined by improper agricultural practices and ill-conceived federal policy. The time had come for new policies that would restore the health of the land and improve the quality of life for the people. The Great Plains Drought Area Committee suggested complete restructuring of land use throughout the stricken area. "The necessary steps are clearly indicated. The region should be divided into sub-areas according to the types of use to which each portion of it may best and most safely be devoted; and, in addition, to determine the kinds of agricultural practice and engineering treatment required to fit each portion to its indicated use." In some areas, the committee's strategy included removing land from private to government ownership. The USDA concluded that "some areas should be retired completely from agriculture." Planners made all of these suggestions believing that experts could succeed in managing the plains where the farming population had failed. [5]

Inherent in each of these schemes was the notion that depopulation of the plains was not necessarily a bad idea. Time and again, writers stressed that the land was being taxed beyond its carrying capacity. There were too many farmers, too much livestock, and too many plowed fields for the health of the land. Equally, the resources of these plains communities did not adequately support the population. In 1937, an author reporting in the *Monthly Labor Review* commented that the "exodus from the Great Plains is clearly desirable, in spite of the distress of the refugees." Furthermore, "to return this area to its best economic use, emigration from the Great Plains would have to proceed continuously at the present rate for more than a decade." The Secretary of Labor, Frances Perkins, testified in 1940 that even those who had fled the drought and had not found new homes on the West Coast were "probably in better circumstances, both temporarily and permanently, than they would be in their former homes on the Great Plains."[6] Although all concerned saw problems with the pell-mell flight of people from drought-stricken areas, many believed that the refugees were quite literally on their way to greener pastures. Federal planners held out little hope for the people and communities of the Great Plains.

Press commentary issuing from outside the Dust Bowl was even more harsh than government criticism. A steady stream of articles about the drought and dust storms appeared in magazines and newspapers as it became apparent that the area's troubles were persisting. In general, writers were unkind in their judgments of the abilities of plains farmers and often more personal than the authors of government reports. Their descriptions of life in the suffering states sometimes challenged credibility. At its height, the Dust Bowl made good copy, and critics exploited the disaster to the fullest extent possible.

Writers looked deep into the Great Plains' past for the roots of the region's problems. In 1935, Chester C. Davis published an article in the *Saturday Evening Post* chiding the nation for its careless use of American resources. "We have been wasteful of our heritage, the land. We have stripped it of forests and have mined its soil."[7] Raymond J. Poole, a writer for *Science*, made the accusations far more specific:

> As a nation and as individuals we have blundered like the vanished races of the earth, in the utilization of our primitive wild-life resources. We have been little concerned about the balances of nature which, if severely disturbed, may bring disaster to large blocks of society. We have boasted too much of our inexhaustible supplies of earth's native goods, and of a growing mastery that gave us every right to *win* in the conquest *against* nature.

This attitude, the author contended, had done immense damage to the lands of the West. "Mother Nature" was "not a nudist by choice," yet "the keen, diagonal blade of the breaking plow scored a snipping symphony with the roots and rhizomes of the prairie grasses and their associates," laying waste to nature's order.[8] Another writer laid the blame upon "man's greed for wheat, wheat, nothing but wheat," which had "rendered millions of acres unfit for habitation. . . . Dust storms are the legitimate result of man's greed and destructive methods. You can't change nature's plans."[9] And yet it seemed to these writers that this was exactly what the people of the plains had been trying to do.

Some critics particularly blamed the American farmer. Farmers had lowered the water table and promoted erosion. They had taken advantage of the wealth to be had in the boom times of World War I, accelerating the destruction of the Great Plains' natural cover. "Gang-plows ripped and chopped the brush and the hardy native grasses. The roots of these plants had been the straw in the brick of the Great Plains' soil. When they were destroyed the soil crumbled."[10] Although the occasional writer claimed that the American farmer had been "practically helpless in the grip of forces over which he had or could have almost no control," this was not the usual argument. Farming practices poorly adapted to the Great Plains were as responsible as human greed in producing the Dust Bowl.

According to some accounts, the American government had been an essential partner in this process. The *Topeka Journal* suggested rather simplistically that the crux of the matter was the Kansas-Nebraska Act of 1854. "An Act of Congress, May 30, 1854, resulted in the state being over-publicized and exploited. Kansas was settled far too rapidly and in the main by men who knew nothing of farming. And so Kansas, the dream state, pays in dust. And pays and pays." The more common analysis followed slightly different lines. A government without a precedent to follow sent its people west to homestead, without consideration of the conditions that those people would find once they crossed the "fatal hundredth meridian." The government handed out patches too small for viable farms to people with very little experience in agriculture. "It was almost as if the government sat like a cynical Zeus bestowing destitution petitioned as a gift."[11] The press analysis of the dust problem laid out a recipe for disaster—human greed, improper farming methods, and federal policies that exacerbated these problems.

Writers described the human implications of this environmental disaster in accounts of daily life in the Dust Bowl. One chose to emphasize the day-to-day drudgery that so much dust imposed upon the people within its reach. Dust permeated and ruined the stock of storekeepers, destroyed the gearshifts of cars, and settled into the butter, "mak[ing] housekeeping, and gradually life itself, unbearable in this swirling drifting dust."[12] This particular description of the situation did not stretch the truth unduly.

Other journalists were more dramatic, exploiting this difficult situation for all it was worth. Writing for the *Christian Century*, Thomas Alfred Tripp examined "a county seat in the southern Great Plains, a town which had a population of about 3,500 in 1924," and concluded that the problems of the thirties had destroyed community life, thwarted the prospects of young adults, and produced class divisions. Young women withered on the vine, for lack of marriageable males. Young men "were found loafing about the streets, slovenly dressed, drinking and telling unprintable yarns in the pool halls and taverns," too poor to marry. The "moral tone" of the townsfolk had evaporated, and couples regularly indulged in "sexual irregularity." The writer concluded that "hating is a thriving industry. Everyone seems to dislike almost everyone else. Few people have many intimate friends. Smiles are infrequent, while frowns are many."[13]

Walter Davenport went several steps further in his infamous article, "Land Where Our Children Die." On a ramble through the Dust Bowl, Davenport found poor farming and hysterical farmers. He wrote of farmers trying to shift the blame for the wind erosion from themselves to a myriad of "fabulous factors," such as atmospheric disturbances caused by the radio, airplanes, moving mountains, and a changing climate. "We began to think the whole Bowl hexed." Although the Dust Bowlers advanced many causes for their problems, Davenport had his own ideas about where to fix the blame. The residents of the Great Plains, in his words, had "perverted Nature until she . . . has gone crazy." Nature, in turn, was taking its revenge, and the storms were driving the population over the edge. Dust-induced hysteria kept the doctors, police, and other angels of mercy busy. Davenport reproduced some alleged messages to the local doctor in his article:

> "Listen, Doctor, this here's Twell Murfick—you know, where you been comin'. It's my wife again. It's like you said—she's bad this time. We got her in her room tied up. Listen, kin you hurry?"
>
> Or, "Doc, kin you come quick? Ackel's gone and done it this time. This here's Jere Hullomon over to Ackel's telephonin' from a fillin' station. Ackel's got the ax. You can hear 'em screamin'. Sure, I'll tell the police. Kin you hurry?"[14]

Davenport's hicks had been driven insane by too much flying dirt. He probably would have agreed with George Greenfield's 1937 article, "Unto Dust," which sounded a death knell for the region. "The last time I was out here, 20 years ago, there was life—birds and trees, cattle and crops. Today I see the cold hand of death on what was one of the richest breadbaskets of the nation."[15]

Those living in the heart of the Dust Bowl could hardly deny that they had a problem, although they were highly indignant about the charges of writers like Davenport. Flying dust choked their cars, their gardens, and their children. The drought robbed them of their crops and income for eight years in succession. Years of dust, however, did not rob them of their love of their communities and their desire to see the Dust Bowl's recovery. They wanted to deal with their problems in their own way, and on their own terms. Business, property values, and pride were at stake.

Papers in Kansas also took exception to this adverse publicity and began by arguing that dust storms were nothing new. The *Dodge City Globe* charged that those who were spreading rumors about the 1930s being "the worst storms ever experienced" were simply trying to impress their relatives back East. More importantly, they needed to get out their history books and learn that the "early travelers over these prairies needed dust masks." Other articles, bearing the titles "Missionary's Journal Proves Black Blizzards Swept Kansas in 1830," "Prehistoric Dust Storms," and "Nothing New," illustrated the commitment of these local newspapers to a long view of the Great Plains' history.[16] When even eastern Kansas newspapers criticized western Kansas, the editor of the *Liberal News* reminisced about a dust storm in 1893 that had sandblasted the area "when hardly a plow had been brought to western Kansas" and concluded by calling contrary arguments "boloney." Dirt storms and drought simply had to be approached with the proper historical perspective. Other western Kansans also resented complaints emanating from farther east. When the dust blew, they expostulated, eastern Kansans who were hardly affected by the dirt yelled the loudest. A little dirt, and "they can't take it." Easterners were softies, and "nobody admires a softy."[17]

Southwestern Kansans also took comfort that people outside the Dust Bowl had problems of their own. Eastern flooding in the spring of 1935 helped the residents of the drought states to examine their troubles in a new light. The *Garden City Daily Telegram* invited photographers to return west after they finished taking pictures of flood-damaged lands. "Pictures depicting the prompt recovery from the dust disaster would look mighty encouraging if printed opposite scenes of flood destruction elsewhere, some of which can never be repaired." When flooding came again in 1936, the Dust Bowlers noted the recurrence and showed their generosity. If so inclined, they could "describe the flood tragedy as 'man-made'" and recommend abandonment of flooded areas as "wasteland," but they instead offered "assistance and sympathy to the area which has suffered far more damage from too much water than the plains region has suffered from having not enough."[18] Editors across southwestern Kansas could be magnanimous when the problem under discussion was not their own.

What Dust Bowlers probably most needed to establish in their own minds, if not for anyone else, was the fact that they were not criminally stupid or half-crazed to farm the Great Plains. They were quick to point out that every area had its drawbacks and that the government's weather summary classified western Kansas as "a very pleasant region in which to live and . . . usually favorable for farming." Not only was western Kansas "usually favorable for farming," but farming was a job that had to be done. Pioneer farmers on the southern plains had discovered land suitable for agriculture. But its development had necessarily involved risks. The settlers as well as latter day farmers were only "right or wrong with the weather." Blaming them for the Dust Bowl made little sense, according to western Kansans. "We might as well charge Hoover with the depression, as many did." There was nothing peculiar, they believed, about the "try, try again" mentality of area farmers and their tendency to forget the trials of the past. Similar selective memory afflicted residents of communities all across the United States. "Cities along the Ohio and Mississippi regularly are flooded and just as regularly rebuild on the same sites. San Francisco didn't move away from earthquakes. . . . Prosperity is the great eraser of lessons taught by misfortune."[19] Dust Bowlers saw no evil intent in their actions, only the attempts of hardworking people to wrest a living from sometimes resisting lands.

Tenacious Kansans maintained that despite their current hardships their region was the best place to live. They contrasted life in the Dust Bowl with the poverty of migrants to the West Coast. A "hardened relief investigator" found conditions among drought refugees shocking. A family from eastern Colorado lived in a broken-down trailer while their children slept in packing-crate huts. A family from Kansas grubbed out a meager living on a seven-acre tract somewhere on the West Coast. The Northwest Regional Planning Commission estimated that the number of farms available throughout the Pacific Northwest would fall two thousand short of the number of needy farmers. On the other hand, western Kansas promised to welcome these people back, if they had the resources to return. Wet years seemed to be on their way, and there would be "important work" for the returning refugees.[20] Rebuilding would require all hands. Southwestern Kansas was on the mend, promised the writers, and there would be work enough, and land enough, for all.

Some southwestern Kansans came to the conclusion that negative advertising was their greatest problem. They had been doing themselves a disservice by publicizing Kansas' dust and drought instead of its prospects. In 1940, the Junior Chamber of Commerce issued a resolution against negative publicity, decrying "publishing or selling postcards and other pictures of dust storms, non-existing giant grasshoppers, and other pictures or material that are detrimental to Kansas and her people." Instead, they encouraged newspaper editors and others to "offer such material as correctly portrays the true beauty of our state, the progress of our industries, the natural beauty or agreeable climate, or the remarkable progress and accomplishments of the people."[21] The members of this organization hoped that a campaign of positive advertising would somehow repair the damage done by nearly a decade of negative images.

Although most residents would have liked to have seen fewer sensational Dust Bowl stories, newspaper editors did not necessarily believe that it was in their communities' best interest to simply quit reporting bad news. By accepting or rejecting the challenge from the Junior Chamber of Commerce, editors defined the role of their newspapers in their communities. Accurately reporting the area's problems fulfilled their role as objective reporters of the day's news and might bring more help from the federal government. However, taking this route might raise the ire of local citizens if business and tourist dollars went elsewhere. Editors could use an alternate strategy and slip back into the role of frontier town booster (which many had never really abandoned) to minimize the true problems facing southwestern Kansas. The editor of the *Garden City Daily Telegram* was ambivalent about reporting the Dust Bowl in his paper. Should he play up the problem in the hope of encouraging increased government aid, or should he follow the dictates of the Chamber of Commerce and "suppress the story of this most depressing of all meteorological phenomena, the plains dust storm?"[22] From his perspective, he and the newspaper faced a hopeless dilemma. As the crises of the 1930s began to ease at decade's end, most newspaper editors were opting for the latter course, emphasizing the positive aspects of southwestern Kansas.

During 1939, most Dust Bowl newspapers published "comeback" issues, which featured articles about oil and gas development, irrigation, and the promise of scientific agriculture. In fact, writers urged their readers to send copies of these issues to their friends and families throughout the country. The *Southwest Daily Times* wanted "the world to know that the area now deserves envy rather than pity" and made additional issues available at their office. The editor published twelve weekly articles under the title "Who Says They Never Come Back?" to advertise the progress that southwestern Kansans had made toward solving their problems. The *Garden City Daily Telegram* printed a "1939 Southwest Resource" edition, "a 56 page review of the wealth of natural advantages this region possesses." The newspaper office provided extra copies, "wrapped for mailing, at 10 cents each." Improved weather, new technology, and government aid had brought beleaguered people a measure of hope and a renewed sense of pride in their region. The area's newspaper editors believed that they could see the light at the end of the tunnel, and wanted to make sure that the rest of the country saw it as well.[23] At roughly the same time, the national press also chose to abandon its negative discussion of the Dust Bowl. Although writers did not endorse a return to the farming methods that had led to the crisis, they did for the most part express faith in the ability of science, government, and individual farmers to rehabilitate the plains.

The faith in technological miracles long embraced by the people of the plains crept into discussions of the future of the Dust Bowl. While some writers insisted that the soil of the Great Plains should remain "right side up," free of agriculture and devoted only to grazing, theirs was a minority opinion. The *Scientific American* urged the study of ecology to reveal the options available in the situation, while an article in the *Saturday Evening Post* expressed a cautious faith in irrigation and careful agriculture. An editorial in *Business Week* revealed the greatest optimism: "Scientific agriculture, utilizing the skill of modern engineering for water supply and water control, will bring the nation through to the stable future. Though distress may be great, panic has no place in our national consideration of this catastrophe. There will be no famines." While no one promised a complete remedy to the problems of the 1930s, writers trusted that a technical and scientific approach to the Dust Bowl would render it fit for human habitation and agricultural use.[24]

Writers also promoted continued government oversight, an innovation of the 1930s, to meet the challenges of the decade. "The answer is planning, planning on a huge scale." They advocated large-scale, collec-tive federal supervision of the area to address the drought and applauded the measures taken to that date. As the *Saturday Evening Post* put it, "Not only justice but also economic advantage are on the side of a great governmental offensive to all[a]y the consequences of the drought."[25]

Former critics also reasserted their faith in the American farmer. In the summer of 1939, an article in the *New York Times Magazine* announced that "a process of natural selection is weeding out the misfits, and those who remain are conforming to the requirements of the situation." Those left on the land had learned some hard lessons but were ready to do things right this time. The *American Magazine* was even more forceful in its endorsement of the farmers' fitness to work the land: "The farmers who remain are the breed and the blood of the American pioneer. Men of God, if you will, with a divine conviction of their ordination to subdue the wilderness. Droughts, grasshoppers, tornadoes, crop blights—they have faced each problem squarely as it came, asking no quarter and giving none. Now it is the dust. But dust or no, this is their frontier; this is their destiny. They'll fight it out." The writer of this piece probably did not see the irony in his or her words. Perhaps it was precisely that "divine convic-tion of their ordination to subdue the wilderness" that had helped to create these problems in the first place. Nonetheless, on the eve of Amer-ica's entry into World War II, the press was ready to put the hard problems of the Dust Bowl on the shelf and to view the state of agriculture on the Great Plains optimistically.[26]

Although the press of the 1930s loudly complained about the human attitudes, farming practices, and government policies that led to the Dust Bowl, in the end it reverted to a less critical opinion of the propriety of farming the plains. The national press eventually endorsed the opinions that Dust Bowl editors had expressed all along. Times were temporarily bad, but the people of the area, with the aid of improved technology and the federal government, would solve their problems and prosper once more. Such a change of heart bespoke an emphasis on the positive and upon a faith in limitless opportunities for development.

These optimistic sentiments reflected the rising expectations of people all over the Dust Bowl. By 1940, the crisis was largely over. Although people were cautious about their prospects, the potential for recovery was more real than it had been in a decade. In that year, many farmers harvested their first paying crop since 1930. The Ford County agricultural extension agent complained that the area's farmers were still dependent upon government aid and that nineteen of fifty-nine rural schools were closed; but, on the brighter side, he wrote that January of 1940 brought a five-inch snow that made the wheat crop more secure. The situation was the same throughout the region. Many families were still dependent upon relief, but there was more moisture and a good chance that there would be a wheat crop and higher prices in 1941. Even in Morton County, hardest hit by the Dust Bowl, hope infused the residents. In May 1939, farmers received nearly ten inches of moisture; in December, eighteen inches of snow fell, followed by another twelve inches in January 1940. The county agent concluded that "Morton County can no longer be called the Dust Bowl."[27] By 1940 the wheat market was booming, the rains had returned to the Great Plains, and the United States had its European allies to feed. It was easy to speak in terms of prospects rather than limitations.

8. TOO POOR TO LEAVE, TOO DISCOURAGED TO STAY

The 1930s presented residents of southwestern Kansas with enormous problems, whether they lived in cities or in the country, whether they made their living directly from the land or indirectly in one of the industries or services that fed off of the local farming economy. Approximately one quarter of the area's population responded to the decade's challenges by leaving. Either because of health problems, financial disasters, or any number of other complications, these people found the cost of remaining too high.

Although levels of persistence varied between counties, the majority of the residents of the Dust Bowl stayed in the area, hoping for better days and the rain that simply had to fall, given enough time and patience. Eighty survivors of the Dust Bowl were asked nearly fifty years later the question, "Why did you stay?"[1] Fifty respondents, or 41 percent of the total, mentioned the lack of money to go anywhere else or having nowhere to go even if they had wanted to leave, essentially negative reasons for remaining. One woman from Kearny County wrote, "We didn't have money to go anywhere so we just *existed* with a few of the people that was left." Another thirty respondents, or 24 percent, commented that they owned land and could not leave or had a job, a precious commodity during depression years. A typical respondent commented that her family "stayed because we didn't have any money to leave and husband had a job, many people did not."[2]

The remaining 35 percent of the answers given by survivors were more positive. Respondents stated that they had endured because of their attachment to the area, their homes, and their families or because of a personal faith that the area would recover from hard times. As Laurie Copeland of Ness County wrote: "We did have faith that the rains would come. We just could not imagine that it would be so long." Some people's reasons for remaining throughout the 1930s were a combination of all of these motivations. One woman summed up the situation for her own family and undoubtedly for dozens more: "Mainly we had our lives savings tied up in the farm and kept thinking 'surely its got to get better' and it did. We had no idea where one could go to start over again when you had no more hard cash than we did. People got real discouraged and talked of leaving but where could they go. That was there home." There were no simple reasons for going or staying. In retrospect, many people believed that the choice had been made for them through a combination of personal and financial attachments to the area, as well as a lack of other opportunities.[3]

Those who answered the questionnaire, however, were a self-selected sample of southwestern Kansans who actually survived the hard years and chose to remain in southwestern Kansas for most, or all, of the next fifty years. Analysis of the characteristics of those Kansans who both stayed and left may give a more accurate picture of the economic and social forces determining persistence in Dust Bowl counties. The ability of individuals and families, as well as whole communities, to persist through a decade of disaster depended upon a variety of factors. Among farm families, land ownership seemed to be the most important determinant of persistence, with farm size, economic sidelines, and family size and linkages playing collateral roles. Those counties that most successfully survived the trials of the 1930s did so for other reasons, such as the size and importance of their major towns, their date of settlement, the location of the county, and the consequent ability of their farmers to continue to make a living. There was no simple formula for survival, but those individuals, families, and communities that best survived did share certain common characteristics.

Although individual-level federal census data is unavailable for these years, the state of Kansas counted its farmers every year throughout the 1930s. Enumerators listed the names of township residents, the size of their farms, the crops they grew, the income they derived from sales of milk, and the number of tractors and combines they owned, among other facts. In most townships, enumerators also recorded family size. Examination of five of these townships, Pleasant Valley Township in Finney County, Pleasant Valley Township in Ford County, Medway Township in Hamilton County, Logan Township in Meade County, and Highpoint Township in Ness County, in 1930, 1935, and 1940 revealed the degree to which factors such as land ownership, farm size, milk and egg production, family size and family networks, and ethnicity affected the ability of members of farming communities to survive the hardships of the decade.[4]

Although part of a single agricultural region, these townships were home to quite diverse aggregations of farming families. Highpoint Township in Ness County was located in the far northeast corner of the Dust Bowl. Settlers arrived in Ness County in advance of much of the rest of southwestern Kansas, and many of those who came to Highpoint Township were German or German-speaking. The 1925 Kansas state census revealed that residents hailed from many other states, as well as Germany, Russia, Switzerland, and Poland.[5] In 1930, 133 farming families lived in the township; approximately two-thirds were ethnic Germans. Among the township's families, 53 percent owned either part or all of the land they farmed. The "average" farmer worked more than 400 acres of land, sowing more than half of it in wheat, with the rest devoted largely to forage crops and pasture. In 1930, each family typically raised roughly two dozen cattle, a couple of pigs, nearly one hundred hens, and provided itself a pound of butter a week, while selling nearly $200 worth of milk per year. The average household was large, with more than five members, and more than half of the families in the township were related to at least one other family, with more than 15 percent related to four or five other families.[6] The farmers of Highpoint Township had the smallest farms, the largest families, and a moderate reliance upon wheat as a primary crop, compared to their counterparts in the other sample townships.[7]

Pleasant Valley Township in Ford County lay directly south of Highpoint Township. Settlers made their way to Ford County, like Ness County, fairly early, since Dodge City was a major cattle town in the 1870s and 1880s. The settlers who built homes in Pleasant Valley Township, not far from Dodge City, were more likely to be native born than their counterparts in Highpoint Township. Most had their birthplaces in the states of Ohio, Oklahoma, and Kansas, although there were a few German families in the area.[8]

In 1930, their farms were fairly large, with the average farmer managing more than 600 acres. Just over half of them, or 52 percent, owned land in the township. They devoted about half of their acres to wheat and about a sixth to pasture. Each owned around fifteen cattle, six swine, and one hundred hens and produced just over a pound of butter a week. In 1930, the average family earned $108.52 from milk sales. The households were smaller in Pleasant Valley Township, with the average just over four

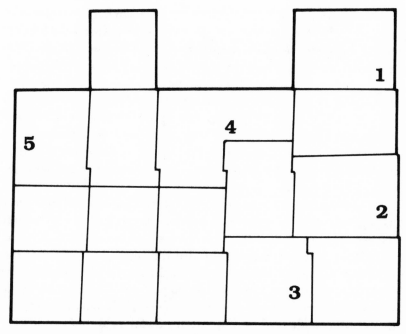

Map 8.1. Study townships: 1. Highpoint, Ness County; 2. Pleasant Valley, Ford County; 3. Logan, Meade County; 4. Pleasant Valley, Finney
County; 5. Medway, Hamilton County.

members instead of five; no family was linked to more than two other
households. These farms were on the small side, compared to others in
this five-township sample, but the farmers on them harvested more wheat
than any but those in Pleasant Valley, Finney County.[9]

This other Pleasant Valley lay a considerable distance to the west of Ness
and Ford counties but was nearly as far north as Highpoint Township. This
township in 1930 had a mixed population of both native-born individuals
of largely northern European descent and a colony of Mennonites, settlers
from the United States, Canada, and Russia. The Mennonite colony made
up approximately one quarter of the township's households.[10]

In 1930 the thirty-seven farming families in this township operated the
largest farms of the five townships, the mean farm being almost 1,000
acres, while the median holding was an entire section, 640 acres. Again,
just over half, or 51 percent, owned land. In this township, there was
quite a disparity between the activities of the largest farmers and those of
the smaller. The mean farm of 1,000 acres devoted nearly 400 acres to

wheat and another 450 acres to pasture. The median holding of 640 acres had 200 acres of wheat and 180 acres of pasture. That a few farmers devoted themselves heavily to livestock is evident in other statistics. The mean farmer had more than twenty-seven cattle, while the median farmer had only seven. The median farmer had two swine, the mean, none. The mean farmer produced twice as much butter as the median and $87.70 worth of milk in 1930, while the median farmer sold no milk. Most families raised roughly sixty hens. Family sizes were approximately equivalent between the mean and the median, with the average family having more than four members. Most families, more than 60 percent, were not related to other families in the township. [11]

The farming community in Logan Township, Meade County, was also a mixed group, with both Mennonite and non-Mennonite farmers. Twenty-nine percent of the households in Logan Township were Mennonite; this area of the county was sometimes called the Settlement because of the high concentration of Mennonites in residence. This group arrived in Meade County in 1906, forming a daughter colony of a larger settlement in Jansen, Nebraska. There were also a number of families of German descent, with family heads born in Austria, Switzerland, and Germany. [12] The farming families in Logan Township had the highest rate of land ownership in the five-township sample: 61 percent of the families held title to at least a portion of their farms.

In this locale there was also a great disparity between the size and composition of mean and median farms. The mean farm in 1930 was over 700 acres, while the median was only 400. The mean farmer planted 205 acres of wheat, the median 170. The major difference was in the amount of pasture land, with the mean farmer using more than 400 acres for his forty cattle and the median farmer using only 100 acres for pasture and owning only fifteen cattle. The mean and median more or less converged, however, in the number of hens owned (around one hundred), the pounds of butter produced (one to one-and-a-third per week), and the amount earned from milk sales in 1930 ($100 to $128). Unfortunately, the census taker in Logan Township did not record household sizes. Information about family linkages, however, reveals extensive kin connections between households, especially among the Mennonites. [13]

Medway Township in Hamilton County was home to the smallest population of the five townships, only twenty-six farming families in 1930. Hamilton County is on the Colorado border at the far western edge of the Dust Bowl, and the majority of the area's farmers arrived quite late in the settlement process. Much of the land remained grazing country well into the twentieth century—the county's residents did not abolish the open range until 1931. In 1925, none of Medway Township's residents were foreign born but were from Missouri, Illinois, Wisconsin, West Virginia, Kentucky, and other areas of Kansas. In this township, considerably fewer of the families owned land, only 23 percent. In 1930, the mean farmer managed 640 acres, while the median farmer had only 370 acres. The mean farmer raised very little wheat, 53 acres, while the median farmer raised none at all. Farmers devoted most of their land to pasture and to forage crops. Some grew broomcorn. The mean farmer had twenty-six cattle, the median eleven. There were few swine, few hens, and little butter or milk produced by this township's residents. Families did not even produce enough butter or keep enough hens for their own needs. Their families were practically as large as those in Highpoint Township, with five members, but only six of twenty-six families had relatives in Medway Township.[14]

The farmers in these five townships operated very different enterprises, in terms of the size of their farms, the crops they planted, the subsistence activities in which they engaged, and the size of their families and kin networks. Likewise, the farmers within these townships had very different persistence histories during the course of the 1930s. Among farm families present in 1930, those living in Highpoint Township were the only ones with greater-than-average persistence in both the period from 1930 to 1935 and from 1935 to 1940. Within the group of families entering the area after the 1930 census and present for the 1935 census, those in Highpoint and Pleasant Valley, Finney County, had greater success in staying than others (see Table A.7). These differences in persistence rates derived from a number of factors, but some of the most important issues in determining whether families remained or left were ownership status, farm size, family linkages, family size, and whether the family engaged in sidelines such as the production of dairy products, chickens, and eggs. Interestingly enough, except in the case of Mennonites, ethnicity appeared to have been a minor factor in determining the degree of family persistence in these farming communities.

Ownership status was probably the greatest determinant in a farming family's survival during the 1930s. For the purpose of this study, a farm owner is defined as the head of a farming family who owned at least part of his or her land, since a large proportion of southwestern Kansas farmers who owned land also rented a few acres (or many acres) on a year-to-year basis. Non-owners rented all of their lands. Land ownership bore a particularly strong relationship to farm survival from 1930 to 1935. Non-owners who were present in 1930 had only an even chance of surviving the first five years of the Great Depression, whereas owners, as a group, had an 85 percent chance of remaining to be counted in 1935.

This relationship weakened in the period between 1935 and 1940, although owners still survived in greater numbers than non-owners. Persistence among those farmers who were present in 1930, for the period between 1935 and 1940, was 37 percent among non-owners, as opposed to 64 percent among owners.

For farmers who arrived in the middle of the drought and depression, there was a lesser relationship between land ownership and persistence. Newcomers in 1935 were less likely than their longer-established neighbors to be landholders, and they were less likely to gain advantage, in terms of persistence, from their investment in the area's land. Within this group, non-owners had a 41 percent chance of staying in their townships, and owners had a 60 percent chance, significantly less than residents who had resided in the township longer (see Table A.8).

Hard times inflicted particular difficulties upon area landholders. Owner-operators bore the brunt of taxation, as well as the costs of maintenance on wind-blown fields. Nevertheless, this did not lead to increased migration out of the Dust Bowl among owners because of other factors. Drought and dusty conditions depressed land values and drove away potential buyers, limiting the chance that a family could even sell their farm. Should a family actually find a purchaser for their land, they were unlikely to recover their original investment, let alone the value of the improvements they had made. For example, land purchased in Hamilton County in 1930 for $18 an acre was worth only $10 an acre in 1935 and $7 an acre in 1940.[15] This deflation in land values was common to the entire Dust Bowl (see Table A.9). Landowners who survived the 1930s felt an attachment to their land that would have made them hesitate before selling their farms, especially at such a reduced price.

Unlike owners, tenants were free to abandon the land and the area when the drought and dust storms intensified. Newcomers for the 1935 census, who had low persistence rates whether they owned land or not, purchased their land at depressed prices and perhaps felt less commitment to area. It is also likely that they entered farming at such a disadvantage that the small incentive of holding onto their land hardly compensated for the trouble. No farmer would have been able to sell a farm at a profit during the 1930s, and those who were the most firmly established had the most to lose from relocation.[16]

Farm size seemed to have less of an impact on a family's ability to remain in farming throughout the Dust Bowl years than did landholding. The only farmers who were clearly at a disadvantage because of the size of their farms were those who worked less than 320 acres. Among the farming families who were in these townships at the outset of the decade, those who made a living on at least 320 acres had a 70 percent or better chance of still being on the land in 1935, whereas the group of farmers with less than 320 acres only had a fifty-fifty chance. Farmers with larger holdings maintained the advantage in the years between 1935 and 1940. Within the group already present in 1930, those on the larger farms had at least a 50 percent chance of persisting until 1940, but only 34 percent of the smaller farmers remained in 1940. The same relationship held with newcomers in 1935. Those with half a section or more had at least a 44 percent chance of remaining, while their neighbors on smaller holdings had only a 17 percent chance of survival (see Table A.10).

A number of factors made farm size a determinant in persistence. Farms of less than 320 acres had a diminished chance of success in a dry environment in general.[17] Farmers in southwestern Kansas learned early in the settlement process that very large farms, combined with heavy mechanization, offered the greatest chance of success. Given the high mean and median farm sizes throughout the region, smaller farm size may have been an indication of economic marginality and a weak commitment to the area's agricultural economy. Federal policy during the 1930s also favored the larger farmer over the smaller, since the AAA and SCS distributed payments on the basis of acreage and Dust Bowl farmers successfully fought any reduction of acreage limits. Size had its advantages, partially because of the stability that larger farmers brought to the depression and government activities that rewarded large-scale operations.

Agricultural sidelines and subsistence activities such as dairying or hen and egg production also seemed to have had a favorable influence on farm persistence to 1935. Families engaging in at least two of these activities— producing fifty-two pounds of butter per year, owning fifty or more hens, or selling more than $52 worth of milk per year—were substantial participants in sidelines and subsistence farming by the standards of the area. Those farm families that did not reach these levels of participation had only a 51 percent persistence rate between 1930 and 1935. Seventy-three percent of those who did participate persisted until 1935, with those who participated most heavily in these activities having the greatest persistence of all, 78 percent.

This work often represented the labors of farming women. Chicken and egg production was traditionally considered "women's work," and the care of cattle was often assumed by women as well. The additions to family income provided by these labors could be critical during these hard times, since the traditional mainstay of southwestern Kansas, winter wheat, failed with the drought. As the experience of the Friesen family showed (Chapter 5), a woman's labors might prove more lucrative in drought years than those of her husband, providing the necessary exchange at the grocery store as well as cash income. [18]

In the years between 1935 and 1940, however, there was very little relationship between engaging in dairy and henhouse production and persistence, except for those present in 1930 who participated on the largest scale. In southwestern Kansas, large-scale barnyard farmers raised or sold per year a combination of two or more of the following: more than 100 pounds of butter, more than one hundred hens, and more than $100 worth of milk. [19] The smaller farmers all suffered attrition rates greater than 50 percent, including those newcomers who arrived in time for the 1935 census. On the other hand, 61 percent of those heavily engaged in subsistence and sidelines survived until 1940.

Heavy participation in milk, cream, and egg production did not provide farmers who entered in 1935 any special security. This group failed at roughly the same rate as those who generally avoided raising chickens and milk cows. Perhaps this was because success in these activities required capital investments in feed, shelter, and perhaps water pumping equipment. Most people who owned cows also owned cream separators. The money for these purchases would have been difficult to come by during hard times. Only large, well-established farmers, who had made the necessary investments prior to the depression, had the resources to maintain their enterprises and to reap the benefits, in terms of greater financial stability. Although prices for eggs, butter, and milk were low during the 1930s, they would have provided these well-established farm families with a small income, despite repeated destruction of field crops. [20]

Other factors that seemed to have a minor influence on household persistence in the period between 1930 and 1935 were family linkages and family size. Those families with no linkages to other families in the township, or only one, had a 66 percent chance of remaining until 1935, whereas families with more extensive networks of relationships had a 77 percent chance of persisting. Family size functioned in much the same way. Those with households of three or less members had a 54 percent persistence rate in the years between 1930 and 1935, while those with four or more members had a 78 percent success rate.

As with the factor of milk, egg, and butter production, family size and family linkages seemed to be less important for the period from 1935 to 1940. Families with more than two kin linkages within the township had a 64 percent survival rate, as compared to 47 percent for those with two or less. Fifty-nine percent of families of four or more people were still in their townships in 1940, as opposed to 43 percent of the smaller families. Family size seems to have had almost no impact upon families migrating into the area in the midst of the drought. Those with larger families had a 51 percent persistence rate, only 5 percent greater than the smaller families. Family linkages may have been a greater determinant of persistence. While only 37 percent of families with one or no households of kin in the township survived, 63 percent of their neighbors with two or more linked families were around to be counted for the 1940 census.

Family size would have affected household mobility in several ways. Larger families may have remained stationary because of the logistical problems of moving greater numbers of people. Although age data was not available for these communities, it is highly likely that a large number of the smaller households were single men, young couples without children, or young families consisting of husband, wife, and one child. Their mobility would not have been hampered in the same way as that of larger families, and small families had other characteristics that encouraged mobility as well. Many young people, without productive land, jobs, or hope of either, left the area for California, Colorado, Oregon, and other points east and west. The young of the farming community were particularly hard hit by the demographic consequences of the Dust Bowl.

Kin linkages between households would have been important because of the tangible and intangible support family members provided each other. In their questionnaires and interviews, many people mentioned the financial and moral support they received from parents, brothers, sisters, and other family members. Support flowed in many directions, from parent to child, between siblings, and from children to their struggling parents, and gave people the option of remaining when their nuclear family's limited resources might have dictated that they go. Family, too, may have represented rootedness. Those with great aggregations of family in one community may have felt themselves a permanent part of that locality and may have had fewer relatives with whom to seek shelter beyond the boundaries of the Dust Bowl.

Ethnicity seemed to play a limited role in determining persistence in these five townships among those who were present in 1930. This population divided fairly easily into three groups: ethnic Germans, Mennonites, and the non-German, non-Mennonite, largely native-born population. Among these groups, those present in 1930 had fairly equal chances of persisting to 1935, with Germans having a 70 percent persistence rate, the Mennonites, 68 percent, and all others, 67 percent. Tracing the groups to 1940, the Germans and the native-born, non-Mennonites had fairly similar success in surviving. Fifty-six percent of the Germans were present, and 50 percent of the "others" had also survived. Only 41 percent of the Mennonite households, however, were still present.

The group of farmers who were newcomers in the 1935 census had a somewhat different history. Among non-German, non-Mennonites, only 38 percent succeeded in surviving until 1940, and only 33 percent of the Mennonites persisted for those five years. Among the Germans, however, there was a 64 percent success rate, largely because many were the children of established residents, taking their position in a large network of related farming families.

The lower persistence rate among Mennonites might come as a surprise to historians who have characterized them as "more determined than almost anyone to stick it out."[21] The high rate of turnover among the Mennonite families reflected characteristics particular to them as an insular and communitarian religious and ethnic group. Whereas German and native-born settlers might relocate as individuals, or in small family groupings, Mennonite farmers tended to move in larger aggregations in order to establish colonies in new locations. In some ways, this discouraged migration, since individual Mennonite families usually would not consider relocation without the group. Elfreda Penner Fast, who grew up in a community of Mennonite Brethren in Gray County, commented that her parents sometimes talked of moving out of the Dust Bowl, but the conversation always came to a close when her mother noted the lack of Mennonite Brethren in the proposed location. David Classen, who grew up in a more conservative Logan Township community, scandalized his fellow Mennonites by working one summer outside Meade County, even though he worked for Mennonites. Given their German language, peculiarities of dress, and religious injunctions against intermarriage and social mixing with non-Mennonites, the Mennonite lifestyle did not easily adapt itself to individual migrations from one locale to another.[22]

On the other hand, this reluctance to relocate without the consent and participation of the group could have a dramatic impact upon persistence when means were found to colonize elsewhere, as happened with the "settlement" in Meade County in the 1930s. Fifteen of twenty-six households in this Mennonite colony relocated during the decade, as members founded two daughter colonies, one in Dallas, Oregon, and the other near Lake Charles, Louisiana. Although it is unclear exactly what caused this division, it is likely that a combination of drought conditions and doctrinal controversies within the community led to the migration of more than half of the settlement's member families.[23] Contrary to historian Donald Worster's assertions that their lifestyle provided Mennonites a degree of stability unavailable to other southwestern Kansans, the experience of Logan township showed that the communal nature of Mennonite life could be powerfully divisive in an economically troubled or doctrinally divided religious community.

Another factor that played only a limited role in determining the level of movement within these townships was the forced sale—foreclosures or tax sales. Bank managers and county officials were not responsible, in the majority of cases, for families relocating. For example, of the twenty-two landowners who left Highpoint Township during the 1930s, eight lost their farms to foreclosures or tax sales. Of those eight, three remained in the township at the conclusion of the decade. One family lost its farm in 1940; another suffered a partial foreclosure in 1934 but remained, only to lose the rest in 1940. The third family experienced a complete foreclosure in 1935, but remained in the community as tenant farmers. The experience of farmers in Highpoint Township was fairly representative of the entire five-township sample.

The farmers who lost their land to forced sales were generally indistinguishable from their neighbors in terms of the size of their farms and the crops and livestock they raised. Of the twenty-eight families losing their farms, five, or just under 20 percent, maintained fairly marginal operations. For example, J. F. Smolik of Medway Township farmed 640 acres of land and planted it all in wheat; he owned no livestock and kept no pasture. Most, however, owned farms that resembled that of Fred Blurton of Pleasant Valley Township, Ford County. He worked 480 acres and planted 300 of them in wheat. He also raised sorghum and kafir corn and left some land in pasture. He owned milk cows, beef cattle, hens, and pigs. In other words, Blurton's operation closely resembled those of his more secure neighbors.[24]

Blurton's weakness, and that of the others who suffered forced sales, generally lay in loans taken out in the prosperous twenties and very early thirties that became too heavy to bear as the depression and drought wore on. In these townships, the average farming family facing foreclosure had taken out a mortgage of nearly $5,000 in 1930 and lost the farm in 1937.[25] In addition to a substantial mortgage, this average family probably would have borne the weight of substantial chattel mortgages. Many owed money to banks, automobile companies, implement manufacturers, and government loan corporations. For example, in 1937 when H. A. Wiebe lost his farm, the bank held a mortgage of $2,000 on his land. Additionally, he owed John Deere more than $500 and the Rock Island Implement Company more than $100, while owing nearly $1,000 to the Reconstruction Finance Corporation. Many of these chattel mortgages were not released until the middle of the 1940s.[26] It is no wonder that he and his neighbors often failed. The costs of running a farm continued to mount whether or not the farmer harvested a crop.

What is perhaps surprising, then, is that on the whole very few families in these five townships in southwestern Kansas lost their farms to forced sales during the decade, as compared to the nation, the region, and the rest of the state. The farmers in these townships experienced an amazingly low level of foreclosures and tax sales per one thousand farms, and even per thousand owners, for the duration of the depression and drought.[27] The low level of forced sales did not necessarily reflect any special economic resilience on the part of families in these townships. Instead, it reflected a number of factors militating against land seizures. First, officials of many county governments placed an unofficial moratorium on efforts to collect outstanding taxes during the depression. The economic and environmental situation provided neither county officials nor bank managers much incentive to seize financially troubled farms. Once in possession of this land, they had little chance of selling it and recovering their losses; unsold land, in turn, became a very heavy financial burden. Owners were liable for taxes on this property and for preventing the soil from blowing, in accordance with soil-drifting resolutions adopted in all of Kansas' Dust Bowl counties. An owner could spend fifty cents an acre to list land following a single storm. No bank manager accepted that responsibility lightly, especially when the drought showed no sign of abating. Finally, what these figures do not reflect is voluntary relinquishment by owners and other special agreements between individuals and their banks. That the banks and counties refused to take ownership of Dust Bowl farms provides a good index of the severity of the depression and drought and the destruction visited upon the land.

The complex pressures affecting families and communities help to explain the variations in persistence from township to township. The people of Highpoint Township consistently enjoyed the highest rate of persistence, with 75 percent of those present in 1930 remaining in 1935, and 60 percent in 1940. Newcomers in 1935 had the best chance of remaining until 1940, 53 percent, as opposed to 44 percent for new entrants in all five townships. Although the residents of Highpoint Township had no special advantages in terms of the number of landowners, they had the largest families, the most extensive kin networks, and a high degree of large-scale participation in milk, egg, and butter production. A large percentage of the newcomers in 1935 were actually life-long residents, the children of established community members. The township's residents entered the depression well-equipped to meet its challenges.

The similarities of the persistence histories of residents of both Pleasant Valleys and Logan Township reflect the similarities of the three townships, each having moderate levels of landholding, average-sized families, fewer kin networks than in Highpoint Township, and moderate participation in economic sidelines. They were the area's average farmers, perhaps more poorly equipped to survive a decade of hardships successfully.

The people of Medway Township, who had a very poor persistence record, also had very low levels of landholding, average-sized families, and no linkages joining more than one family to another. Twenty of twenty-six families had no family relationships with their neighbors. In 1930, milk, butter, and egg production was foreign to area residents, with only one family producing enough to meet its own basic needs. Their experience could not have been more different from that of the people of Highpoint Township. Perhaps because of the late date of the township's settlement and its location so very far to the west the people of Medway township faced the 1930s without the benefits that the residents of the other four townships enjoyed.

Certainly, other factors influenced the decisions of individual families to stay or leave during hard times. Assessment of the intangible, but extremely important, support that people drew from family and neighbors is very difficult. This type of support makes survival possible for people in almost impossible situations. One family lost their farm in 1930 but made their way through the decade largely because of all-important aid from relatives and friends. Although they "wanted to go it alone," they were grateful for the aid of friends and family. When they could not afford their own home, they borrowed a basement house from a neighbor and raised geese from eggs given by relatives and hens from eggs a neighbor offered. They heated their home with cow chips gathered from a neighbor's field and fed the few cattle they owned with feed borrowed from the same neighbor who lent them their home. It was a meager existence—as the woman remembered it, "no telephone, no newspaper, no radio"—but they managed. "It was poverty, and I didn't know it." The odds were against it, but they endured and persisted.[28] This family was not the only one to maintain its resolve at least partly through the love and support of friends and family.

Just as individuals and families had characteristics which made them more or less prone to migrate during the 1930s, the region's counties had variable experiences with migration as well. The differences were considerable. Finney County lost 8 percent of its total population during the 1930s, twice the rate of depopulation experienced by the state of Kansas during the decade. Nonetheless, it was a considerable feat for a Dust Bowl county to lose only 8 percent of its population, given the disastrous conditions facing the area for the larger part of a decade. At the other end of the spectrum was Morton County, which thoroughly succumbed to the drought and depression and lost 47 percent of its total population. Both the experience of Morton County and that of Finney County were extreme. The average county in the study sample lost 24 percent of its people. The considerable variation between the best case, Finney County, and the worst case, Morton County, suggests that the people in those counties and the fourteen in between experienced the problems of the thirties in significantly different ways.[29]

The urban counties all remained above the median population decline. They include Ford County, which sported the largest city in the area, Dodge City. It was the oldest, best-established urban area in the region—more than 10,000 people lived there in 1930. Finney County, too, had a fairly large city, Garden City, which had a population of just over 6,000. Seward County brought up the rear. Its major city, Liberal, had just over 5,000 residents at the outset of the Great Depression. Over the course of the decade, Finney County lost 8 percent of its population, while Garden City grew by 3 percent. Ford County lost 17 percent of its people; Dodge

City, 16 percent. Liberal shrank by 17 percent, and the county had a 19 percent population loss, both figures perhaps a reflection of a major tornado that destroyed a good deal of the town in 1933. On the whole, however, the people of these counties sustained themselves somewhat better than those in other locales.

That the residents of these urban counties did better than many of their neighbors is most likely attributable to the relatively large cities within their borders. The times dictated that people would be attracted to towns. The dust was generally less severe in town, and farming families moved to urban areas to escape the worst of the dust storms and to send their children to school. Rural schools were closing, and transporting children to town each day could be difficult or impossible, given poor weather conditions and the cost and difficulty of keeping of vehicles operating. For families with children, towns offered certain advantages over badly blown rural neighborhoods. Once in town, families could support themselves by commuting to the farm to work or by locating jobs in factories or with relief projects.

The area's largest cities had other advantages as well. Each of these cities was a regional trading center, and much of the business for outlying

A woman outside her home, which was devastated by Liberal's 1933 tornado. (Photo by James Harvey Riney; by permission of Elsie Riney)

rural communities passed through them. Each was on at least one major rail line, either the Atchinson, Topeka, and Santa Fe or Rock Island—or both—and handled freight for more remote areas. Southwestern Kansas had little industry, but that which it did have was centered in the larger towns. Garden City had its sugar plant, the largest manufacturing concern in the area. The company paid out $1,000 a week to workers during the three months of beet harvesting and processing and spent another quarter of a million dollars in the other nine months of the year. Residents of Liberal were engaged in broomcorn processing, and wage earners in Dodge City processed poultry, milled flour, and worked in railroad shops. There were nine manufacturing companies in Finney County, twenty in Ford County, and six in Seward County. Morton and Kearny counties had five and four manufacturers, respectively, but employed only a fraction of the workers involved in manufacturing in the three largest counties.[30] Factory employment was scarce and generally only available in the largest of towns, Garden City, Dodge City, and Liberal.

These communities also operated more active relief distribution networks. Large towns generally had sewing rooms and hot lunch programs that other communities lacked or established them in advance of other towns. Most WPA projects were centered in towns, and poor commissioners in most counties directed their share of federal funds toward swimming pools, stadiums, and other urban projects. Dodge City was able to sponsor an enormous relief garden and operated a federal transient camp, as did Liberal. The major towns were also large enough that their citizens could more effectively canvass for private relief than in smaller communities, although the results were not always encouraging. As previously discussed, residents of Finney County created and maintained their own private relief network for more than a year. Red Cross volunteers in Liberal maintained an active relief distribution center for the duration of the decade. C. C. Isely, a Dodge City businessman, was able to appeal for enough federal money to realize a personal dream, a subsistence farming community for the unemployed of Dodge City and Ford County. These programs stumbled and sometimes fell, but they were more extensive and farther reaching than those most smaller communities could muster. Even if these cities could not always carry through on what they promised, life in them may have seemed more hopeful than to residents of the area's sandblasted rural communities.

In addition to Finney, Ford, and Seward counties, another five non-urban counties fell below the median population loss of 20 percent. Clark,

This abandoned land near Syracuse once produced forty bushels to the acre. (Farm Security Administration photo by Russell Lee; Library of Congress)

Hodgeman, and Wichita counties lost 15 percent of their populations. Eighteen percent of the residents of Ness County left or died, as did 19 percent of those in Meade County. Some characteristics defined these counties and helped to shape their migration histories.[31] None of the residents of these counties had the geographic misfortune of being at the heart of the Dust Bowl. Four of these five counties were on the fringes of the Dust Bowl, lying either farther north or farther east of the most severely affected areas. Only Meade County was surrounded by counties experiencing very severe drought.

Better weather conditions affected the earning potential of farmers in these five counties. Between 1931 and 1939, the mean value of products produced on these farms was $1,916.44. In no year during the 1930s did the value of products produced per farm fall below $1,000 a year, before government payments. Farm income was fairly consistent and generally higher than in other parts of southwestern Kansas.[32] Additionally, none of these five counties was marked by above average population growth in the years between 1920 and 1930. The people were a little more seasoned, and perhaps a little more rooted, than their contemporaries to the south and west. Also, compared to other counties in the area, more of their residents were foreign-born, or second-generation residents of the

United States, a characteristic that tended to create lower levels of mobility.[33] The demographic characteristics of these counties, in addition to environmental and economic conditions, provide at least a partial explanation of the lower rates of depopulation in these five counties.

The 1930s were not quite so forgiving for the people of Grant, Gray, Hamilton, Haskell, Kearny, Morton, Stanton, and Stevens counties. In each, the population fell by more than 20 percent over the course of the decade. Hamilton and Kearny counties each lost 21 percent of their people; Gray County lost 23 percent. Twenty-six percent of the population of Haskell County migrated. Stevens and Stanton counties lost 31 and 33 percent, respectively. The population of Grant County shrank by 37 percent. Morton County experienced the steepest decline. By the decade's end, 47 percent fewer people lived within its borders. The 1930s were not a hopeful period in their collective histories.

Just as the counties that managed fairly well had certain characteristics in common, those counties that lost a greater proportion of their people had similarities as well. Geographically, they were in the center of the Dust Bowl, surrounded by other counties experiencing very severe drought. Five of the counties most severely depopulated, Haskell, Stevens, Stanton, Grant, and Morton, formed a block in the southwestern corner of the Dust Bowl where rainfall was naturally lower, even prior to the drought. Although the borders of the drought shifted throughout the decade, that particular area never escaped its grasp.[34]

As a result of the very severe drought conditions in the heart of the Dust Bowl, the value of agricultural products harvested by area operators was considerably lower than on less severely affected farms. The mean value of products produced per farm was $1,498.86 between 1931 and 1939, more than $400 less per year than for farms outside this most troubled zone. Additionally, farmers in the hardest hit areas suffered some very bad years in the late 1930s. In 1937 in Stanton County, the value of products per farm was $471.97, and in 1938, $733.47. In Morton County, the situation was considerably worse; farmers there suffered terribly during the period from 1936 to 1938. In 1936, the average value of products produced was $573.10, in 1937, $351.88, and in 1938, $304.41.[35] It was no wonder that farmers, even those whose land was not purchased by the government, left in droves.

Residents of this hard-hit zone may well have been unprepared for the economic downturn during the 1930s. A 1910 census bureau map of Kansas showed that four of the five worst hit counties were also four of the five last counties in Kansas to attain population levels of more than two people to the square mile. A good proportion of their populations arrived in the 1920s, in the midst of prosperous times. Haskell County grew by 93 percent in the 1920s, Stanton County by 137 percent, and Grant County by 184 percent. These three counties were among those hurt worst by depopulation in the 1930s. The five counties with the highest levels of depopulation also lacked the strengthening infusion of an immigrant population. Newcomers arrived just in time for a decade of discouragement.

Not all of the factors affecting individual decisions to remain or to migrate from southwestern Kansas are quantifiable. The "spirit" or commitment within a community to maintain business as usual, or the failure of that spirit and consequent community disintegration, is difficult to gauge. Agricultural extension agents, who were in a unique position to comment upon the mental state of the residents of the communities they served, noted that this process was under way in various Dust Bowl counties. In 1939, the home demonstration agent, or home economist, in Ford County wrote that there were not "quite so many 'next yearers'" in the county, a condition which tended to encourage migration. In the same year, the agricultural extension agent in Morton County commented that the extreme conditions in that corner of the Dust Bowl had mentally and financially "crushed" the people to the extent that they could not, or would not, cooperate in the fight against the effects of drought and blown dust. In desperation, he warned that unless residents learned to work together, "it might seem that the Soil Conservation Service might just as well return this county to a grazing area." Crushed, contentious people would be more likely to migrate than those who learned to cooperate with each other and who gained strength from the effort.[36]

What becomes evident is that not all farming families and not all localities entered the 1930s with equal chances of survival. The conditions of the decade were to the advantage of practically no one, but financial stability and community connections helped some residents to survive more or less intact, while the same conditions forced others to retreat.

Southwestern Kansas was home to a fairly large population of Mexican citizens, who worked in the fields and along the railroad tracks of the area, and an African American population, which was spread throughout a number of rural locations but with its greatest concentration in the towns of Garden City and Dodge City. For these southwestern Kansans, racial and ethnic differences removed them from the mainstream of their communities and compounded their problems during the decade. Mexicans and African Americans experienced the drought and Great Depression much differently than the other inhabitants of southwestern Kansas.

The region's Mexican population suffered terribly from the problems of the 1930s. Most were not citizens of the United States but had come to southwestern Kansas to fill jobs with the railroads and at the Garden City Company's sugar plant. As railroad employees, most worked in track maintenance or performed other manual labor. In the beet fields, they planted, hoed, thinned, and topped—again, all hard manual labor.[37] Although wages were not high, the jobs attracted enough Mexicans to southwestern Kansas for them to become the largest group of foreign-born residents in the area. In 1930, enumerators counted nearly 2,000 Mexicans in southwestern Kansas, ranging from a high of 614 in Ford County to none in Morton, Stanton, and Stevens counties. The troubles of the 1930s devastated the Mexican community, reducing their numbers in southwestern Kansas to 460 by 1940, a 74 percent decline (see Table A.11).

The economic downturn caused unemployed native-born workers to look more favorably on jobs that they would have scorned in better times. The managers of the Garden City Company, who normally hired Mexican workers for the hardest labor in the sugar beet fields, eliminated them from their payroll in 1932 in order to provide jobs for non-Mexicans on the relief rolls. J. W. King, a county commissioner, said that "he found no difficulty in securing the men for the jobs and that when more jobs were found he had plenty of men willing to work and very much in need of funds." Native-born workers seemed to prefer jobs normally reserved for Mexicans to no job at all, given their straitened circumstances. In future years, the company continued to reserve these jobs as relief work, although they occasionally provided them to Mexicans who were receiving welfare. Although relief officials were disturbed by the increasing numbers of Mexican families on the relief rolls, they preferred to save the pride of white workers by providing them jobs. County and federal relief administrators were unwilling to provide Mexicans with welfare; but they were equally unwilling to see available work, however menial, given to Mexican laborers when citizens were unemployed.[38]

Mexican men also had trouble keeping their jobs with the railroads. On

November 17, 1930, J. F. Lucey, the southwest regional director of President Hoover's emergency committee on unemployment, wrote to Kansas governor Clyde M. Reed, requesting that the railroads in the state discontinue their practice of hiring Mexican workers: "It occurs to me that a request from you as Governor of the State to the railroads responsible for bringing this class of labor into Kansas to return them to Mexico . . . would materially help the unemployment situation. In any event, it occurs to me that citizens of our own country should receive preference to employment as against those of a foreign nation." The governor, in turn, contacted the six major railroads and requested that they employ only "home labor." Although the presidents of several of the railroads protested that they did not employ very many Mexican laborers, most agreed that they would not do so in the future, as far as was feasible. The president of the Chicago, Rock Island, and Pacific believed that he was bound to honor aliens covered by union contracts and those satisfactorily performing jobs that they had held for years, but he promised to hire "unemployed American labor" for any new positions. Carl R. Gray, president of the Union Pacific System, informed the governor that Mexican laborers "who have not had several years service with us" were being dropped in favor of "American labor to the extent that it is available."[39]

The president of the Atchinson, Topeka, and Santa Fe was more concerned about the welfare of his company's Mexican workers than about Gov. Reed's directive. Although the company had attempted to increase its hiring of "white men," one of the two experimental gangs had not performed satisfactorily (only two of eighty native-born men continued to work), leaving the company to ponder the wisdom of using non-Mexican laborers. "When spring work opens up and we begin to lay new rails we shall be glad to use our own citizens just as far as they can be had for this work," wrote W. L. Story, president of the company. The Santa Fe Railroad was evidently unable to find adequate non-Mexican laborers in the following years; the company acquired a bunkhouse for Mexican workers from Kearny County in 1933 and 1934 and paid the rent into the county poor fund. Although this small window of opportunity remained for Mexican workers, their most reliable source of work began to dry up as employers consciously attempted to provide jobs to unemployed native-born workers.[40]

Given these conditions, it is not surprising that the number of Mexicans in southwestern Kansas fell dramatically. They lost their jobs, and they had limited access to relief. When Mexican families became impoverished and asked for aid, they risked deportation, even if their local county government was not actively or consistently engaged in repatriation. Apparently only one case of deportation occurred in Ford County, but the knowledge that this was a possibility may have kept Mexican families from asking for help, even when it was desperately needed.[41] There was some private aid available to Mexican residents, both from their own fraternal organizations and from the Garden City Ministerial Association in Finney County. The Ministerial Association helped settle the debts of the city's Mexican mission, and the Methodist church agreed to oversee and support its work. Private money, however, was scarce in the 1930s, and most Mexican families were forced to look to the cities and counties for aid. But relief dollars stretched only far enough to cover the needs of a few residents, and administrators had little to spare for individuals who were not citizens. As the numbers showed, many Mexicans chose to move on or return to Mexico, rather than fight a losing battle against the competition for jobs and relief money provided by unemployed native-born workers.[42]

The African American population experienced the 1930s much differently than the area's Mexicans, losing a quarter of its people instead of three quarters, a similar figure to the general population. Their numbers fell from just over 1,000 in 1930 to 762 in 1940, a decline of 24 percent. This decline, however, was unevenly distributed throughout the group as a whole. African Americans in cities and towns were much more likely to survive the 1930s than their rural counterparts. The African American population of Garden City fell from 252 to 199, while in Dodge City their population rose from 205 to 218. The increase in Liberal was much more remarkable: The African American population rose from three to forty-six. Overall, their numbers in the towns and cities of southwestern Kansas fell by 18 percent across the decade.

Urban African Americans faced their own set of problems, many of them similar to those faced by the Mexican population. Many men in urban areas supported themselves and their families by working at odd jobs. In depressed times this was an unreliable source of income, because "people began to do all of their own work that they could," and "the odd jobs became fewer and fewer." African American women who worked as domestics faced the same problems. They increasingly came into competition with white women of all ages who, because of the depression, were working as servants. The supply of jobs that black women counted on was diminishing because the jobs were "filled by girls of other races who were willing to work for their room and board or the families have taken care of their own work." Like Mexicans, African Americans found that white workers were taking jobs that they had scorned in good times, forcing them out of the job market.[43]

Like the white rural population, the African American rural population suffered disproportionate decreases in numbers. The white rural population, farming and nonfarming, shrank by 28 percent in the 1930s. The African American rural population diminished by 42 percent. Although those in Ford County essentially held their own and their numbers in Meade County increased, this was not typical of the area as a whole. Of the three counties with more than fifty African American rural residents, all saw their numbers diminished by 45 percent or more.[44] Rural African Americans faced the same problems as all other rural residents, namely the drought and dirt storms that destroyed their crops and their opportunity to make a living in agriculture. Additionally, they were handicapped by the same problems that had hampered their agricultural settlements since the Exoduster migration into Kansas in the post–Civil War years—lack of capital and low rates of land ownership.[45]

Probably the only reason that African Americans did not suffer migration rates as high as Mexicans was that they had relatively greater access to relief money. Unlike the Mexicans, they were citizens and could not be deported for requesting relief. In 1934, in Finney County, 133 African American people, or approximately 45 percent of their total population, received relief. In Ford County, it was 115 people, or 50 percent. They worked at relief jobs ranging from mattress making to road work to sewing, and some rural families joined the state's Homestead Rehabilitation program, initiated in Kansas in June 1934. Farm families enrolled in the program to improve their farms and become self-sustaining. The program was replaced by the FSA.[46]

Although African Americans had an easier time obtaining relief relative to the local Mexican population, this is not to imply that relief disbursal was color-blind. Chester Brown, an African American resident of Garden City, wrote to Congressman Clifford Hope to protest the poor treatment of Finney County's African American residents by relief administrators. Brown alleged that local officials had discriminated against people of color; he believed that an African American administrator "would be more sympathetic and helpful than a white person could be under the same circumstances."[47] If relief administration in Finney County and throughout southwestern Kansas operated in the same manner as it did elsewhere, Brown was probably right. The one-quarter of the African American population that relocated during the 1930s probably did so in response to diminishing job opportunities and limited access to local and federal relief dollars, in addition to the difficulties associated with the drought and dust storms which affected all.[48]

There was no single "persistence history" for all of the people of southwestern Kansas. Analysis of the agricultural census records of farming families of five townships shows that they were helped by their status as landowners, the large size of their farms, their subsistence activities, and the family and kin connections to others in their township that they enjoyed. In some ways, these characteristics define rootedness and prosperity, which could only help people to maintain their farms in the face of serious economic dislocations. Localities benefited from the presence of industry, favorable geographic situation, and the lack of recent, heavy migration into the county. Again, prosperity and a longer period of community establishment worked in favor of population maintenance. Mexican and African American families, lacking the financial stability or equal access to public resources, suffered proportionally greater hardships and heavier population losses. In many ways, the experience of the 1930s confirmed the obvious: It was best to enter hard times with financial and emotional resources large enough to provide a cushion against economic and environmental disintegration.

EPILOGUE:
THE DUST SETTLES

Despite the hardships of the decade, the 1930s finally ended, and beleaguered southwestern Kansans heaved a collective sigh of relief. The fortunes of the area's residents were not long in changing, once the process of mending began. The most important element in this process was the return of more normal patterns of rainfall. Although "normal" southwestern Kansas rainfall would look meager to most midwesterners, the 1940s were bountiful years for area farmers. In fact, in terms of moisture, they were the best years southwestern Kansans had seen since the turn of the century.[1] Without this increase in rainfall, it would have been impossible for local farmers to take advantage of the conditions created by the war in Europe.

Even though the drought had lowered production considerably, American farmers had for years been producing far more grain than the people of the United States could consume or the U.S. could profitably export. The drought reduced, but did not eliminate, that overproduction. The war, which made it necessary for the U.S. to support its European allies, provided more than adequate markets for American farm products. Although production limitation had been the USDA's main goal during the thirties, this concern gave way to the exigencies of wartime, and the government encouraged farmers to produce and produce extravagantly. The combination of greater yields and higher prices meant a return to prosperity for people who had wondered if that day would ever come. The average southwestern Kansas farmer, who had produced only one or two thousand dollars worth of products per year during the 1930s, experienced a bonanza in the early forties. In 1942, with the benefit of abundant moisture and war-stimulated prices, that same farmer produced $11,183.33 in crops and livestock, a sum that would have seemed incomprehensible but a few years before.[2] World War II meant an astoundingly swift economic recovery for the region's battered population.

The return of prosperity could be gauged by the increase in the value of farm land throughout southwestern Kansas. In 1940, an enterprising and far-sighted individual could have purchased land in Hamilton County for a mere $7 an acre; by 1945, that investment would have been worth $14 an acre, and in 1950, $43 an acre. An investor in Morton County would have had a similar experience, purchasing land for only $8 an acre in 1940 and seeing its value rise to $49 an acre by 1950. These were substantial increases in land values, even when adjusted for inflation.[3] Hard times had driven down farm incomes and land values, problems which were corrected by the relative prosperity of the following years.

Improvements in the farm economy inspired a return trickle of population to southwestern Kansas. When Dust Bowl conditions were at their height in 1937 the area's population reached its lowest point. The number of inhabitants in southwestern Kansas increased between 1938 and 1940, but in 1940 the region was still only at 75 percent of its population of the previous decennial census. In fact, six of the sixteen Dust Bowl counties have never regained the population levels of 1930. One of these is Morton County, which began the 1940s with 2,186 inhabitants, down from 4,092 in 1930. In 1940, a writer for the *Elkhart Tri-State News* cheerfully predicted that "500 to 1000 old timers may again take up their homes in Morton County, thus repeating the historical colonizing waves of the late '8os and from 1907 to 1910."[4] For Morton County, like several others, this was not to be; in 1990, 3,480 people lived there. Although the urban counties, Finney, Ford, and Seward, enjoyed fairly substantial increases in the number of residents in the ten or twenty years following the Great Depression, the size of most counties has either increased or decreased at a fairly modest rate. The 1930s initiated a period of winnowing and stabilization for the people of the region. The wild up and down fluctuations in total population that characterized the settlement period as well as the hard times of the thirties were over.

Those southwestern Kansans who endured the 1930s or returned at the decade's end envisioned changes for their counties in a new and improved future. They hoped to rebuild their communities in ways that would allow them to withstand any future economic and environmental shocks. People believed that one of the elements of this future should be an industrial base for southwestern Kansas. A 1937 editorial in the *Southwest Daily Times* outlined a three-point plan to capture manufacturing business that they hoped would shore up the local economy and stave off future depressions. First, residents needed to advertise their community in the most positive light, particularly its low gas rates. Second, all residents, but especially county and city officials, should make Liberal attractive to firms by "fostering the industries we already have, by demonstrating that we are sympathetic toward industries and are willing to go more than half way in giving them every possible advantage in Liberal." And finally, they should hope and pray that industrial decentralization would occur in the postdepression economy. Only through concerted effort could the people of southwestern Kansas' towns expect to create an industrial base and ensure a more prosperous and stable future.[5]

Many southwestern Kansans also believed that agricultural reform was necessary to a more secure future for the region. The key to improved farming, in the words of agricultural extension agents, was diversification. The Ford County agent argued that dependence upon wheat was down-right dangerous and left farmers vulnerable to repeated failure. His counterpart in Morton County wanted the individual farmer to establish "a truly diversified economic farm and forget the cash grain idea except as a minor sideline." Another agent in Gray County suggested that farm operators should make their farms their homes—become more self-sufficient. The development of a livestock industry to complement cash grain sales would lead to "a more stable business system and a better community with happier people," he predicted.[6]

Diversification also concerned newspaper editors, who presented their readers with reasons to stay in southwestern Kansas and ways in which to accomplish that goal. The editors of the *Ulysses News* argued that gas wells and carbon black plants in Grant County were not enough to ensure the county's future: "Too much dependence is still placed on the easy, big profits of wheat. Diversification is the chief challenge before all farmers who won't wait to be forced from wheat." The editor of the *Garden City Daily Telegram* agreed and pointed to the successes of farmers under the FSA's rehabilitation program as evidence. The "balanced farming" on FSA farms brought those families greater stability and promised to bring the same security to farmers throughout the region.[7] Improving weather conditions gave farmers the chance to start over again and to alter their practices in order to ensure continued good times in the years ahead.

Southwestern Kansans placed the most hope for the future, however, in irrigation, a logical conclusion on their part, since they believed that their most vexing problems would be solved "if it would only rain." They

Getting ready to put in the pumping machinery for an irrigation well in the Garden City vicinity in 1939. (Farm Security Administration photo by Russell Lee; Library of Congress)

described their groundwater supply as bountiful, never-ending, never failing, and flowing unimpaired, despite years of drought on the plains. Tapping into that reserve, many farmers believed, would provide the region with enough moisture to secure their futures, even in the driest of years.[8]

A number of people suggested ways the irrigation of southwestern Kansas should be accomplished. J. C. Hopper, former resident of Ness County and a migrant to Glendale, California, wrote Congressman Clifford Hope with a fanciful solution to the region's ills. Instead of relying upon groundwater, Hopper proposed that the federal government dig a "great canal, from the Black [H]ills to the Gulf of Mexico," in order to bring water to the plains. Owen K. Sheldon of Liberal wrote to Hope with a more reasonable solution. He believed that deep wells powered by wind chargers would provide water at a minimal cost to the parched fields of southwestern Kansas. Additionally, the windmills would provide power for numerous other home and farm chores. As he put it, "The very cause of the trouble out here may be the means of solving the difficulties. That cause is the wind."[9]

Although few others mentioned the possibility of harnessing the wind for pumping and electricity, the Chambers of Commerce in Stevens, Seward, and Clark counties endorsed deep well irrigation and suggested that the federal government sponsor such irrigation projects in their counties. H. A. Kinney, secretary of Liberal's Chamber of Commerce, went on record in favor of deep well irrigation. He believed that in conjunction with terracing, contour farming, and improved listing, the "unlimited supply of water from a few feet . . . underground" would make Seward County "the garden spot of the southwest." It was a dream that many southwestern Kansans shared, as they channeled their energies into pilot irrigation projects in 1938, 1939, and 1940.[10]

These visions reflected the hopes and dreams of people emerging from a ten-year nightmare and determined not to repeat the past. They desired a more secure economic future, based on industry and sound agricultural practices. They wanted to insure themselves against the recurrence of drought and Dust Bowl conditions. And they wanted to take these actions themselves and be as free from government interference as possible. A writer, discussing an irrigation project in Morton County, summed up the attitude of many southwestern Kansans as they faced the future: "Regardless of success or failure these men are to be praised for their courage and initiative. Instead of sitting on their haunches and howling, waiting for the government to decide their fate, they have taken action and are shaping their own destinies."[11]

From the vantage point of the late twentieth century, southwestern Kansans have watched the progress of the dreams of the late 1930s. Some, like hopes for an industrial future for the region, have remained only dreams. In 1930, at the Great Depression's outset, only 5.5 percent of all employed southwestern Kansans worked for manufacturing firms. Predictably, higher concentrations of industrial workers made their homes in the area's most urban counties. In Finney County, 7 percent of the employed population worked in manufacturing, as did 10 percent in Ford County and 9 percent in Seward County. They worked mainly for companies engaged in refining agricultural products, such as millers, sugar refiners, and broomcorn processors. In other counties, between 1 and 5 percent of the working population found employment with a few small manufacturing firms.[12]

Very little has changed, and still very few southwestern Kansans work in manufacturing. In 1987, only 35 manufacturers employed more than 20 persons; only three employed more than 99 persons; and four had more than 250 employees. These seven largest firms are all located in Finney, Ford, and Seward counties.[13] Although companies have come and gone over the years, most of these workers still process agricultural products. The Garden City Company's sugar plant no longer operates, and Liberal is no longer the broomcorn capitol of the southwest, but meat packing plants have taken their place, with Iowa Beef Packers, among others, owning and operating plants and feed lots in Garden City, Dodge City, and Liberal. Ulysses, in Grant County, has also made the transition to a more industrial economy, unlike most of the region's other cities and towns. During the 1930s, entrepreneurs took advantage of the abundant natural gas in the area and constructed two carbon black plants, which remain the industrial base of the county. In 1980, the situation in the twelve other counties was essentially as it was in 1930—between 2 and 5 percent of their working populations earned their living in manufacturing, with the rest in agriculture, retail and wholesale trade, and other service occupations. For the most part, industrial development has been confined to a few locations, and there has been little or no increase in the total amount of manufacturing in the other counties. The vision of an "industrial revolution," which many people hoped would provide a more secure future, has not been realized.[14]

For the residents of those counties with an industrial base, the years

Finishing an irrigation well on a farm in the Garden City vicinity in 1939. (Farm Security Administration photo by Russell Lee; Library of Congress)

following the Great Depression have been a little brighter as they have continued to grow. Of the sixteen counties in southwestern Kansas, nine experienced growth between 1980 and 1990. For four of these counties, Grant, Gray, Haskell, and Morton, however, growth was small, 5 percent or less. Finney, Ford, and Seward counties all had large numbers of new residents in 1990, probably because of the industrial employment available. Stevens County, with its enormous reserves of natural gas and attendant pumping stations, has grown since the 1930s, but more modestly than Finney, Ford, and Seward counties. Kearny County was the only predominantly agricultural county that grew substantially in the last decade. The dreamers were right; industrial development has meant sustained growth for the citizens of those communities lucky enough to attract industry. Unfortunately for the rest, the lack of industry and opportunities outside of agriculture has meant a steady migration of young people to other locations where they perceive opportunities to be better.[15]

Agricultural change also did not progress in the ways that reformers envisioned. Agricultural extension agents wanted farmers in southwestern Kansas to make their farms "places to live," from which their residents would derive their sustenance, as well as a cash income. In 1940, had an agricultural extension agent looked over the census reports on farmers who had survived the thirties, he might have been encouraged about the possibilities for such a program. "Old timers" seemed to appreciate the idea of diversification. Although the drought depleted their flocks of chickens and numbers of cattle and swine were somewhat diminished, many still maintained sufficient livestock to provide their families with food and to sell for profit.

The old-timers, however, were not the only farmers in the area. Those farmers who arrived after the 1930 agricultural census farmed far differently. They planted a larger percentage of their lands in wheat and fewer acres of other grains and forage crops. Among those who arrived after 1935, cattle were almost a thing of the past, as were swine, and they owned just a third of the number of hens that the average "old-timer" raised. The operations of these newer farmers were indicative of things to come.[16]

Over the next fifty years, farmers moved farther and farther away from the ideals reformers espoused at the end of the Great Depression. Farm size grew during the depression and continued to grow thereafter. Farmers planted considerably less diverse crops, shifting more heavily into wheat and plowing up pastures as they decided to eliminate cattle and swine for home consumption from their operations. Although some farmers diversified into corn and sorghum, these decisions generally reflected the availability of irrigation water. The range of crops has diminished, rather than expanded.

Rural districts throughout southwestern Kansas appear far different to-day. A visitor would be hard-pressed to find a flock of chickens on a farm, much less a milk cow or a pig. There are few gardens that would yield fifty, one hundred, or two hundred quarts of food to feed a family through the winter. Many rural neighborhoods are no longer neighborhoods, but vir-tually empty districts. Families have left the land for other occupations, and many of the farmers who remain have moved to the county seats in order to enjoy the amenities of town life. They have become "sidewalk farmers," commuting to their land much as city-dwellers commute to their workplaces.[17] The more remote county seat towns, like many rural districts, are succumbing to the aging and migrations of their populations as well. For example, Jetmore, the county seat of Hodgeman County, was home to 1,028 people in 1960. In 1990, only 855 people lived there, down from 862 in 1980.[18] The same reductions in population affected Ashland, Syracuse, Ness City, and Meade. In six of the Dust Bowl coun-ties, individuals over sixty-five years of age make up more than 15 percent of the total population.[19] Transported to the present, the agricultural agents of the 1930s would hardly recognize the farms and communities they tried to reform so many years ago.

Farms without the usual garden, milk cow, chickens, and pig might have been considered poor farms fifty years ago, but not so today. Al-though entire rural neighborhoods are empty, or fading fast, the farmers apparently are not impoverished.[20] As compared to the rest of the state, southwestern Kansas is a high-income farming area. In 1970, 1980, and 1990, the value of agricultural products produced by the farmers of south-western Kansas was at least 65 percent higher than that produced on the average farm in the state. As in the 1930s, farm income seems to have affected the ability of farmers to maintain their holdings in southwestern Kansas. Of the nine counties that have grown very little since the 1930s, seven showed consistently lower than average value of farm production in 1970 and 1980. The exceptions are Kearny County and Wichita County, whose farmers produced well, yet left anyway. Both counties are within a very short distance of major towns, Scott City and Garden City, and farmers may be commuting to their land from these population centers. Most counties that showed consistent population growth had a stronger agricultural income base, in addition to some industrial activity. As in the "dirty thirties," some counties were better equipped to deal with fluctuations in the economy and therefore able to hold their people more successfully.[21]

The high farm incomes throughout most of southwestern Kansas essentially reflect the one dream of the late 1930s that came true—irrigation. Irrigated farmland yields more abundantly, and in turn, farmers who irrigate their land depend on the correspondingly higher income to pay the cost of machinery and fuel for pumping.[22] Farmers made investments in irrigation early in the history of southwestern Kansas, but accelerated their pace following the Dust Bowl. Between 1940 and 1954, they installed a good deal of irrigation equipment, as a report from the Kansas State Finance Council showed. In 1954, the amount of irrigated farmland in southwestern Kansas ranged from a low of 285 acres in Clark County, to 81,800 acres in Finney County, the most highly irrigated county in all of Kansas. Farmers in Finney County rely upon water from the Arkansas River, in addition to groundwater. In 1954, 80 percent of all irrigated acres in Kansas were in the nineteen counties in the southwestern corner of the state.[23]

Since that year, the number of southwestern Kansas farmers irrigating their lands has increased rapidly. The drought of 1953 and 1954, which temporarily brought the "filthy fifties" to the old Dust Bowl, inspired farmers to even greater efforts to make use of groundwater. The most highly irrigated portion of the state is still the southwest. By the early 1980s, the number of irrigated acres in the region, according to SCS personnel, ranged from a low of 2,600 acres in Clark County, to a high of 259,300 in Finney County, with a total of 1,936,100 acres under irrigation. This water has become so essential to the operations of farmers in southwest Kansas that the authors of a recent history of agriculture in Kansas defined nine of sixteen Dust Bowl counties as prime agricultural land only in the presence of irrigation, a judgment that would have surprised most of the region's farmers fifty years before.[24] This intense reliance upon irrigation by farm operators is an enduring legacy of the Dust Bowl. The land is dry and hard to manage, and since the 1930s, farmers have understood the astounding costs of a prolonged drought. By tapping the Ogallala Aquifer, in addition to the area's rivers, they have attempted to prevent a recurrence of the disastrous 1930s. In doing so, they have increased the short-term productivity of their farms. In 1990, on average, the farmers of southwestern Kansas reaped an extra eleven bushels per acre on irrigated lands, above and beyond the yields of summer fallowed fields.[25]

Memories are persistent. Many of the individuals interviewed for this project clearly recalled those years and have come to interpret their experiences during the thirties as positive. When asked to relate their most vivid memories of the decade, many respondents mentioned the all pervading dust, but many also cast the experience in terms of what they learned or gained from living through hard times. The depression and Dust Bowl were years that built character, they believed.

Horace Malin, a longtime resident of Seward County, commented that the Dust Bowl "turned out to be quite a challenge. . . . It separated the sheep from the goats. The people who just had a little pride and a little grit stayed with it." Elfreda Penner Fast, who grew up in Gray County, also remembered the decade in terms of its strengthening qualities. "I think through all of this time I had a sense of security. . . . We were always challenged and optimistic, we knew there was something to do." Survivors also remembered the closeness with family and friends that made those years livable and even enjoyable. The trials of the 1930s also set them apart from a younger, softer generation, born too late for the Dust Bowl. Hazel Steenis Shriver spoke for a number of older Kansans when she commented, "I don't know what young people would do in that situation now." In many ways, the Dust Bowl years defined older southwestern Kansans. Like combat veterans, they had been through the worst that the region had to offer and had emerged stronger for the experience.[26]

The Dust Bowl may have changed survivors in other ways, shaping their understanding of the way in which their lives and their children's lives should be lived. A 1965 survey of students at Kansas State Agricultural College (now Kansas State University) revealed that many were attending college at least partially because of their parents' Dust Bowl experiences. Given the deprivations of the 1930s, parents wanted their children "to acquire something that can't be lost, to 'acquire security.' . . . Education is seen by our students' parents, and hence by the students, as a means to security—as acquiring tangible facts, skills and information that are not destroyed by economic conditions nor 'blown away' by the quirks of nature."[27] From the perspective of these researchers, the experience and memory of the 1930s made Kansas parents more education-oriented and committed to providing their children a hedge against unpredictable nature. Whether this caution applied to other areas of their lives outside of their children's education is unclear, but this example illustrates the degree to which the 1930s colored survivors' actions in the following decades.

The Dust Bowl lingers in other ways and has become integral to the area's remembered past. Local histories recount those days for the residents too young to remember. Although a writer prefaced a description of the dust storms in a history of Stevens County with the words "we would like to forget about the 'dirty thirties,'" it would seem that the region's people cannot. County and local histories cannot be written without extensive reference to rabbit drives, dust storms, and other trials of the 1930s, complete with photographs and eyewitness accounts. Centennial editions of local papers go to press with the first page of text devoted to the Dust Bowl, indicating the prominence of those events in the sweep of local history. A writer for the Southwest Daily Times concluded one such article with the following words: "The days when even the sunshine could be blotted out of the Seward County sky would always hang in Liberal's consciousness as a nightmare no one wants to repeat." H. Don Hazell, local writer and Dust Bowl survivor, published a small book of recollections and photographs that can be found in numerous southwestern Kansas homes.[28] Unpleasant as the experience may have been, the dusty years were the single time in the area's remembered past when it had the undivided attention of the nation. Consequently, the story of the storms and the stubborn folk who endured them is told and retold.

Anniversaries of the Black Sunday dust storm of April 15, 1935, also bring out the storytellers of southwestern Kansas. The Wichita Eagle Beacon of April 15, 1984, sported a picture of a "black roller" and included interviews with residents who had witnessed the storm. The Southwest Kansas Senior Beacon, a newsletter for the area's senior citizens, published a front-page story about Black Sunday in April 1985. As Tim Wenzel, editor of the Senior Beacon, wrote, Black Sunday was "a day that would forever be etched on the memories of those who experienced it." Given the importance of that day in the memories of older Kansans, Mr. Wenzel surely had no trouble finding people to recount their experiences.[29]

The periodic droughts that plague the area also bring the Dust Bowl back to the center of public discourse. The most recent period of serious drought occurred from the fall of 1988 through the spring of 1989. The dry conditions that fall, winter, and spring, during which the residents of the southern plains saw almost no rain or snow, precipitated a dust storm on March 14, 1989, that diminished visibility to one block in Garden City, closed Interstate 70 from the Colorado border to Hays, and disrupted air traffic as far away as Kansas City. Although the storm did not compare to the "rollers" of the 1930s, at least in the judgment of some older Kansans, it was enough to rekindle memories and bring the 1930s back to the front pages of local newspapers.[30]

The storm made the news all across Kansas, from the Colorado border to Kansas City. Not surprisingly, the largest headline in the *Garden City Daily Telegram* on March 15, 1989, read "Conditions Ripe for Rerun of 'Dirty '30s.'" The article was subtitled, "Two or three more days of this and we can cash it in." On page two, a writer asked, "Will It Be the Dirty '80s?" Other papers boasted similar headlines. The front page of the *Dodge City Globe* read "Dust storm brings small example of Dirty 30s to Ford County area." The *Wichita Eagle Beacon* informed its readers that "Yellow Haze Rekindles Dust Bowl Memories." The *Hutchinson News* quoted Tom Roberts, executive vice president for the Wheat Quality Council, as saying that the conditions were ripe for a return of the Dust Bowl. Roberts, implying that hard times were right around the corner, commented, "I hate to be the guy who cries 'wolf' but . . . ."[31] People were expecting the worst, a rerun of the "dirty thirties."

In a small way, these dire predictions were borne out. The drought continued until the last day of April, leaving the wheat too stunted to make a decent yield. Then it began to rain and rained from April 30 through the end of June, depositing as much as fifteen inches of moisture in some parts of southwestern Kansas. The drought was broken, but not in time for the area's wheat farmers. Dry conditions early in the growing season dwarfed the wheat, which was then choked by the weeds that grew up around it, encouraged by rains late in the growing season. Those farmers irrigating their crops suffered equally, having lost most of their wheat to several unexpectedly hard freezes in January. Many farmers left their combines parked during the harvest of 1989. Fortunately, the late rains of 1989 meant a much more abundant crop in 1990, rescuing the farmers of southwestern Kansas from a repetition of the hard times of the 1930s. Farmers, and all of the area's residents, could lay their fears of a return of the Dust Bowl to rest for another season.

Nevertheless, memories of the Dust Bowl and fears of its recurrence are never far from the surface in southwestern Kansas. Despite the availability of crop insurance and federal aid to farmers, no one wants to repeat the past. These fears are not unreasonable. The Dust Bowl was not simply a phenomenon of the 1930s. As long as Euro-Americans have inhabited the area, they have witnessed the repeated occurrence of drought and dust storms. The Wichita *Eagle* published the following notice in 1872: "Real estate for sale at this office, by the acre or bushel. We have no disposition to infringe upon the business of our friends down the street, but owing to the high winds and the open condition of our office, and not being ready for internment just yet, necessity compels to us [*sic*] dispose of the fine bottom land now spread over our type and presses."[32] Similar comments peppered the presses from the 1850s well into the present century. The problem has not disappeared, even in the years since the Dust Bowl. Despite government attempts to control the dust storms of the 1930s through improved farming methods, blowing dust returned in the 1950s and threatened in the 1970s. Partly, this was due to farmers abandoning the conservation measures of the thirties and plowing more acres to meet high wartime demand. As rain returned and the conditions of World War II made their abandonment profitable, use of conservation measures diminished.[33] In fact, dust storms are natural to the region, with its light, sandy soils, dry climate, and high spring winds. Dry soil can and does still blow, as it has done in the past.

Many farmers now irrigate their lands, but this is hardly a long-term solution to the problem of aridity on the southern plains. Groundwater pumping has significantly lowered the water table throughout southwestern Kansas, threatening the long-term viability of irrigation as a solution to dry conditions. Farmers are slowly but surely exhausting the Ogallala Aquifer, the source of water for much of the area's agricultural and household use. In some places, the water level has fallen one hundred feet below that of fifty years ago, and water quality has also diminished.[34] As one writer has described the situation, "Everything hinges on one constant—the weight of water—and two variables: the cost of energy and the price of food."[35] Groundwater pumping is expensive and becomes more expensive with every foot the water table subsides. Whether farmers will be able to afford to pump what water remains during the next twenty years is anyone's guess. One issue, however, seems sure. The underground water which southwestern Kansans depend upon in good years, as well as bad, is probably not a reliable foundation upon which to continue to build an agricultural future for the region.[36]

Some observers have forecasted a very bleak future for the people of southwestern Kansas. Frank J. Popper and Deborah Epstein Popper of

Rutgers University have predicted that the Great Plains will support only one more generation of agricultural settlement before succumbing to problems generated by an exhausted water supply and depleted soil: "We believe that over the next generation the Plains will, as a result of the largest and longest running agricultural and environmental miscalculation in America, become almost totally depopulated."[37] The authors suggest that the government tear down the fences, replant the short grass prairies, and restock wild animals, including bison, in order to create a "Buffalo Commons," a proposal that inspired anything but enthusiasm from the people of the plains.[38]

Marc Reisner, author of Cadillac Desert, a study of the West and its problems with water, was no more optimistic than the Poppers. Reisner has predicted a second Dust Bowl in the near future, at least as devastating as the first and without a 1940s-style recovery. He wrote that as the Ogallala Aquifer becomes depleted, economic realities will force farmers to plow again the marginal land they retired in the presence of irrigation. Sandy soils, unanchored by irrigated greenery, will take to the air in the grandest Dust Bowl fashion. Reisner described the present and future of the southern plains: "This, then, is the plains region today—a place that is reverting, slowly and steadily, into an amphitheater of natural forces toying with its inhabitants' fate." This description would have seemed quite familiar to the southwestern Kansans of the 1930s.[39]

John Opie in his book Ogallala: Water for a Dry Land explores the potential for sustainable agriculture throughout the southern plains. High Plains farmers, Opie asserts, are depleting the groundwater at a horrific pace, taking water at ten times the natural rate of replenishment.[40] Failure to rethink water-mining agricultural practices could be devastating for the region. "At worst, if Ogallala water becomes inaccessible over the next ten to thirty years, the region will become unmanageable and revert to a deserted land." Opie, however, does not believe that this has to be. "At best, rethinking the Ogallala and reworking High Plains agriculture could provide America with a model for sustainable development."[41] The potential exists, he argues, for either outcome.

It is too early to tell if the people of southwestern Kansas, after weathering the Dust Bowl and the enormous changes it wrought, will see their land revert to the buffalo or to an unmanageable desert. Farmers, and indeed all the region's people, face enormous challenges as the water table drops. It remains to be seen if they will meet these problems with workable, effective solutions. Much depends, too, on the market for the crops produced by southwestern Kansas farmers. At some time in the future, if prices and government subsidies fail to meet the cost of producing irrigated crops, farmers on the southern plains will likely choose to plant more drought-resistant crops or move out of agriculture altogether.

Given the primacy of meat packing in the economy of the area and the migration of people out of smaller county seat towns and into the larger cities of Garden City, Dodge City, and Liberal, the future of the region may very well be as a "cattle commons," with a few processing centers in its midst. The future of southwestern Kansas could look very much like its distant past, when its people depended upon grazing, trail drives, and the cattle towns as the cornerstones of their local economy.[42]

The dire predictions of the Poppers and of writers like Marc Reisner are not foregone conclusions, however. Those who hastened to respond to the Poppers' article suggested that the people of the plains would not give in so easily. One man wrote that "the people of the Great Plains are quite aware of the region's problems, and most are working to correct them." A member of the City Planning Commission in Hutchinson argued that the resilience of the people of the plains would carry the day. In his words, the actions of residents during the Dust Bowl suggested a "stubborn adaptability" that would have to be worked into any equation predicting the area's future. A woman, born and raised on the plains, suggested that the Poppers had "completely underestimated the vitality, ingenuity, and prosperity of the Plains people." Indeed, these critics are probably at least partially correct. Any evaluation of the future of the old Dust Bowl will have to take into account the extreme adaptability and stubbornness of people under stress, qualities that southwestern Kansans demonstrated so well during the 1930s.[43]

That the water upon which southwestern Kansas has staked its future will eventually become depleted seems certain, but that this means life there will end does not. The hardships of the 1930s encouraged residents to change their ways of farming, in the hope of avoiding another decade of bone-dry, dirty conditions. This does not mean, however, that the farm operators of southwestern Kansas must continue to plant corn and alfalfa, to irrigate their crops, and to continue to farm using the techniques that the circumstances of the 1930s encouraged. Southwestern Kansas is not a desert; it is a semiarid land, and from the 1880s through the 1930s, farmers made a living planting drought-resistant crops, expecting to lose the occasional crop to dry conditions.[44] In the late twentieth and early twenty-first centuries, accepting these conditions will be difficult, and there may be many who will prefer to leave farming altogether, rather than live through the ups and downs such an environment has to offer. Nonetheless, it might be done.

The people of southwestern Kansas endured the "dirty thirties," the most serious and sustained agricultural crisis to visit itself upon rural America, and did so with a great deal of grit, determination, and imagination. The odds against survival and the maintenance of viable communities were not favorable, and yet with cooperation and government assistance, they endured. Circumstances have periodically disrupted the purposes and plans of the people of southwestern Kansas, but they have yet to be driven en masse from the southern plains.

APPENDIX A:
QUESTIONNAIRE AND
ORAL HISTORY PROJECT

Oral history has been an invaluable resource for this project. I was unable to find more than a handful of letters and diaries recounting personal experiences of the Dust Bowl. Oral history is probably the only way to capture and preserve these experiences, and the time left to record these recollections is limited. Those remembering the Dust Bowl are, at the youngest, in their sixties. Cognizant of this, I constructed a questionnaire and oral history project in order to learn as much as I could about people's experiences of the Dust Bowl in their family and working lives.

During the fall of 1988, I distributed 144 questionnaires to residents of southwestern Kansas who had lived in the area during the 1930s (see copy of questionnaire at end of this appendix). My method in distributing these questionnaires was not particularly scientific. I sent informational flyers describing my project to relatives, libraries, and historical societies throughout the area and sent letters to the editors of some local papers. I then mailed questionnaires to those individuals who responded to my informational notice or letters. Of the 144 distributed, 125 were returned and 114 were usable. (Some were incomplete or the individual had not lived in one of the sixteen study counties during the 1930s.) Nevertheless, it was a surprisingly good response, which I attribute to one factor in particular. Those individuals who lived through the thirties in southwestern Kansas have very vivid memories of those years and have had little opportunity to share those memories. My project confirmed the personal importance survivors placed upon their experiences during the Great Depression.

I did not attempt to secure information from individuals who left southwestern Kansas during the 1930s to settle elsewhere, since my focus was on those who stayed behind.

These questionnaire responses were the basis for selecting seventy-one individuals for oral histories. I selected the individuals for the interviews on the basis of geographic, social, and occupational diversity. I also took into account the degree of willingness to be interviewed that the subject seemed to display in the questionnaire. Undoubtedly, there were many fascinating stories I did not hear because of time restrictions.

Each interview lasted from one-half hour to two hours. Most lasted forty-five minutes to an hour. In some I interviewed two people at once, usually married couples, siblings, or friends. Some sample questions were:

How did you make a living during the thirties?
Were you able to keep your job through the decade?
What are some ways in which you economized?
Were friends and family important to your decision to remain in south-
western Kansas?

My purpose was to learn as much as possible about the fabric of everyday life under the stresses imposed by the drought and dust storms. The interviews were by no means entirely comprehensive.

I have indexed the tapes used in this project. The indexes and tapes, as well as a number of the questionnaires, will eventually find a home at the Kansas State Historical Society. The survey questions read as follows:

Did your family come from southwestern Kansas?
If yes, when did they move to the area?
If not, where did your family live?
Did any members of your family live near you during the 1930s?
Please tell how many, and their relation to you.
Did they remain in the area throughout the 1930s?
Did your family in any way help or encourage you to remain in south-
western Kansas during the thirties?
Where did you live in 1930?
Where did you live in 1940?
How many moves (if any) did you make between 1930 and 1940?
Where did you move each time? Please include moves made both inside
and outside southwestern Kansas.
Briefly explain why you made these moves.
Are you, or have you ever been, married?
Date of marriage:
Are you now married, single, divorced, or widowed?

Do you have any children? Please list the date and location of birth for each child.

What occupations did you have during the 1930s?

Did you or anyone in your family participate in government work programs, such as the Works Progress Administration, the C.C.C., or the N.Y.A.?

Did you or your family participate in any other assistance programs between 1930 and 1940?

Did your community offer any type of local assistance?

If you were a farmer, or lived on a farm, did your family own the farm?

If so, when was the farm purchased?

If the farm was rented, who owned the land?

Did the land belong to a relative?

Did your family retain the farm through the 1930s?

Did you, or anyone else in the family, work off the farm for extra income during the 1930s?

Did you or your family participate in any government programs for farmers, such as the Agricultural Adjustment Administration, the Soil Conservation Service, or use the services of the local extension agent? Please list the years participated, and the services used.

Do you believe that these programs were important in helping your family to remain in farming?

Did your community have a farmers' cooperative? If so, did you or your family belong? Why or why not?

Did you belong to a church between 1930 and 1940?

If yes, to which church or churches did you belong?

How often did you attend?

Did you belong to any other organizations, such as the Masons, women's clubs, 4-H, or scouting? Please list the organizations to which you belonged, and the dates of your activity with them.

Did local churches or other organizations offer any programs to aid the community during the Depression?

In your opinion, what effect did the Depression and Dust Bowl have upon local organizations?

What is your impression of the impact of the Depression and Dust Bowl on banks and businesses in your area?

Did most of the people that you knew stay in southwestern Kansas through the Depression, or did they leave?

If you remained in the area between 1930 and 1940, why did you stay?

APPENDIX B:
USE OF THE KANSAS
STATE AGRICULTURAL CENSUS

One of my primary concerns in developing this project was that I be able to analyze persistence on a more detailed level than is possible using aggregate census data. Use of the federal manuscript census for this purpose was not possible; the Census Bureau adheres to a "seventy year rule," and individual level census data for 1930 and 1940 will not be available until the years 2000 and 2010, respectively. That left me with few options. I could attempt to reconstruct some sort of profile from tax records, as Richard Bremer did in *Agricultural Change in an Urban Age*. Unfortunately, such reconstructions offer little information about tenant farmers. I wanted to find an alternative source of data.

To my great elation, such a source exists for the state of Kansas. Each year throughout the 1930s and for a number of years both before and after the state counted its farmers, then recorded and stored the information in manuscript form. Ledgers are available for the years prior to 1937, and microfilm is available for the years since. The census is available in the Archives and Manuscripts Division of the Kansas State Historical Society in Topeka.

In the pages of this census, enumerators recorded the names of farmers, the size of their farms, what crops they grew and in what acreages, the number and kind of animals they raised, total butter and egg production, and income earned from milk and cream. The census also reveals the degree of mechanization on individual farms, recording numbers of tractors and combines. In many cases, the enumerator also listed household size.

Unfortunately, many bits and pieces of useful information were omitted. The age of the farm operator, land descriptions, and length of tenure were not available. Ownership status (owner, part-owner, or tenant) was stricken from the census in the late 1920s. Nevertheless, this census provides the most detailed information currently available for farms throughout Kansas.

On a completely random basis, I selected five southwestern Kansas townships for study. I then collected from the census all of the information available about farmers in each of the townships in 1930, 1935, and 1940. I followed data collection at the Kansas State Historical Society with visits to the county courthouses serving each of these townships. From transfer and deed records I ascertained which farmers owned land and whether they lost that land to a bank or the county during the study decade.

On my return from field work, I entered each case into the computer using DBase 3. I then transferred these files into SPSS PC+ for analysis, in order to calculate means and medians and to cross tabulate persistence with a number of other factors. The results of this analysis are presented in Chapter 8.

Undoubtedly, these records (and my analysis of them) have their limitations. There is no way of knowing if the census enumerator was careful, thorough, and unbiased in data collection. Because only the name of the head of household was listed, it was impossible to trace kin connections except by surname, leaving connections through females unexamined. And because I did not track the residents of these townships for every year of the 1930s (a truly daunting task), movements in the intervening years between sample dates went unrecorded. Much remains to be studied in these records; I have made only the most preliminary of forays into their depths.

APPENDIX C:
TABLES

Table A.1. Rural Rate of Total Population Increase per Decade, by County,
1900–1930 (in percentages)

County	1900–1910	1910–1920	1920–1930
Clark	+ 141	+ 22	− 4
Finney	+ 100	+ 3	+ 22
Ford	+ 100	+ 10	+ 21
Grant	+ 99	+ 2	+ 36
Gray	+ 130	+ 13	+ 15
Hamilton	+ 136	− 23	+ 29
Haskell	+ 117	+ 47	+ 93
Hodgeman	+ 44	+ 27	+ 11
Kearny	+ 190	− 18	+ 22
Meade	+ 220	+ 10	+ 24
Morton	+ 304	+ 138	+ 29
Ness	+ 30	+ 27	+ 12
Seward	+ 398	− 36	+ 7
Stanton	+ 216	+ 12	+ 37
Stevens	+ 296	+ 61	+ 18
Wichita	+ 68	− 8	+ 39
Mean change	+ 162	+ 17	+ 26

Source: U.S. Department of Commerce, Bureau of the Census, Thirteenth, Fourteenth, and Fifteenth censuses.

Table A.2. Change in Total Population per Decade, by County, 1880–1930 (in percentages)

County	1880– 1890	1890– 1900	1900– 1910	1910– 1920	1920– 1930
Clark	—	− 28	+ 141	+ 22	− 4
Finney	—	+ 4	+ 99	+ 11	+ 44
Ford	+ 70	+ 4	+ 107	+ 25	+ 45
Grant	—	− 68	+ 158	0	+ 184
Gray	—	− 48	+ 147	+ 51	+ 32
Hamilton	—	− 30	+ 136	− 23	+ 29
Haskell	—	− 58	+ 117	+ 47	+ 93
Hodgeman	+ 41	− 15	+ 44	+ 27	+ 11
Kearny	—	− 30	+ 190	− 18	+ 22
Meade	—	− 38	+ 220	+ 10	+ 24
Morton	—	− 58	+ 338	+ 138	+ 29
Ness	+ 33	− 8	+ 30	+ 27	+ 12
Seward	—	− 45	+ 398	+ 52	+ 30
Stanton	—	− 68	+ 216	− 12	+ 137
Stevens	—	− 68	+ 216	+ 281	+ 18
Wichita	—	− 34	+ 68	− 7	+ 39

Source: U.S. Department of Commerce, Bureau of the Census, Fourteenth and Fifteenth censuses.

Where percentage changes are not included for periods of first settlement, increases in population were too large to make statistical comparisons meaningful.

Table A.3. Population Changes in Towns of More Than 2,500 Inhabitants, 1930–1940

Town	Population in 1930	Population in 1940	Percentage Change	Percentage Change in Share of Total Population
Garden City, Finney County	6,121	6,285	+ 3	+6
Dodge City, Ford County	10,059	8,487	− 16	0
Liberal, Seward County	5,294	4,410	− 17	+1

Source: U.S. Department of Commerce, Bureau of the Census, Fifteenth and Sixteenth censuses.

Table A.4. Rural Populations, Nonfarm and Farm, as Percentages of
Total Population

County	Nonfarm[a]			Farm		
	1930	1940	Change	1930	1940	Change
Clark	49	53	+ 4	51	47	− 4
Finney	4	7	+ 3	40	32	− 8
Ford	23	23	0	28	28	0
Grant	45	47	+ 2	55	53	− 2
Gray	39	42	+ 3	61	58	− 3
Hamilton	49	56	+ 7	51	44	− 7
Haskell	38	45	+ 7	62	55	− 7
Hodgeman	29	32	+ 3	71	68	− 3
Kearny	40	45	+ 5	60	55	− 5
Meade	46	48	+ 2	54	52	− 2
Morton	54	61	+ 7	46	39	− 7
Ness	39	43	+ 4	61	57	− 4
Seward	5	8	+ 3	30	25	− 5
Stanton	37	48	+11	63	52	−11
Stevens	36	51	+15	64	49	−15
Wichita	38	43	+ 5	62	57	− 5

[a] Includes populations of towns of less than 2,500 inhabitants.

Source: U.S. Department of Commerce, Bureau of the Census, Fifteenth and Sixteenth censuses.

Table A.5. Total Rural Population, 1930 and 1940, and Percentage Change over Decade

County	1930	1940	Percentage Change
Clark	2,424	1,929	−20
Finney	4,427	3,201	−28
Ford	5,817	4,783	−18
Grant	1,702	1,034	−39
Gray	3,819	2,761	−28
Hamilton	1,692	1,160	−31
Haskell	1,752	1,153	−43
Hodgeman	2,972	2,388	−20
Kearny	1,919	1,385	−28
Meade	3,698	2,886	−22
Morton	1,890	860	−54
Ness	5,122	3,896	−24
Seward	2,390	1,643	−31
Stanton	1,347	755	−55
Stevens	2,965	1,580	−53
Wichita	1,611	1,239	−23
All	45,547	32,653	−28

Source: U.S. Department of Commerce, Bureau of the Census, Fifteenth and Sixteenth censuses.

Table A.6. Changes in Total Population in the 1890s and 1930s (in percentages)

County	1890–1900	1930–1940
Clark	−28	−15
Finney	+ 4	− 8
Ford	+ 4	−16
Grant	−68	−37
Gray	−48	−23
Hamilton	−30	−21
Haskell	−58	−26
Hodgeman	−15	−15
Kearny	−30	−21
Meade	−38	−19
Morton	−58	−47
Ness	− 8	−18
Seward	−45	−19
Stanton	−68	−33
Stevens	−68	−31
Wichita	−34	−15

Source: U.S. Department of Commerce, Bureau of the Census, Fourteenth, Fifteenth, and Sixteenth censuses.

Table A.7. Persistence Rates by Township (in percentages)

| Township | Farmers Present in 1930 | | Farmers Entering in 1935 and Remaining in 1940 |
	Remaining in 1935	Remaining in 1940	
Highpoint	75	60	53
Logan	65	50	22
Medway	65	38	25
Pleasant Valley (Finney County)	66	39	51
Pleasant Valley (Ford County)	67	48	41
All	70	52	44

Source: Statistical Rolls, Agricultural Census, 1930, 1935, 1940, Archives, KSHS.

Table A.8. Relationship between Persistence and Ownership of Land

Township	Present in 1930 and Remaining to 1935				Present in 1930 and Remaining to 1940				Entering in 1935 and Remaining to 1940			
	Non-owners		Owners		Non-owners		Owners		Non-owners		Owners	
	Stay	Leave	Stay	Leave	Stay	Leave	Stay	Leave	Stay	Leave	Stay	Leave
Highpoint (Ness)	37 (59)	26 (41)	63 (87)	9 (13)	30 (48)	33 (52)	50 (69)	22 (31)	18 (50)	18 (50)	9 (75)	3 (25)
Logan (Meade)	14 (41)	20 (59)	42 (79)	11 (21)	9 (26)	25 (74)	34 (65)	19 (35)	3 (21)	11 (79)	2 (33)	4 (67)
Medway (Hamilton)	11 (55)	9 (45)	6 (100)	0 (0)	6 (30)	14 (70)	4 (67)	2 (33)	4 (29)	10 (71)	0 (0)	4 (100)
Pleasant Valley (Finney)	8 (44)	10 (56)	17 (89)	2 (11)	5 (28)	13 (72)	10 (53)	9 (47)	13 (37)	22 (63)	14 (70)	6 (30)
Pleasant Valley (Ford)	16 (50)	16 (50)	28 (82)	6 (18)	12 (37)	20 (63)	20 (59)	14 (41)	9 (56)	7 (44)	4 (67)	2 (33)
All Townships	86 (51)	81 (49)	156 (85)	28 (15)	62 (37)	105 (63)	118 (64)	66 (36)	47 (41)	68 (59)	29 (60)	9 (40)

Source: Statistical Rolls, Agricultural Census, 1930, 1935, 1940, Archives, KSHS.

Figures in parentheses are percentages.

Table A.9. Land Values in Southwestern Kansas ($ per acre)

County	1925	1930	1935	1940
Clark	22	23	18	14
Finney	23	27	20	14
Ford	38	47	32	26
Grant	22	35	22	16
Gray	25	38	24	20
Hamilton	17	18	10	7
Haskell	20	38	23	18
Hodgeman	25	31	18	15
Kearny	19	20	14	11
Meade	23	33	19	19
Morton	16	22	14	8
Ness	30	34	21	17
Seward	24	30	19	14
Stanton	16	23	15	8
Stevens	25	30	22	14
Wichita	16	18	11	9

Source: Wilfred H. Pine, *100 Years of Farmland Values in Kansas,* Bulletin no. 611 (Manhattan: Agricultural Experiment Station, Kansas State University, 1977), Table 2.

Table A.10. Persistence by Size of Farm (in acres)

	Farmers Present in 1930				Farmers Entering in 1935 and Remaining to 1940	
	Remaining to 1935		Remaining to 1940			
Farm Size	Stay	Leave	Stay	Leave	Stay	Leave
Less than 320	31	32	21	41	3	15
	(49)	(51)	(34)	(66)	(17)	(83)
320–479	77	33	63	47	18	23
	(70)	(30)	(57)	(43)	(44)	(56)
480–639	51	14	36	30	8	7
	(78)	(22)	(55)	(45)	(53)	(47)
640–959	48	17	35	30	10	8
	(74)	(26)	(54)	(46)	(56)	(44)
960 or more	36	14	26	26	7	8
	(72)	(28)	(50)	(50)	(47)	(53)

Source: Statistical Rolls, Agricultural Census, 1930, 1935, 1940, Archives, KSHS.

Figures in parentheses are percentages.

Median farm size of farmers present in 1930 was 480 acres; the mean farm size, 630 acres. The median farm size of farmers entering in 1935 was 320 acres; the mean farm size, 584 acres.

Table A.11. Mexican Population, 1930 and 1940, and Percentage Change over Decade

County	1930	1940	Percentage Change	Percentage Change, All Groups
Clark	22	11	−50	−15
Finney	571	167	−71	− 8
Ford	614	151	−75	−16
Grant	33	5	−85	−37
Gray	103	24	−77	−23
Hamilton	87	11	−87	−21
Haskell	30	2	−93	−26
Hodgeman	6	2	−66	−15
Kearny	134	58	−57	−21
Meade	28	3	−89	−19
Morton	0	4	•	−47
Ness	30	5	−83	−18
Seward	83	7	−92	−19
Stanton	0	3	•	−33
Stevens	0	0	—	−31
Wichita	81	7	−91	−15
Total	1,800	460	−74	−24

Source: U.S. Department of Commerce, Bureau of the Census, Fifteenth and Sixteenth censuses.

•Numbers in excess of 100 percent.

NOTES

INTRODUCTION

1. Interviews with Lawrence R. Smith, Elkhart, June 5, 1989; Hazel Steenis Shriver, Deerfield, June 14, 1989; Bonna L. Sutton, Elkhart, June 2, 1989.

2. I chose these counties because they form a contiguous area of very severe drought and dust activity in the southwestern corner of Kansas. These people were quite literally in the heart of the Dust Bowl. The federal government classified fifteen of the sixteen counties (Clark, Finney, Ford, Gray, Hamilton, Haskell, Hodgeman, Kearny, Meade, Morton, Ness, Seward, Stanton, Stevens, and Wichita) as "very severe drought" areas in 1936. The only county not so designated, Grant County, sits in the interior of the area and was also seriously affected by the climate conditions of the 1930s. Francis D. Cronin and Howard W. Beers, *Research Bulletin: Areas of Intense Drought Distress, 1930–1936* (Washington, D.C.: WPA, Division of Social Research, 1937).

3. The Joads' story, although told as a Dust Bowl story, was actually more of a tale of the southern states during the 1930s, when thousands of sharecroppers and tenants lost their farms to mechanization and landowners desiring to keep government crop payments for themselves. John Steinbeck, *The Grapes of Wrath* (New York: Viking Press, 1939).

4. Although census data showed that Kansas as a whole lost just over 4 percent of its population during the 1930s, these sixteen counties on average lost a quarter of their populations. The largest proportion of this loss occurred within the farm population, especially its young. U.S. Department of Commerce, Bureau of the Census, *Sixteenth Census of the United States, 1940: Population*, pts. 2 and 3.

5. Interview with Opal Musselman Burdett, Ness City, May 13, 1989.

6. Interview with George and Laurie Copeland, Ness County, May 13, 1989.

7. Interview with Ona Libertus, Coolidge, June 10, 1989.

8. R. Douglas Hurt's book *The Dust Bowl: An Agricultural and Social History* (Chicago: Nelson-Hall, 1981) deals admirably with the abundant information about agricultural practices on the southern plains and New Deal farm policies but leaves the social history to a short chapter entitled "Life in the Dust Bowl." Although Hurt's conclusion that "physical and psychological stamina, humor, and regional pride enabled Dust Bowlers to endure, adapt and survive" is certainly correct, a single twenty-page chapter could hardly provide an adequate examination of the many ways people endured, adapted, and survived. Paul Bonnifield, author of *The Dust Bowl: Men, Dirt,*

and Depression (Albuquerque: University of New Mexico Press, 1979), also left his discussion of "living through it all" to one short concluding chapter. The best known of the Dust Bowl studies is Donald Worster's book *Dust Bowl: The Southern Plains in the 1930s* (New York: Oxford University Press, 1979), which provides a highly impressionistic examination of the ecological and social dimensions of the problems of the 1930s. Worster touches only lightly on the social history of the Dust Bowl. His research drew rather narrowly from the findings of federal studies of the drought area made in the 1930s, and only rarely did he allow the affected individuals to speak for themselves.

9. Many historians of rural America have found a high degree of cooperation within farming neighborhoods. Effective cooperation tended to mitigate the harsh effects of economic depressions. This cooperation appeared to be an important factor in cementing people to their communities in established areas, such as Ness County, but it was less of a factor in newer areas such as Hamilton County (see Chapter 8). In newer communities, farming families had fewer connections to kin, and they often had more tenuous ties to their land. See Nancy Grey Osterud, *Bonds of Community: The Lives of Farm Women in Nineteenth-Century New York* (Ithaca, N.Y.: Cornell University Press, 1991); Mary Neth, "Preserving the Family Farm: Farm Families and Community in the Midwest, 1900–1940" (Ph.D. diss., University of Wisconsin–Madison, 1987); Hal S. Barron, *Those Who Stayed Behind: Rural Society in Nineteenth-Century England* (New York: Cambridge University Press, 1984).

CHAPTER ONE. HARDLY A CLOUD IN THE SKY

1. C. B. Erskine, "Gray County History Pantomimed by Women," Gray County Agricultural Extension, Kansas Annual Report, 1933, 26–27; Stanton County Agricultural Extension, Kansas Annual Report, 1934, 15. (All agricultural extension documents are manuscript copies of annual reports, consulted in county extension offices.)

2. U.S. Department of the Interior, Census Office, *Tenth Census of the United States, 1880: Population* (Washington, D.C.: Government Printing Office, 1883), 60–61.

3. Craig Miner, *West of Wichita: Settling the High Plains of Kansas, 1865–1890* (Lawrence: University Press of Kansas, 1986), 96–97, 224–225.

4. Commissioner of the General Land Office, *Annual Report of the Commissioner of the General Land Office for the Year 1885* (Washington, D.C.: Government Printing Office, 1885), 79.

5. Daniel Fitzgerald, *Ghost Towns of Kansas: A Traveler's Guide* (Lawrence: University Press of Kansas, 1988), provides informative and entertaining sketches about the rise and fall of these communities, as well as other ghost towns throughout Kansas.

6. Ibid., 260–300.

7. Census Bureau maps for 1890 showed a population of at least two inhabitants per square mile for all but Morton County, in the extreme southwestern corner of the state, and a portion of Stevens County, just to the east of Morton County. Similar maps published in 1900 showed an aggregate population of fewer than two people per square mile for much of the area that became the Dust Bowl in the 1930s.

8. Frank S. Sullivan, *A History of Meade County, Kansas* (Topeka, Kans.: Crane and Company, 1916), 21–22; "English Firm Once Owned 51,000 Acres in Kearny County," *History of Kearny County, Kansas*, vol. 1 (Dodge City, Kans.: Rollie Jack,

1964), 97; "Why the Bubble Burst," *History of Kearny County, Kansas*, vol. 2 (North Newton, Kans.: Mennonite Press, 1973), 36.

9. Increases and decreases in the area's population were the product of changes in the birth and death rates, as well as in- and out-migration. Richard Easterlin has argued that the end of settlement could be defined as the point soon after the rural rate of total increase fell below 20 percent. Given high nineteenth-century fertility rates, an increase of less than 20 percent showed that outward migration was outstripping natural increase. It is likely that Easterlin's estimate of 20 percent is a generous figure when applied to the twentieth century, given the decrease in fertility between the nineteenth and twentieth centuries. "Population Change and Farm Settlement in the Northern United States," *Journal of Economic History* 36, 1 (Mar. 1976): 45–75.

10. In his report for 1930, the agent commented that the homes of the area attested to its frontier status: "Many of the homes are only what could be built easily and without much expense. These farms are being gradually improved. The homes of those who have been in the county for several years are modern and comfortable." Grant County Agricultural Extension, Kansas Annual Report, 1930, 24.

11. Carl C. Taylor, Helen W. Wheeler, and E. L. Kirkpatrick, *Disadvantaged Classes in American Agriculture*, Social Research Report No. 8 (Washington, D.C.: USDA, Apr. 1938), 50; Leslie Hewes, *The Suitcase Farming Frontier: A Study of the Historical Geography of the Southern Great Plains* (Lincoln: University of Nebraska Press, 1973), 202. In 1936, nonresidents owned 57.9 percent of the acres in Stanton County, 68.2 percent in Hamilton County, and 64.2 percent in Haskell County. Although these figures were somewhat above those for the rest of southwestern Kansas, a high degree of tenancy existed throughout the region.

12. Hewes, *Suitcase Farming Frontier*, 3; Lynnell Rubright, "Development of Farming Systems in Western Kansas, 1885–1915" (Ph.D. diss., University of Wisconsin–Madison, 1977), 264–265.

13. A suitcase farmer was one who lived more than one county away, returning to his land only to plant and harvest. Essentially, they were absentee or nonresident farmers. Hewes, *Suitcase Farming Frontier*, 4, 30.

14. U.S. Census Office, *Twelfth Census of the United States, 1900: Agriculture*, pt. 1 (Washington, D.C.: U.S. Census Office, 1902); U.S. Department of Commerce, Bureau of the Census, *Fifteenth Census of the United States, 1930: Agriculture*, pt. 1 (Washington, D.C.: Government Printing Office, 1932).

15. In 1940, census-takers asked respondents how long they had been on the land they farmed. Full owners had been on the land, on the average, since 1921, part owners since 1923, and tenants since 1933. The mean year of occupance for all farmers was 1927. U.S. Department of Commerce, Bureau of the Census, *Sixteenth Census of the United States, 1940: Population* pt. 2, Characteristics of the Population, pt. 3.

16. Kansas State College of Agriculture, Agricultural Experiment Station, *Kansas Weather and Climate* (Topeka: Kansas State Printing Plant, 1942), 85.

17. Carter Goodrich et al., *Migration and Economic Opportunity: The Report of the Study of Population Redistribution* (Philadelphia: University of Pennsylvania Press, 1936), 700–703.

18. Interview with Earl Owens, Liberal, May 3, 1989.

19. Paul Bonnifield has argued that the area that would become the Dust Bowl was home to two separate frontiers during the 1920s. One was a rural frontier based on agriculture; the other was an urban frontier based on the development of oil and gas reserves. *The Dust Bowl: Men, Dirt, and Depression* (Albuquerque: University of New Mexico Press, 1979), 31.

20. "About Our Population," *Hugoton Hermes*, Sept. 19, 1930, 3.

21. "Ulysses Sets Record Pace in Southwest This Census," *Grant County Republican*, June 19, 1930, 1.

22. J. A. Hodges, "Important Factors Affecting Migration of Rural Population in Kansas," U.S. Congress, House, *Hearings before the Select Committee to Investigate Interstate Migration of Destitute Citizens*, pt. 4, 76th Cong., 3d Sess., Sept. 16, 17, 1940, 1752.

23. Bonnifield, *Dust Bowl*, 30–37.

24. Pauline Toland, ed., *Seward County, Kansas* (Liberal, Kans.: K.C. Printers, 1979), 80.

25. Stevens County History Association, *The History of Stevens County and Its People* (Hugoton, Kans.: Stevens County History Association, 1979), 139.

26. "Looks Like Boom Days," *Clark County Clipper*, May 22, 1930, 1.

27. "Development to Continue for Many Years," *Hugoton Hermes*, Aug. 29, 1930, 1.

28. "Much Building in Hugoton City," *Hugoton Hermes*, Sept. 19, 1930, 1.

29. "Grant County's Wheat in 1929 Worth Over 2 Million," *Grant County Republican*, Jan. 9, 1930, 1; "Progress and Vision," *Clark County Clipper*, Jan. 2, 1930, 2; "The New Year," *Clark County Clipper*, Jan. 1, 1931, 2; "Stanton Counting on a Big Year Again," *Johnson Pioneer*, June 19, 1930, 1.

30. "More Homes Needed," *Liberal News*, Aug. 21, 1930, 2.

31. "Enormous Gain in Rail Shipments," *Hugoton Hermes*, Jan. 10, 1930, 1. Oil and gas development slowed considerably during the 1930s, due to a depression in prices. It did, however, continue to bring a slow but steady amount of business into communities such as Hugoton. Bonnifield, *Dust Bowl*, 97.

32. "Prosperity King," *Liberal News*, Jan. 10, 1930, 1, 5; "Dependable Merchants of a Dependable Town Are Progressing through Our So-Called Business Depression," *Liberal News*, Nov. 17, 1930, 1.

33. "P.O. Doubles Its Business," *Johnson Pioneer*, June 19, 1930, 1; "Growth of Post Office Receipts Show Prosperity of Hugoton," *Hugoton Hermes*, Jan. 10, 1930, 1.

34. Frank Greene, "The Map of the Nation's Business," *Nation's Business* 18 (Jan., Feb., 1930): 34, 40.

35. "In the Heart of the Most Prosperous Section of the U.S.," *Garden City Daily Telegram*, Jan. 17, 1930, 2; "This Section Fortunate," *Garden City Daily Telegram*, Apr. 23, 1930, 2.

36. The maps for the spring of 1935, the height of the dust storms, graphically explained the reluctance of newspaper editors to report this news. Virtually the only sections of the country showing "quiet" business conditions were those areas of the plains states buffeted by dust storms. Business conditions in southwestern Kansas, of course, were quiet. "Changes in the Map mainly reflect less activity in textile lines, floods in Arkansas and a clearer delimitation of the dust storm trouble." Frank Greene, "The Map of the Nation's Business," *Nation's Business* 23 (Mar., Apr., May, 1935): 51, 51, 46.

37. *History of Stevens County*, 139; "A Review of the Year Just Closed," *Ness County News*, Jan. 3, 1931, 1; "Stanton County Continues Its Growth," *Johnson Pioneer*, Dec. 31, 1931, 1; "More Room Will Be Needed Soon," *Liberal News*, Feb. 26, 1930, 1.

38. "It Is Different in Stevens Co. Now," *Hugoton Hermes*, Jan. 3, 1930.

39. "The Prosperity of Western Kansas," *Garden City Daily Telegram*, Oct. 1, 1930, 2.

40. "The Second Generation," *Garden City Daily Telegram*, May 4, 1931, 6.

41. "Southwest Kansas Looks Great," *Liberal News*, Sept. 6, 1930, 2.
42. "Southwest Is Indeed Changing," *Liberal News*, Apr. 8, 1930, 5.
43. "The Census Vindication," *Garden City Daily Telegram*, May 23, 1930, 1.

CHAPTER TWO. TRIALS, TESTS, AND HARD TIMES

1. *Crops and Markets* (USDA) 8, 8 (Aug. 1931): 293; *Agricultural Situation* (Bureau of Agricultural Economics, USDA) 15, 9 (Sept. 1931): 5.
2. USDA, *Yearbook of Agriculture, 1932* (Washington, D.C.: Government Printing Office, 1933).
3. The farmer began feeding kafir corn to his fish when the water level in his lake fell. When the price of wheat fell, he began feeding them that, too: "Like other livestock, the fish seem to thrive on this diet." "Feeding Wheat to Fish," *Fowler News*, Aug. 14, 1930, 1.
4. "The Passing of 1931," *Agricultural Situation* 16, 1 (Jan. 1, 1932): 25.
5. *Agricultural Situation* 15, 9 (Sept. 1931): 5; *Crops and Markets* 8, 9 (Sept. 1931): 360.
6. "Building Big Bins," *Bucklin Banner*, July 23, 1931, 1.
7. Clark County Agricultural Extension, Kansas Annual Report, 1931, 8.
8. "Meeting Here for Dollar Wheat," *Liberal News*, May 13, 1931, 1.
9. "Want $1 Wheat," *Liberal News*, May 14, 1931, 1.
10. "Stanton Wheat Raisers Cut Acreage 35 to 40 Percent," *Johnson Pioneer*, July 23, 1931, 1.
11. Interview with Kathleen Jenkins, Bucklin, May 9, 1989.
12. Kansas State College of Agriculture, Agricultural Experiment Station, *Kansas Weather and Climate* (Topeka: Kansas State Printing Plant, 1942), 13–15, 85, 93, 97, 101; USDA, *Climate and Man: 1941 Yearbook of Agriculture* (Washington, D.C.: Government Printing Office, 1941), 873–875.
13. Ford County Agricultural Extension, Kansas Annual Report, 1940, 9; Stanton County Agricultural Extension, Kansas Annual Report, 1939, 8. On the far western border of Kansas, even with less rain than was optimal, farmers could grow wheat if they received a few well-timed rains in the spring and early summer. Although they did not expect to harvest a good crop every year, they could generally hope for a really good crop one year in seven. They also experimented with more drought resistant crops, such as grain sorghum and broomcorn.
14. Martha Schmidt Friesen, Diary, Feb. 18, 1937. By permission of Thelma Warner and Verna Gragg, Syracuse. All names used in connection with the Friesen diary are pseudonyms, at the request of the diary's owners. All quotations from the diary are produced exactly as written, without corrections to grammar or spelling.
15. "Diaries of Iman C. Wiatt," in Kearny County Historical Society, *History of Kearny County, Kansas*, vol. 2 (North Newton, Kans.: Mennonite Press, 1973), 282.
16. "Stops at 100 Degrees," *Garden City Daily Telegram*, July 23, 1934, 1.
17. James C. Malin, "Dust Storms, Part One, 1850–1860," "Part Two, 1861–1880," and Part Three, 1881–1900," *Kansas Historical Quarterly* 14 (May, Aug., Nov., 1946).
18. U.S. Department of Commerce, Bureau of the Census, *United States Census of Agriculture, 1925*, pt. 1, The Northern States.
19. U.S. Department of Commerce, Bureau of the Census, *Fifteenth Census of the United States, 1930*, Agriculture, vol. 3, pt. 1, Type of Farm, The Northern States.

20. Ford County Agricultural Extension, Kansas Annual Report, 1940, 228.

21. Friesen Diary, Mar. 22, 1937, and Aug. 5, 1937, to June 18, 1938.

22. "Diaries of Iman C. Wiatt," 283–284.

23. *Topeka Journal*, Mar. 23, 1935.

24. I interviewed approximately sixty Dust Bowl survivors in the summer of 1989. All of them remembered the particulars of that dirt storm. When I visited a meeting of the Ford County Historical Society in Dodge City in May 1989, the "old timers" present recounted their memories of that day. Only one could not remember where she had been on Black Sunday. April 14, 1935, was obviously a day that made a great impression upon them, in the same way that the bombing of Pearl Harbor and the assassination of John F. Kennedy are remembered by many other Americans.

25. Letter to author from Opal Musselman Burdett, Ness City, Dec. 9, 1988; "Wind Sunday Was Worst Yet," *Meade Globe-News*, Apr. 18, 1935, 1, 8; interview with Leota Swafford Lambert and Elsie Swafford Riney, Liberal, Mar. 19, 1989.

26. Adjusted for deflation, farm products valued at $1,663.68 per farm in the 1930s would have bought nearly $2,000 worth of products at the prices of the 1920s. Nonetheless, the average farmer found his purchasing power cut roughly in half. Kansas State Board of Agriculture, *Biennial Report of the State Board of Agriculture*, vols. 28–32, 1933–1941 (Topeka: Kansas State Printing Plant).

27. Interview with Thelma Warner, Syracuse, June 9, 1989.

28. Interview with Opal Musselman Burdett, Ness City, May 13, 1989; interview with Gaylord Haflich, Garden City, June 12, 1989.

29. Ford County Agricultural Extension, Kansas Annual Report, 1935, 4.

30. Letter to author from Daniel S. Penner, Hillsboro, Fall 1988.

31. Interview with Lois Patton, Syracuse, June 10, 1989.

32. "Found under the Drifts," *Garden City Daily Telegram*, Apr. 11, 1935, 1, 7; "Dust Storm," *Bazine Advocate*, Mar. 22, 1935, 1.

33. "Dust Causes Big Damage in Meade," *Meade Globe-News*, Apr. 4, 1935, 1.

34. Ibid.

35. "Salome," "Dust," *Bucklin Banner*, Apr. 25, 1935, 1.

36. Pauline Winkler Grey, "Dust to Dust," Patricia Mueller, ed., *Kansas Author's Club Bulletin Year Book*, 1934, vol. 10, 1934, 50.

37. Interview with Elfreda Penner Fast, Hillsboro, Apr. 15, 1989.

38. Interview with Lois Patton, Syracuse, June 10, 1989.

39. "Diaries of Iman C. Wiatt," 279.

40. Friesen Diary, Mar. 19, 1937.

41. More than fifty years later, the owner of an older home in Ness City raises dust clouds when she pounds nails into walls. Interview with Opal Musselman Burdett, Ness City, May 13, 1989; interview with Esther Beasley and Fontell Litrell, Hugoton, May 22, 1989; "Yields 13 Buckets of Sand," *Liberal News*, May 14, 1935, 1; "Dust Fills Local Home As Silt-Laden Plaster Falls," *Garden City Daily Telegram*, May 3, 1935, 1.

42. E. M. Dean and Bertha Carpenter, "Morton County History," n.p., n.d., City Library, Elkhart.

43. *Liberal News*, Apr. 1, 1933, 1.

44. "Officials Claim Conditions Grave," *Liberal News*, Apr. 29, 1935, 1.

45. "Comes to Aid," *Liberal News*, Apr. 25, 1935, 1.

46. Ten of sixteen counties had much higher numbers of pneumonia deaths than were common for the 1930s, either before or after 1935. Only the residents of Stevens and Wichita counties escaped the scourge entirely. Kansas State Board of Health,

Biennial Report of the State Board of Health of the State of Kansas, vols. 16–20 (Topeka: Kansas State Printing Plant, 1932, 1935, 1937, 1939, 1942).

47. "Physical Defects in Children Increase," *Garden City Daily Telegram,* July 6, 1934, 1; "Find Physical Defects," *Garden City Daily Telegram,* May 4, 1935, 1; "Comes to Aid," *Liberal News,* Apr. 25, 1935, 1; E. Fredericka Beal, R.N., WPA Office Memorandum, WPA, Central Files, Kansas, Box 1374, Record Group 69, Central Branch, National Archives and Records Administration, Washington, D.C.

48. Edith Stanforth, public health nurse, Ulysses, July 1938, "A Sunday in June," Kansas Collection, Spencer Research Library, University of Kansas, Lawrence.

49. "Hysteria Accompanies Measles," *Grant County Republican,* May 2, 1935, 1.

50. Friesen Diary, Nov. 24, Dec. 29, 1936; Jan. 5, 8, May 28, June 6, 1937; Jan. 13, 1938; May 25, 1939.

51. A. B. Madison, "Mere Existence," *Fowler News,* Apr. 25, 1935, 1.

52. Warren Zimmerman to Clifford Hope, Jan. 31, 1934, Clifford R. Hope Papers, Correspondence, 1934–1935, W–Z, Collection 50, Box 46, Manuscripts Division, KSHS, Topeka.

53. Stanton County Agricultural Extension, Kansas Annual Report, 1935, 4; Meade County Agricultural Extension, Kansas Annual Report, 1937, 91; Ford County Agricultural Extension, Home Demonstration Agent, Kansas Annual Report, 1939, 4; Morton County Agricultural Extension, Kansas Annual Report, 1939, 113.

54. In these sixteen counties, there were 1.6 divorces per thousand of population in 1933, 1.7 in 1934, 1.6 in 1935, and 1.9 in 1936 and 1937. Kansas State Board of Health, *Nineteenth Biennial Report of the State Board of Health of the State of Kansas* (Topeka: Kansas State Printing Plant, 1939), 226–227.

55. "Diaries of Iman C. Wiatt," 282.

56. Lillian Foster, Scrapbook, February–May 1935, Manuscripts Division, KSHS.

57. "Western Kansas Dust," *Hugoton Hermes,* Feb. 26, 1937, 4; "Wanted—the Impossible," from *Grant County Republican,* printed by the *Liberal News,* Sept. 29, 1933, 4.

58. "Shoulders the Blame," *Liberal News,* Apr. 17, 1933, 1; "Dirty Paragraphs," *Clark County Clipper,* Apr. 11, 1935, 5; "Poultry Man Disgusted," *Bucklin Banner,* Apr. 11, 1935, 1; "Didn't Need Any Help," *Liberal News,* Apr. 20, 1935, 1.

59. During interviews of survivors of the Dust Bowl, I lost track of the number of times people told me that "everyone was in the same boat" and that they were all "as happy as if they had good sense." Most interviewees acknowledged that the thirties had been difficult and that they would not want to go through those years again, but they also insisted that what they remembered most vividly were the good times and the closeness they felt to friends and family.

60. Counties in neighboring states experiencing extreme drought distress suffered similar population losses. Baca County, Colorado, lost 41 percent of its population. The following counties in the Oklahoma panhandle also experienced the Dust Bowl and lost population: Cimarron (32 percent), Texas (30 percent), Beaver (24 percent), Harper (17 percent), and Ellis (20 percent). The first tier of states in the Texas panhandle showed the same patterns of depopulation: Dallam (17 percent), Sherman (12 percent), Hansford (22 percent), Ochiltree (20 percent), and Lipscomb (17 percent). Those Texas counties experiencing extreme drought distress below this first tier of states showed a much more diverse pattern of population movement, perhaps due to the presence of a major city, Amarillo. All of these counties with extreme drought distress showed a mean population loss of 3 percent. When only those counties closest

to Kansas are counted (Baca County, Colorado, the Oklahoma panhandle, and the first tier of counties in the Texas panhandle), the mean population loss was 20 percent. U.S. Department of Commerce, Bureau of the Census, *Fifteenth Census of the United States, 1930: Population*, pt. 1, and *Sixteenth Census of the United States, 1940: Population*, vol. 2, pt. 3.

61. James C. Malin made this argument in his article "The Turnover of Farm Population in Kansas," *Kansas Historical Quarterly* 4 (Nov. 1935): 339–372.

62. U.S. Department of Commerce, Bureau of the Census, *Fifteenth Census of the United States, 1930: Population*, pt. 1, and *United States Census of Agriculture, 1935, 1, 1, The Northern States*.

63. USDA, "Human Side of Land Use Changes," *Report of the Secretary of Agriculture, 1939* (Washington, D.C.: Government Printing Office, 1939), 66; "Farm Population Increase Less Pronounced during 1933," *Agricultural Situation* 18, 4 (Apr. 1934): 2.

64. N. A. Tolles, "A Survey of Labor Migration between States," *Monthly Labor Review* 45 (July 1937): 8–9; "Farm Population Reaches All-Time Peak," *Agricultural Situation* 17, 5 (May 1933): 2–3.

65. U.S. Department of Commerce, Bureau of the Census, *Fifteenth Census of the United States, 1930: Population*, pt. 1, and *Sixteenth Census of the United States, 1940: Population*, pts. 2, 3.

66. U.S. Department of Commerce, Bureau of the Census, *Fifteenth Census of the United States, 1930: Population*, pt. 1, and *Sixteenth Census of the United States, 1940: Population*, pts. 2, 3. Richard Bremer's study of the Loup River country revealed essentially the same pattern, with young people taking the brunt of the depressed economic and environmental conditions of the decade. *Agricultural Change in an Urban Age: The Loup Country of Nebraska, 1910–1970* (Lincoln: University of Nebraska Press, 1976), 125–139.

67. U.S. Department of Commerce, Bureau of the Census, *Sixteenth Census of the United States: 1940: Population*, vol. 2, *Characteristics of the Population*, pt. 3: Kansas–Michigan (Washington, D.C.: Government Printing Office, 1943), 17, 45–65.

68. Dorothy Schweider and Deborah Fink, in their study of Boone County, Nebraska, and Lyman County, South Dakota, found evidence of similar fertility restriction during the Great Depression. "Plains Women: Rural Life in the 1930s," *Great Plains Quarterly* 8 (Spring 1988): 79–88.

69. This finding runs counter to those of Paul Bonnifield in *The Dust Bowl: Men, Dirt, and Depression* (Albuquerque: University of New Mexico Press, 1979), 66–67.

70. "Mechanization Reduces Labor in Growing Wheat," *Agricultural Situation* 21, 4 (Apr. 1937), 12–14.

71. Wilfred H. Pine, *Mid-Century Farm Tenure in Kansas*, Agricultural Economics Report no. 53 (Manhattan: Agricultural Experiment Station, Kansas State University, May 1953), 60 and Figure 23.

72. In a six-county sample consisting of Anderson, Comanche, Kingman, Kiowa, Scott, and Stafford counties, farmers purchased tractors at a far higher rate than farmers in the Dust Bowl. Although they made these purchases during the thirties, their net decrease in population was only 10 percent, compared to 25 percent in the Dust Bowl. These counties were all outside of the very extreme drought region (two each from the slight, moderate, and extreme drought areas). Each of these counties, like the Dust Bowl counties, had no city of greater that 10,500 residents and a rural-farm population that composed 50 to 60 percent of its total population. U.S. Department of Commerce, Bureau of the Census, *Fifteenth Census of the United States, 1930:*

Population, vol. 3, pt. 1, and *Agriculture*, vol. 2, pt. 1; *Sixteenth Census of the United States, 1940: Population*, vol. 2, pt. 3, and *Agriculture*, vol. 1, pt. 2.

73. R. A. Paden to Arthur M. Capper, May 24, 1937, Arthur M. Capper Papers, Collection 12, Box 32, Agricultural General Correspondence, 1918–1939, KSHS.

74. U.S. Department of Commerce, Bureau of the Census, *Sixteenth Census of the United States, 1940: Population, Internal Migration, 1935–1940*.

75. Information for the migration of the American population from 1935 to 1940 is drawn from the U.S. Department of Commerce, Bureau of the Census, *Sixteenth Census of the United States, 1940: Population, Internal Migration, 1935–1940*. Testimony of Frances Perkins, Secretary of Labor, U.S. Congress, House, *Hearings before the Select Committee to Investigate Interstate Migration of Destitute Citizens*, pt. 4, 76th Cong., 3d Sess., Sept. 16–17, 1940, 4,119.

76. "Still No Exodus," *Garden City Daily Telegram*, Aug. 29, 1934, 6.

77. "Western Dry Fog Blows in As State Is Promised Rain," *Garden City Daily Telegram*, Mar. 21, 1936, 1.

78. "Church of God Notes," *Grant County Republican*, Aug. 27, 1936, 1; "Several Families Leave Elkhart during Past Week," *Elkhart Tri-State News*, Sept. 2, 1937, 1; "30," *Grant County Republican*, Aug. 12, 1937, 1.

79. The mean price per bushel for hard winter wheat at Kansas City was $1.32 for the period from 1920 to 1929. In 1929, the price was $1.20; one year later, it had fallen to $.76. Wheat reached its lowest price for the decade in 1931, at $.47 per bushel. Prices rebounded in 1935, 1936, and 1937, to $1.05, $1.21, and $1.11 per bushel, respectively, and then fell again. Newspaper reports indicated that the prices at local elevators were significantly lower. The highest local price recorded for wheat in 1931 was only $.35. The decade's highest prices for wheat corresponded with the worst years of the drought, when southwestern Kansas farmers experienced near total crop failures. USDA, *Agricultural Statistics: 1941* (Washington, D.C.: Government Printing Office, 1941), 26.

CHAPTER THREE. A COW IN EVERY YARD

1. The problems described in this chapter are very similar to those experienced by urban areas, large and small, throughout the country. On the Great Plains, however, these problems were aggravated by the drought, which provided an additional layer of complications. For an excellent description of the impact of the Great Depression upon an urban area see Lizabeth Cohen, *Making a New Deal: Industrial Workers in Chicago, 1919–1939* (New York: Cambridge University Press, 1990), 213–250.

2. "Grant County Bank Closes," *Grant County Republican*, Nov. 13, 1930, 1; "Business At a Standstill As a Result of Banks Closing," *Johnson Pioneer*, Mar. 9, 1933, 1; "Englewood Bank Closed," *Clark County Clipper*, Jan. 5, 1933, 4; "Bank May Reorganize," *Grant County Republican*, Jan. 12, 1933, 1; "First National Bank in Voluntary Liquidation," *Hugoton Hermes*, May 21, 1937, 1.

3. Chattel Mortgage Records, vol. 19, book 2, Register of Deeds Office, Ness County Courthouse, Ness City.

4. Ibid.

5. "Gray and Rosel Closing Out," *Johnson Pioneer*, Dec. 1, 1932, 1; "Penney Store Closes Doors," *Elkhart Tri-State News*, June 17, 1938, 1; "Home Cafe Sale Saturday Not So Good," *Grant County Republican*, Aug. 4, 1932, 1.

6. "Fail to Get Enough Guarantors for Next Year's Chautauqua," *Johnson Pioneer*,

Aug. 6, 1931, 1; "Grocery Stores on Cash Basis," *Bucklin Banner,* May 4, 1933, 1; "Budget Is Cut," *Liberal News,* Feb. 4, 1932, 1.

7. Interviews with Lois Patton and Fern Patton Royer, Syracuse, June 10, 1989; Earl Owens, Liberal, May 3, 1989; "Dr. C. C. Bennett Takes His Life," *Bazine Advocate,* Apr. 28, 1934, 1.

8. "Stantonians Appreciate Subscription Offer of Pioneer," *Johnson Pioneer,* Sept. 10, 1931, 1; "Your Wheat Is Worth 50 Cents at This Office," *Grant County Republican,* July 23, 1931, 1; "Chicken! Chicken! Where's the Chicken!" *Hugoton Hermes,* Sept. 17, 1937, 1.

9. "Business Men Offer Premium," *Fowler News,* July 23, 1931, 1; "Eggs 1 Cent Each," *Bucklin Banner,* March 6, 1933, 2.

10. Interviews with Earl Owens, Liberal, May 3, 1989; Lois Stringfield Harmon, Garden City, June 13, 1989; and Gaylord Haflich, Garden City, June 12, 1989.

11. Commissioners' Journal, Seward County, vol. 4, Feb. 17, 1933, 463, and vol. 5, Mar. 25, 1937, 296.

12. "Farmers-Merchants Supper Good," *Grant County Republican,* June 11, 1931, 1; "Trade Merit Specials Saturday and Monday," *Clark County Clipper,* Jan. 9, 1930, 1; "Confidence in the Future," *Clark County Clipper,* Feb. 22, 1934, 2.

13. "Johnson Merchants Sponsor a 'Million Dollar' Auction," *Johnson Pioneer,* Jan. 3, 1935, 1; "Make Dollar More Value," *Grant County Republican,* Feb. 23, 1933, 1; "Expect Large Crowd Here for First Goodwill Day," *Southwest Daily Times,* Sept. 24, 1936, 1.

14. "Morton County People Coming to Hugoton," *Hugoton Hermes,* Apr. 1, 1938, 1.

15. *Grant County Republican,* Dec. 4, 1930, 2; "Itinerant," *Bazine Advocate,* May 15, 1930, 1; "Open Season," *Southwest Daily Times,* Dec. 12, 1937, 2; "Liberal Homes Displaying 'No Peddler' Cards," *Southwest Daily Times,* Apr. 8, 1937, 1.

16. "Stores Take On Yuletide Atmosphere," *Grant County Republican,* Dec. 1, 1932, 1; "Show Your Loyalty Now!" *Grant County Republican,* Nov. 23, 1933, 1; "Wanted—Co-Operation," *Grant County Republican,* June 22, 1933, 1.

17. Editorial, *Elkhart Tri-State News,* Sept. 26, 1935, 2.

18. "Chasing Job Mirages," *Liberal News,* Apr. 29, 1931, 2.

19. Commissioners' Journal, Ford County, vol. G, Jan. 19, 1933, 638.

20. "391 Placements in Relief Work over the County," *Hugoton Hermes,* Dec. 29, 1933, 1.

21. "Finney County Has 333 Unemployed—156 at Work on U.S. Projects," *Garden City Daily Telegram,* Jan. 18, 1938, 1.

22. "Chasing Job Mirages," *Liberal News,* Apr. 29, 1931, 2.

23. "Work Program Now in Force," *Liberal News,* Nov. 14, 1931, 1; "Establishing Transient Camp," *Liberal News,* June 21, 1934, 1; "Liberal Becoming a Mecca for the Jobless," *Southwest Daily Times,* Sept. 16, 1938, 1.

24. "Appeal for Home Workmen," *Clark County Clipper,* Mar. 26, 1931, 1.

25. Gray County Agricultural Extension, Kansas Annual Report, 1934, 49; "Relief People Ask for Farms," *Johnson Pioneer,* Feb. 7, 1935, 1; interview with Pauline Renick Owens, Liberal, May 3, 1989.

26. "Ways to Utilize Leftovers," *Garden City Daily Telegram,* Nov. 9, 1933, 3.

27. Interview with Eula Reath Wilson, Jetmore, May 11, 1989; interview with Esther Beasley and Fontell Littrell, Hugoton, May 22, 1989.

28. Ford County Agricultural Extension, Home Demonstration Agent, Kansas Annual Report, 1933, 1, 20.

29. "Demonstration of Family Menu," *Liberal News*, Sept. 15, 1933, 3; "Farm Bureau News," *Clark County Clipper*, Jan. 12, 1933, 6; "17 Tons Surplus Food Aids County's Relief Load," *Johnson Pioneer*, Nov. 23, 1939, 1.

30. Clifford R. Hope to Mr. W. W. Coons, Plains, Apr. 22, 1935, Clifford R. Hope Papers, Correspondence, 1934–1935, C, Collection 50, Box 44, KSHS.

31. Interviews with Esther Beasley and Fontell Littrell, Hugoton, May 22, 1989; Bonna Sutton, Elkhart, June 2, 1989; Leota Swafford Lambert and Elsie Swafford Riney, Liberal, Mar. 19, 1989.

32. Questionnaire response, Thelma Warner, Syracuse, Fall 1988; interview with Eula Reath Wilson, Jetmore, May 11, 1989.

33. Interview with Opal Musselman Burdett, Ness City, May 13, 1989.

34. Although federal law lifted prohibition in 1933, state laws kept Kansas a "dry" state until November 1948. Interview with Carl Clare, Dodge City, May 8, 1989.

35. Interview with Lois Stringfield Harmon, Garden City, June 13, 1989.

36. Interview with Esther Beasley and Fontell Littrell Hugoton, May 22, 1989; questionnaire response, Fontell Littrell, Hugoton, Fall 1988.

37. "Help It Along," *Liberal News*, Feb. 26, 1932, 5; "Many Register," *Liberal News*, Mar. 1, 1932, 1; "Feed Children," *Liberal News*, Feb. 6, 1933, 1; "Raymond Lloyd, Welfare Pres.," *Southwest Daily Times*, Jan. 8, 1939, 1.

38. "Thirty-seven Needy Families Are Aided by the Lions Club," *Garden City Daily Telegram*, Dec. 23, 1935, 1; "Will You Help?" *Clark County Clipper*, May 7, 1936, 1.

39. "Boy Scouts Repair Toys," *Liberal News*, Dec. 10, 1931, 1; "Made 33 Little Dolls," *Liberal News*, Dec. 19, 1930, 1; "Baskets Appreciated," *Liberal News*, Dec. 12, 1934, 4.

40. "Needy Family List Will Not Be Published," *Southwest Daily Times*, Dec. 19, 1939, 1.

41. "Endeavoring to Find Jobs," *Southwest Daily Times*, Oct. 2, 1938, 1; "Registering Home Labor," *Garden City Daily Telegram*, Nov. 11, 1930, 1; "Civic Group to Register Home Labor," *Garden City Daily Telegram*, Nov. 12, 1930, 1.

42. "Free Ads for the Unemployed," *Grant County Republican*, Dec. 18, 1930, 1; "A Free Service to the Unemployed of Garden City," *Garden City Daily Telegram*, Dec. 30, 1930, 2; "Farmers Swap Column Fills Need for Rural Subscribers," *Elkhart Tri-State News*, Aug. 8, 1935, 1.

43. "Children Are Examined Free," *Liberal News*, Sept. 7, 1934, 4.

44. "Briefly Speaking," *Garden City Daily Telegram*, Sept. 1, 1934, 6; "How Would You Feel If Santa Claus Missed You Christmas?" *Hugoton Hermes*, Dec. 13, 1935, 1; "Place Your Contributions under Local Direction," *Liberal News*, Aug. 18, 1932, 1.

45. "Red Cross in Enthusiastic Meeting Here," *Garden City Daily Telegram*, Oct. 24, 1930, 1; "Red Cross Assists Local Relief Administration," *Clark County Clipper*, Feb. 27, 1936, 1.

46. *Liberal News* and *Southwest Daily Times*, Dec. 5, 1930, Dec. 17, 1930, Jan. 6, 1931, Oct. 6, 1939, Nov. 8, 1940.

47. "Pleasant Valley Church," *Bucklin Banner*, Feb. 2, 1933, 3; "Meetings Postponed," *Meade Globe-News*, Mar. 1, 1934, 1; "Methodist Episcopal Church," *Bucklin Banner*, July 20, 1933, 6.

48. "Churches Will Sponsor Public Auction to Raise Tax Money," *Syracuse Journal*, Apr. 10, 1936, 1; "Additional Funds Needed to Save Churches," *Garden City Daily Telegram*, Jan. 8, 1938, 5.

49. Church Notice, Epworth Memorial Church, Elkhart, 1936; Virgil M. Hayes, minister, Letters to Congregation, Epworth Memorial Church, Elkhart, Apr. 5, 1935,

Jan. 1, 1937, Sept. 8, 1937; Record of Membership, Epworth Memorial Church, Elkhart, 1915–1936, United Methodist Church, Elkhart.

50. A. L. Jantzen to J. M. Suderman, Ransom, Jan. 20, 1937, Box 11, File 118, and A. S. Bechtel to J. M. Suderman, Deer Creek, Okla., March 5, 1937, Box 7, File 55, Mennonite Church, Western District, Home Mission Committee Field Files, Mennonite Library and Archives, Bethel College, Newton, Kansas.

51. Abe A. Schmidt to Brother Kaufman, Montezuma, March 10, 1939, Box 9, File 91, Mennonite Church, Western District, Home Mission Committee Field Files.

52. R. O. Thomas to Jess C. Denious and C. C. Scates to Jess C. Denious, Jess C. Denious Papers, Collection 25, Box 3, Correspondence, 1930–1940, Manuscripts Division, KSHS.

53. Rudolph Schmidt, Western District Conference Home Mission Worker's Report, Nov. 1939, Box 8, File 76, Mennonite Church, Western District, Home Mission Committee Field Files; "Pleasant Valley Church," *Bucklin Banner*, July 28, 1932, 1.

54. Kansas Emergency Relief Committee, *Public Welfare Service in Kansas: A Ten Year Report, 1924–1933*, KERC Bulletin no. 127, Dec. 1, 1934, 2–32, 111–560.

CHAPTER FOUR. "EVERYTHING COMES FROM WASHINGTON"

1. Commissioners' Journal, Haskell County, vol. C, Jan. 6, 1930, 437; July 6, 1931, 477; Dec. 7, 1931, 485.

2. Commissioners' Journal, Stanton County, Dec. 7, 1931, 89; Stevens County, vol. E, Nov. 2, 1931, 559; Hamilton County, vol. 5, Apr. 4, 1932, 163.

3. Kansas Emergency Relief Committee, "Poor Farms," (Topeka: Kansas State Printing Plant, n.d.), x; "County Will Build Homes for the Poor," *Garden City Daily Telegram*, Nov. 7, 1931, 1; "Cabins Will Be Built for Poor," *Garden City Daily Telegram*, Dec. 2, 1932, 1.

4. Commissioners' Journal, Hamilton County, vol. 5, July 5, 1932, 168; June 5, 1933, 189.

5. "$12,000 in Bank—Broke," *Liberal News*, Apr. 20, 1933, 1; "Livewire Volunteer Is Needed in Johnson Public Works Program," *Johnson Pioneer*, Oct. 5, 1933, 1.

6. "Notice," *Grant County Republican*, Aug. 17, 1933, 1; "They Need Your Assistance Now," *Johnson Pioneer*, Apr. 7, 1932, 2; "Clothing Needed for the County Poor," *Ness County News*, Jan. 16, 1932, 1.

7. This material appeared in slightly different form in Pamela Riney-Kehrberg, "Hard Times, Hungry Years: Failure of the Poor Relief in Southwestern Kansas, 1930–1933," *Kansas History* 15, 3 (Autumn 1992): 154–167.

8. The state of Kansas defined the mother's pension as follows: "Mothers Pensions. Granted to women with children under 14, who are widowed, divorced, or deserted, or whose husbands are unable to support them; total sum not to exceed $50 a month; administered by board of county commissioners, assisted by an investigating board of three reputable women of the county or the board of public welfare, if there be such a board." Commission of Labor and Industry, *Annual Report of the Commission of Labor and Industry, State of Kansas, 1932* (Topeka: Kansas State Printing Plant, 1932), 56.

9. Arthur Woods, chairman, President Hoover's Emergency Committee for Employment, "Give a Neighbor a Job," *Garden City Daily Telegram*, Feb. 21, 1931, 2.

10. "Provident Association Aid," *Garden City Daily Telegram*, Apr. 15, 1931, 2; "Approval for New Charity Organization," *Garden City Daily Telegram*, June 9, 1931, 1.

11. "It's the Poor That Worries Commission," *Garden City Daily Telegram*, July 8, 1931, 1.

12. "Volunteers of America Doing Community a Good," *Garden City Daily Telegram*, Oct. 14, 1931, 6; "Send Hungry to Volunteers," *Garden City Daily Telegram*, July 6, 1931.

13. "Local Junior Red Cross to Aid Needy by Canning Food," *Garden City Daily Telegram*, Nov. 17, 1931; "Relief Show Will Feature Miss Bennett," *Garden City Daily Telegram*, Nov. 17, 1931, 1; "None Will Go Hungry Here on Christmas," *Garden City Daily Telegram*, Dec. 24, 1931, 1.

14. "Plan Drive to Get Funds for Poor in County," *Garden City Daily Telegram*, June 3, 1932, 1.

15. Commissioners' Journal, Finney County, vol. G, June 7–8, 1932, 561.

16. "A Problem, Not Experiment," *Garden City Daily Telegram*, June 14, 1932, 6.

17. "Concentrated Effort to Aid Unemployed," *Garden City Daily Telegram*, June 14, 1932, 1, 5.

18. "A Problem, Not Experiment," 6.

19. "Schulman to Be Leader of Charity Board," *Garden City Daily Telegram*, June 18, 1932, 1.

20. "Hear Relief Report," *Garden City Daily Telegram*, Oct. 5, 1932, 1; "Committee Aids Needy Families," *Garden City Daily Telegram*, Sept. 2, 1932, 1; "Welfare Group Hears Reports," *Garden City Daily Telegram*, Aug. 3, 1932, 1–2.

21. "Relief Group Approves $3,456 Fund for Work on Local Improvement," *Garden City Daily Telegram*, Oct. 13, 1932, 1; "25 Are Working at Relief Jobs," *Garden City Daily Telegram*, Oct. 19, 1932, 2.

22. "Lack of Interest in Relief Work Is Shown Last Night," *Garden City Daily Telegram*, Dec. 9, 1932, 1.

23. "It Cannot Die," *Garden City Daily Telegram*, Dec. 12, 1932, 4.

24. "County Board Gives $150 Monthly for Relief Organization," *Garden City Daily Telegram*, Jan. 4, 1933, 1.

25. "Help Needed," *Garden City Daily Telegram*, Feb. 11, 1933, 4; "Relief Association Pledges, Donations Not Coming in Fast," *Garden City Daily Telegram*, Feb. 3, 1933, 1; "Relief Association Plans to Sponsor Community Garden," *Garden City Daily Telegram*, Feb. 21, 1933, 1; "Demands for Relief Double during Month of February," *Garden City Daily Telegram*, Mar. 3, 1933, 1.

26. "Cut Relief to Allow More Laborers a Job," *Garden City Daily Telegram*, Apr. 13, 1933, 1–2; "Volunteers to Cut Transient Menu," *Garden City Daily Telegram*, June 13, 1933, 1.

27. Commissioners' Journal, Finney County, vol. G, Mar. 7, 8, 10, 1933, 610.

28. "Relief Association Votes to Wind Up Its Work and Quit," *Garden City Daily Telegram*, Sept. 13, 1933, 1.

29. "Number of Relief Cases in a Rapid Increase of Late," *Garden City Daily Telegram*, June 27, 1934, 1; "Uncle Sam Bears Bulk of County's Poor Relief Load," *Garden City Daily Telegram*, Oct. 3, 1934, 1.

30. "Board of Education Cuts Budget of $12,000," *Hugoton Hermes*, Mar. 25, 1932, 1; "Ulysses Grade School in Sweeping Reduction," *Grant County Republican*, Apr. 14, 1932, 1; "We Wish to Suggest As Commendable," *Johnson Pioneer*, Jan. 5, 1933, 2; "Open Sept. 4," *Liberal News*, Aug. 24, 1933, 1–2.

31. Commissioners' Journal, Seward County, vol. 5, Aug. 22, 1938, 468; Haskell County, vol. D, Oct. 1939, 118; Morton County, book 3, Sept. 4, 1939, 14.

32. Real estate agents were actually selling homes in Elkhart to residents of other

counties and moving the homes to their buyers. People also left town and took their homes with them. It was cheaper to buy a home in Elkhart and move it to a new location than to construct new homes in other locations. Commissioners' Journal, Morton County, book 3, May 15, 1939, 8.

33. "Relief Load Makes Big Gain in a Year," *Johnson Pioneer*, July 11, 1940, 1; "Ness County Courthouse Official News Notes," *Ness County News*, Aug. 3, 1939, 1.

34. Kansas ranked sixteenth of the forty-eight states based on state and local contributions to total relief expenditures. Kansas Emergency Relief Committee, *Fundamental Policies of the Ka: sas Emergency Relief Committee and Summaries of Obligations for Relief, 1924–1936* (Topeka: KERC, 1936), 69–70.

35. Kansas Emergency Relief Committee, *Work Relief in Kansas, April 1, 1934–June 30, 1935*, vol. 1 (Topeka: KERC, July 31, 1935); "Home Advisors Demonstrate Helpful Household Methods," *Kansas Relief News Bulletin* 23 (May 27, 1935): 4; "Summer Program Is Outlined for Haskell County Residents," *Kansas Relief News Bulletin* 24 (June 10, 1935): 4.

36. Arthur Meyer, State Garden Supervisor, *Relief Garden Program, State of Kansas, 1935* (Topeka: KERC, 1935), 19–29; "Distribution of Free Garden Seed Added As Relief Project," *Johnson Pioneer*, Mar. 29, 1934, 1.

37. The Civilian Conservation Corps and Tennessee Valley Authority are the best examples of these values expressed on a larger scale. David E. Shi, *The Simple Life: Plain Living and High Thinking in American Culture* (New York: Oxford University Press, 1985), 232–247.

38. Meyer, *Relief Garden Program*, 19–29, 48–49.

39. Kansas Emergency Relief Committee, *Report on Proposed Leather and Wool Program, The State of Kansas* (Topeka: KERC, June 1, 1935).

40. Kansas Emergency Relief Committee, *Report: Drought Cattle Operations, The State of Kansas* (Topeka: KERC, May 1, 1935), 17, 40.

41. Ford County defined acceptable direct relief clients as the elderly, the handicapped, and widows with children. Commissioners' Journal, Ford County, vol. H, Dec. 23, 1935, 27–28.

42. "Will Put 135 Men to Work Here," *Liberal News*, Oct. 24, 1935, 1.

43. "Sewing Room Busy Place," *Liberal News*, May 8, 1935, 4; "Household Aid to Six Families," *Southwest Daily Times*, Apr. 11, 1939, 1.

44. "$330,000 Spent in Improvements Here in '37," *Ulysses News*, Jan. 13, 1938, 1.

45. "Leave for CCC Camps," *Liberal News*, Apr. 30, 1935, 1; "To Work Soon on Barracks for Lake Construction Corps," *Garden City Daily Telegram*, Oct. 4, 1933, 1.

46. "Call Is Issued for New or Used Toys," *Southwest Daily Times*, Dec. 21, 1939, 1; "Federal Funds to Help Needy College Students," *Garden City Daily Telegram*, Sept. 5, 1935, 1; "Benefits of NYA Recreational Program Show," *Ness County News*, July 9, 1936, 1; "College Work Gets Started," *Southwest Daily Times*, Feb. 5, 1937, 1.

47. "Don't Give Up," *Liberal News*, Feb. 6, 1931, 2.

48. "Limited Direct Relief Work Given As CWA Program Ends," *Johnson Pioneer*, Mar. 22, 1934, 1.

49. "Helping Themselves," *Clark County Clipper*, July 19, 1934, 2.

50. "Voters Turn Thumbs Down School Bond Proposition," *Grant County Republican*, May 15, 1930, 1; Commissioners' Journal, Hamilton County, vol. 5, July 6, 1931, 148.

51. "Proposed Swimming Pool for Ulysses Receives WPA Approval," *Grant County Republican*, July 16, 1936, 1; "Council Seeking Projects to Provide Work Relief,"

Elkhart Tri-State News, Aug. 1, 1935, 1; Clark County Republican Committee, advertisement, *Clark County Clipper,* Oct. 1, 1936, 5.

52. Commissioners' Journal, Ford County, vol. G, Aug. 5, 1931, 607.

53. Commissioners' Journal, Ford County, vol. H, Aug. 25, 1938, 152; vol. H, Aug. 21, 1939, 196.

54. "Taxpayers Invited to Meet with Commissioners," *Syracuse Journal,* Aug. 7, 1931, 1.

55. Questionnaire response, Thelma Warner, Syracuse, Fall 1988.

56. "Send Them to the City Clerk," *Liberal News,* Jan. 13, 1931, 2; "Stop Feeding Them," *Liberal News,* June 15, 1933, 1; "Not Feeding Transients," *Liberal News,* Apr. 7, 1932, 1; "Give Work to Home Men," *Liberal News,* Sept. 6, 1930, 1; "Poor Commissioner Grants Relief in Deserving Cases—Not to 'Vacationers,'" *Garden City Daily Telegram,* Aug. 28, 1933, 1.

57. Commissioners' Journal, Stanton County, June 5, 1933, 118; Commissioners' Journal, Hamilton County, vol. 5, Jan. 5, 1932, 159.

58. "Notice," *Elkhart Tri-State News,* Sept. 10, 1935, 1.

59. Commissioners' Journal, Ford County, vol. H, Apr. 9, 1936, 45, and Mar. 9, 1939, 180; Commissioners' Journal, Hodgeman County, vol. F, Nov. 24, 1930, 225; Commissioners' Journal, Seward County, vol. 5, May 9, 1936, 203.

60. Commissioners' Journal, Seward County, vol. 5, Mar. 11, 1937, 294; Commissioners' Journal, Hamilton County, vol. 5, Jan. 12, 1931, 1938; "Here's How Relief Fund Will Be Used," *Ness County News,* Nov. 19, 1932, 1; "No Further Aid to Able Bodied Men," *Hugoton Hermes,* Sept. 11, 1931, 1.

61. "Notice to Relief Clients in Bazine," *Bazine Advocate,* May 24, 1935, 1.

62. Commissioners' Journal, Gray County, vol. 4, Feb. 1, 1932, 290; "Variety of Foods from Relief Aid," *Johnson Pioneer,* Mar. 16, 1933, 1; "Relief Agency in Need of Gifts," *Ness County News,* Sept. 8, 1934, 1.

63. "Public Aid Clients Must Give Up Cars," *Bucklin Banner,* Mar. 2, 1939, 1; Commissioners' Journal, Ford County, vol. H, Feb. 10, 1939, 177.

64. "Notice to County Poor and Relief Workers," *Johnson Pioneer,* Oct. 12, 1933, 3.

65. "Commissioners Proceedings," *Elkhart Tri-State News,* Oct. 15, 1937, 6; "Welfare Head Answers Chamber's Charges," *Southwest Daily Times,* Aug. 25, 1938, 1.

66. Interview with Elfreda Penner Fast, Hillsboro, Apr. 15, 1989.

67. Interview with Leota Swafford Lambert and Elsie Swafford Riney, Liberal, Mar. 19, 1989.

68. Commissioners' Journal, Ford County, vol. H, Dec. 23, 1935, 26–27; Ford County Agricultural Extension, Kansas Annual Report, 1933, 1; "Yuletide Spirit Prevails, Merchants Report Increase in Sales," *Grant County Republican,* Dec. 21, 1933, 1.

69. Joe "Gloomy Dan" David, "Dustitis," *Leoti Standard,* 1936, as quoted in Wichita County History Association, *History of Wichita County, Kansas,* vol. 1 (North Newton, Kans.: Mennonite Press, 1980), 331.

CHAPTER FIVE. THE HARDEST OF TIMES

1. A prime example of this appeared in a back-to-the-land manual first published in 1935. The author stressed that urban-dwelling, wage-earning individuals would come

to appreciate the virtues of rural life during depressions. "When hard times arrive and his savings steadily melt away he begins to appreciate the advantages of a home which does not gobble up his hard-earned money but produces its up-keep, especially in the way of food for the family." M. G. Kains, *Five Acres and Independence: A Practical Guide to the Selection and Management of the Small Farm* (New York: Greenberg, 1935), 4–5.

2. Carl C. Taylor, Helen W. Wheeler, and E. L. Kirkpatrick, *Disadvantaged Classes in American Agriculture*, Social Research Report 8 (Washington, D.C.: USDA, FSA, and Bureau of Agricultural Economics, Apr. 1938), 114–123.

3. Clark County Agricultural Extension, Kansas Annual Report, 1930, 7; Grant County Agricultural Extension, Kansas Annual Report, 1930, 24.

4. Taylor et al., *Disadvantaged Classes*, 11; Kansas State Board of Agriculture, *Biennial Report of the State Board of Agriculture*, vol. 27 (Topeka: Kansas State Printing Plant, 1931).

5. "Prosperity King," *Liberal News*, Jan. 10, 1930, 1, 5; "Grant County's Wheat in 1929 Worth Over 2 Million," *Grant County Republican*, Jan. 9, 1930, 1; "Past Twelve Months Were Full of Important Events," *Garden City Daily Telegram*, Jan. 1, 1931, 1.

6. Gray County Agricultural Extension, Kansas Annual Report, 1930, 4; Clark County Agricultural Extension, Kansas Annual Report, 1930, 7; Meade County Agricultural Extension, Kansas Annual Report, 1930, 16–17.

7. "Fewer Hands Needed Here," *Johnson Pioneer*, June 18, 1931, 1.

8. "As I See It," *Clark County Clipper*, Jan. 7, 1932, 2.

9. Meade County Agricultural Extension, Kansas Annual Report, 1932, 39.

10. "Grant County Wheat Harvest Averaging Low," *Grant County Republican*, July 14, 1932, 1; Grant County Agricultural Extension, Kansas Annual Report, 1932, 9.

11. "Proceedings of Meeting Held at Guymon, Oklahoma, June 16, 1933," Alfred M. Landon, Governor's Papers, Box 3, Folder 11, Manuscripts Division, KSHS.

12. "Harvest in Stanton is About [8],000 Bushels," *Johnson Pioneer*, July 18, 1935, 1.

13. Kansas State Board of Agriculture, *Biennial Report of the State Board of Agriculture*, vols. 27, 30 (Topeka: Kansas State Printing Plant, 1931, 1937).

14. Ness County Agricultural Extension, Kansas Annual Report, 1935, 8; "What About 1934," *Grant County Republican*, Dec. 28, 1933, 1.

15. Interviews with Minnie Hirn Hoag, Liberal, May 4, 1989, and Gaylord Haflich, Garden City, June 12, 1989.

16. Kansas Emergency Relief Committee, *Report: Drought Cattle Operations, The State of Kansas* (Topeka: KERC, May 1, 1935).

17. Stanton County Agricultural Extension, Kansas Annual Report, 1935, 4.

18. Kansas Emergency Relief Committee, *Report: Drought Cattle Operations*.

19. Interview with David A. Classen, Hillsboro, Apr. 15, 1989.

20. Morton County Agricultural Extension, Kansas Annual Report, 1936, 3–4.

21. "Report Shows Crop Increase," *Southwest Daily Times*, Aug. 13, 1937, 1; "Big Drive against Hoppers Starts Monday," *Southwest Daily Times*, July 15, 1937, 1; Meade County Agricultural Extension, Kansas Annual Report, 1937, 5.

22. Letter from W. G. West, Live Stock Sanitary Commissioner, to Walter A. Huxman, Oct. 29, 1937, Walter A. Huxman, Governor's Papers, Box 1, Drouth File, Manuscripts Division, KSHS.

23. Martha Schmidt Friesen, Diary, Dec. 10, May 19, and July 20, 1937.

24. "Wheat Averages About 10 Bushels," *Southwest Daily Times*, June 28, 1938, 1; "9 Bu. Average As Harvest Ends," *Ulysses News*, July 7, 1938, 1; Stanton County Agricultural Extension, Kansas Annual Report, 1939, 2.

25. "Diaries of Iman C. Wiatt, Kearny County Historical Society, *History of Kearny County, Kansas,* vol. 2 (North Newton, Kans.: Mennonite Press, 1973), 284.

26. Meade County Agricultural Extension, Kansas Annual Report, 1932, 37; Gray County Agricultural Extension, Kansas Annual Report, 1931, 7; Grant County Agricultural Extension, Kansas Annual Report, 1932, 29.

27. Grant County Agricultural Extension, Kansas Annual Report, 1930, 13–15; Stanton County Agricultural Extension, Kansas Annual Report, 1935, 36; Morton County Agricultural Extension, Kansas Annual Report, 1936, 5; Meade County Agricultural Extension, Kansas Annual Report, 1934, 15; Gray County Agricultural Extension, Kansas Annual Report, 1936, 125.

28. Meade County Agricultural Extension, Kansas Annual Report, 1937, 8; Gray County Agricultural Extension, Kansas Annual Report, 1935, 158; Morton County Agricultural Extension, Kansas Annual Report, 1936, 41; Grant County Agricultural Extension, Kansas Annual Report, 1937, 43; "Chicken Canning," *Johnson Pioneer,* July 19, 1934, 5.

29. Clark County Agricultural Extension, Kansas Annual Report, 1932, 145; "Proceedings of Meeting Held at Guymon, Oklahoma, June 16, 1933," Landon Governor's Papers; Stanton County Agricultural Extension, Kansas Annual Report, 1935, 136.

30. Pamela Riney-Kehrberg, "Separation and Sorrow: A Farm Woman's Life, 1935–1941," *Agricultural History* 67, 2 (Spring 1993): 187–189.

31. Riney-Kehrberg, "Separation and Sorrow," 189.

32. Friesen Family, Expense Accounts, 1935. See also Deborah Fink, "Sidelines and Moral Capital: Women on Nebraska Farms in the 1930s," in Wava G. Haney and Jane B. Knowles, eds., *Women and Farming: Changing Roles, Changing Structures* (Boulder, Colo.: Westview, 1988): 55–70.

33. Letter from Otto Feldman, Meade, to Sen. Arthur M. Capper, Mar. 10, 1937, Arthur M. Capper Papers, Collection 12, Box 32, Agricultural General Correspondence, 1918–1939, KSHS.

34. "Farm Garden Saves Family's Budget $114," *Johnson Pioneer,* Jan. 13, 1938, 1.

35. Although historian Paul Bonnifield argued that the economic patterns of Dust Bowl counties showed no signs of mass outmigration and James Ware, in a doctoral dissertation written at Oklahoma State University, wrote that most Dust Bowl migrants "came from urban areas, not from rural ones," this was not the case among the farmers of southwestern Kansas. Paul Bonnifield, *The Dust Bowl: Men, Dirt, and Depression* (Albuquerque: University of New Mexico Press, 1979), 94–95; James Wesley Ware, "Black Blizzard: The Dust Bowl of the 1930s" (Ph.D. diss., Oklahoma State University, 1977), 105.

36. Andrew Gulliford, *America's Country Schools* (Washington, D.C.: Preservation Press, 1984), 43; "No Finney County Schools Forced to Close Their Doors," *Garden City Daily Telegram,* Feb. 16, 1935, 1.

37. "Most Schools over County in Good Shape," *Elkhart Tri-State News,* Sept. 24, 1937, 1; "Close Two Schools Next Year," *Elkhart Tri-State News,* Jan. 13, 1939, 1.

38. Friesen Diary, Mar. 19, 1937, and Apr. 3, 1937.

39. Friesen Family, Expense Accounts, 1935.

40. Friesen Diary, Jan. 17, 1937, and Feb. 27, 1937.

41. For a more detailed discussion of this issue see Riney-Kehrberg, "Separation and Sorrow."

42. This is a direct contradiction to historian Paul Bonnifield's assertions that the federal government essentially caused the migration of the 1930s. He stated, "The

often tragic Okie migration from the heartland of the dust bowl to California and elsewhere was largely caused by policies of the federal government." In his analysis of the impact of federal programs upon the farm population, Bonnifield claimed that the federal government, in essence, conspired against the residents of the Dust Bowl. In his opinion, federal aid was the key element in a malevolent plan to depopulate the Great Plains. Federal officials offered farm families the "bait" (aid), addicted them, and then removed their support, forcing them to flee the Dust Bowl. *Dust Bowl*, 188, 201, 137.

43. Gilbert Fite, *The Farmers' Frontier, 1865–1900* (New York: Holt, Rinehart, and Winston, 1966), 130.

44. Value of products per farm and benefit payment per farm calculated from the Kansas State Board of Agriculture, *Biennial Report of the State Board of Agriculture*, vols. 29–32, 1933–1940. Per capita rates of aid are drawn from Taylor et al., *Disadvantaged Classes*, 98.

45. Taylor et al., *Disadvantaged Classes*, 18. Leonard J. Arrington also made this argument in his article "Western Agriculture and the New Deal," *Agricultural History* 44 (Oct. 1970): 337–353.

46. Mortgage Records and Chattel Mortgage Records, vols. 9–19, both in Register of Deeds Office, Hamilton County Courthouse, Syracuse.

47. Case no. 18-68-64478, Farmers' Home Administration, Rural Rehabilitation Case Files, Region 7, Ness County, Kansas, Boxes 97–107, Record Group 96, National Archives and Records Administration, Central Plains Region, Kansas City, Kans.

48. A. D. Edwards, *Influence of Drought and Depression on a Rural Community: A Case Study in Haskell County, Kansas*, Social Research Report no. 7 (Washington, D.C.: USDA, Jan. 1939), 6, 7, 17n.

49. Carl C. Taylor, Bushrod W. Allin, and O. E. Baker, "Public Purposes in Soil Use," *United States Department of Agriculture Yearbook, 1938* (Washington, D.C.: Government Printing Office, 1938), 54.

50. Frances Perkins, Statement, U.S. Congress, House, *Hearings before the Select Committee to Investigate Interstate Migration of Destitute Citizens*, pt. 8, 76th Cong., 3d Sess., Nov. 29 and Dec. 2, 3, 1940, 3195.

51. USDA, "Aftermath of the Drought," *Report of the Secretary of Agriculture*, 1935 (Washington, D.C.: Government Printing Office, 1935), 51.

52. Grant County Agricultural Extension, Kansas Annual Report, 1933, 19; "Diaries of Iman C. Wiatt," 278; "Allotments for Counties Fixed," *Liberal News*, July 17, 1933, 1.

53. Gray County Agricultural Extension, Kansas Annual Report, 1933, 5; "Yuletide Spirit Prevails," *Grant County Republican*, Dec. 21, 1933, 1.

54. Morton County Agricultural Extension, Kansas Annual Report, 1936, 32–33.

55. In 1936, the Supreme Court ruled that the processing tax that funded wheat and corn-hog allotments was an unconstitutional delegation of congressional taxing power. Congress followed the Supreme Court's action with amendments to the AAA. See Theodore Saloutos, *The American Farmer and the New Deal* (Ames: Iowa State University Press, 1982), 131–133.

56. Morton County Agricultural Extension, Kansas Annual Report, 1937, 4, and 1939, 114; Stanton County Agricultural Extension, Kansas Annual Report, 1937, 7; Meade County Agricultural Extension, Kansas Annual Report, 1937, 91; Ness County Agricultural Extension, Kansas Annual Report, 1935, 76.

57. "Rural Resettlement at Work in County," *Ness County News*, Feb. 18, 1937, 1;

"Who Said They Never Come Back," *Southwest Daily Times*, Feb. 26, 1939, 4–6; "FSA Announces Loans for 4-H Project Work," *Southwest Daily Times*, Mar. 30, 1940, 1; "FSA Inaugurates Cooperative Buying," *Garden City Daily Telegram*, Feb. 14, 1940, 1; "Group Health Succeeds," *Garden City Daily Telegram*, Apr. 23, 1940, 8.

58. "Seward County Farm Woman Has a 'Grocery Store' in Cave," *Southwest Daily Times*, Nov. 7, 1939, 4.

59. "Families to Benefit from Group Buying," *Johnson Pioneer*, June 3, 1937, 1, 8; "Accomplishments of the Homemakers under the Farm Security Administration in Ness County, Kansas, for the Year of 1937," *Ness County News*, Dec. 30, 1937, 1; Case no. 18-68-2482, Farmers' Home Administration, Rural Rehabilitation Case Files, Region 7, Ness County, Kansas, Boxes 97–107, Record Group 96, National Archives and Records Administration, Central Plains Region, Kansas City, Kans.

60. Cases nos. 18-68-62546 and 18-68-2482, Farmers' Home Administration, Rural Rehabilitation Case Files, Region 7, Ness County, Kansas, Boxes 97–107, Record Group 96, National Archives and Records Administration, Central Plains Region, Kansas City, Kans.

61. Commissioners' Journal, Seward County, vol. 4, Dec. 18, 1933, 551; "Farmers Off Relief," *Liberal News*, Apr. 29, 1935, 1; "Ness County Official News Notes," *Ness County News*, Feb. 4, 1937, 1; Commissioners' Journal, Hodgeman County, vol. F, Jan. 6, 1936, 444.

62. Letter from Gray County Board of Commissioners to Harry Hopkins, May 8, 1936, WPA Central Files, Box 1374, Kansas, 1935–1944, Record Group 69, National Archives and Records Administration, Central Branch, Washington, D.C.; letter from Aubrey Williams, Deputy Administrator, WPA, to Sen. George McGill, Dec. 11, 1936, WPA Central Files, Box 0296, File 201.32, Kansas, General, 1935–1944, Record Group 69, National Archives and Records Administration, Central Branch, Washington, D.C.

63. Letter from John Cavanaugh, Arthur Capper, George McGill, Clifford Hope, and Phil Ferguson to Lt. Col. F. C. Harrington, Asst. Admin., WPA, June 16, 1938, and memorandum from John Wray to Lt. Col. Harrington, June 16, 1938, WPA Central Files, Box 0295, File 201.31, General, 1935–1944, Record Group 69, National Archives and Records Administration, Central Branch, Washington, D.C.

CHAPTER SIX. DOWN BUT NOT OUT

1. Portions of this chapter appear in slightly different form in Pamela Riney-Kehrberg, "From the Horse's Mouth: Dust Bowl Farmers and Their Solutions to the Problem of Aridity," *Agricultural History* 66, 2 (Spring 1992): 137–150.

2. Lawrence Svobida, *An Empire of Dust* (Caxton, Idaho: Caxton Printers, 1940); reprint, *Farming the Dust Bowl: A First-Hand Account from Kansas* (Lawrence: University Press of Kansas, 1986), 57, 233.

3. Interviews with Earl Owens, Liberal, May 3, 1989, and Katherine Scheer Wilson, Leoti, June 17, 1989.

4. During the 1930s, the jackrabbit population multiplied out of control and destroyed or threatened to destroy what little crops were raised. In order to combat this menace, communities organized rabbit drives to gather and kill the rabbits. Interview with Elfreda Penner Fast, Hillsboro, Apr. 15, 1989; Gray County Agricultural Extension, Kansas Annual Report, 1934, 71; letter to author from Daniel Penner, Hillsboro, Fall 1988.

5. Interview with Dean McVicker, Beeler, May 12, 1989.

6. Ford County Agricultural Extension, Home Demonstration Agent's Report, Kansas Annual Report, 1939, 187.

7. Interviews with Katherine Scheer Wilson, Leoti, June 17, 1989; Doreen Jacobs, Ashland, July 2, 1989; Eula Reath Wilson, Jetmore, May 11, 1989; and Opal Musselman Burdett, Ness City, May 13, 1989.

8. Interview with Leota Swafford Lambert and Elsie Swafford Riney, Liberal, Mar. 19, 1989.

9. Interview with Minnie Hirn Hoag, Liberal, May 4, 1989.

10. Interview with David A. Classen, Hillsboro, Apr. 15, 1989.

11. Martha Schmidt Friesen, Diary, Nov. 5, 1936.

12. Interview with Leota Swafford Lambert and Elsie Swafford Riney, Liberal, Mar. 19, 1989.

13. Interview with Pauline Renick Owens, Liberal, May 3, 1989.

14. Interviews with Hazel Steenis Shriver, Deerfield, June 14, 1989, and Louise Schroeder, Jetmore, May 10, 1989.

15. "Local Merchants Report Only Slight Trade Jump," Elkhart Tri-State News, Dec. 24, 1936, 1.

16. Interview with Minnie Hirn Hoag, Liberal, May 4, 1989.

17. Donald Worster, Dust Bowl: The Southern Plains in the 1930s (New York: Oxford University Press, 1979), 26–27.

18. Interview with Elfreda Penner Fast, Hillsboro, Apr. 15, 1989.

19. "The Nation Goes Democratic," Hugoton Hermes, Nov. 11, 1932, 1; "First Tabulation of Rural Ballots Shows Farmers Voting 2 to 1 Roosevelt," Garden City Daily Telegram, Oct. 12, 1936, 1.

20. "The Farmer Is Grateful," Garden City Daily Telegram, Feb. 11, 1936, 6.

21. Office of the Secretary of State, Biennial Report of the Secretary of State, vol. 32 (Topeka: Kansas State Printing Plant, 1941), 100.

22. "Getting Closer to Home," Liberal News, Feb. 15, 1933, 2; petition to Henry J. Wallace et al., received Sept. 25, 1936, WPA Central Files, 1935–1944, Box 0297, File 201.33, Record Group 69, National Archives and Records Administration, Central Branch, Washington, D.C.; "Morton County Farmers Voice Dissatisfaction on Crop Yield Adjustments," Elkhart Tri-State News, Sept. 24, 1936, 1.

23. Meeting of the Farm Practice and Legislative Committee of the Southwest Agricultural Association, Elkhart, Apr. 30, 1937, Walter A. Huxman, Governor's Papers, Box 1, Dust Bowl File, Manuscripts Division, KSHS.

24. Telegram to Walter Huxman from Giles Miller and H. A. Kinney (copy of the telegram sent to Franklin Roosevelt), Apr. 23, 1937, Walter A. Huxman, Governor's Papers.

25. H. A. Kinney to Walter Huxman, Apr. 29, 1937, Walter A. Huxman, Governor's Papers.

26. Walter Huxman to H. A. Kinney, May 4, 1937, Walter A. Huxman, Governor's Papers.

27. "Assn. Asks an Authority for the Dust Bowl," Southwest Daily Times, May 13, 1937, 1; "Action Demanded in the Five State Dust Bowl Area," Hugoton Hermes, May 28, 1937, 1.

28. "Up and Down Again," Southwest Daily Times, May 19, 1937, 2.

29. Ray Jackson to Clifford Hope, May 25, 1937, George McGill Papers, Collection 43, Box 65, Dust Bowl File, Manuscripts Division, KSHS.

30. "Petition," Elkhart Tri-State News, Apr. 22, 1937, 1.

31. David E. Shi, *The Simple Life: Plain Living and High Thinking in American Culture* (New York: Oxford University Press, 1985), 233.

32. Ford County Agricultural Extension, Kansas Annual Report, 1940, 255–257.

33. Letter from C. C. Isely, Ford County Housing Authority, Dodge City, to John G. Stutz, Kansas Emergency Relief Committee, Apr. 24, 1935; and letter from C. C. Isely to Rep. Clifford Hope, Apr. 24, 1935; Clifford R. Hope Papers, Collection 50, Box 52, C. C. Isely Correspondence, Manuscripts Division, KSHS; C. C. Isely to Mr. Robert Laubengayer, June 6, 1933, Alfred M. Landon, Governor's Papers, Box 12, Folder 1, Relief Matters, Manuscripts Division, KSHS; "Disclose Expansion Plans at Wilroads Deed Party," *Dodge City Daily Globe*, Oct. 15, 1943.

34. Settlements such as Wilroads Gardens sprang up around the country, often with the same lack of success. A similar program that was tested at Austin, Minnesota, was intended for the workers at the Hormel Packing Company. As a housing project, it worked; as a settlement of subsistence homesteads, it did not. Shi, *The Simple Life*, 239.

35. For a more detailed description of soil-saving farming methods, see R. Douglas Hurt, *The Dust Bowl: An Agricultural and Social History* (Chicago: Nelson-Hall, 1981), 65–86.

36. "Program Started to Prevent Dust," *Ness County News*, Dec. 21, 1935, 1.

37. See Hurt, *The Dust Bowl*, 75–76, for a more comprehensive discussion of local soil-drifting resolutions and their successes and failures.

38. "To Act against Erosion," *Garden City Daily Telegram*, Jan. 27, 1936, 6; "Farmer Can List a Neighbor's Land," *Garden City Daily Telegram*, Mar. 11, 1937; "Non-Resident Land Owners Sue the County," *Garden City Daily Telegram*, Nov. 4, 1937, 1.

39. E. A. Keply to George McGill, Jan. 11, 1938, George McGill Papers, Collection 43, Box 65, Agriculture Committee, second file, Manuscripts Division, KSHS.

40. Ray Jackson to Clifford Hope, May 25, 1937, George McGill Papers.

41. "Farmers Again Reject Soil District Plan," *Johnson Pioneer*, Sept. 1, 1938, 1; "Farmers Vote Conservation District Out," *Southwest Daily Times*, Sept. 16, 1937, 1; "Farmers Turn Thumbs Down on SC District," *Elkhart Tri-State News*, Nov. 5, 1937, 1; USDA, *Farmers in a Changing World: Yearbook of Agriculture*, 1940 (Washington, D.C.: Government Printing Office, 1940), 413–414.

42. "Indifferent to Land Purchases," *Hugoton Hermes*, Mar. 15, 1935, 1; "Controlling the Nation's Unproductive Acres," *Johnson Pioneer*, Feb. 7, 1935, 2; "Land Buying Welcome," *Garden City Daily Telegram*, Nov. 22, 1937, 8.

43. "Recommendations for Soil Control in Dust Bowl Area Adopted by the Farm Practice Committee of the Southwest Agricultural Association, Guymon, Oklahoma, June 25, 1937," Walter A. Huxman, Governor's Papers, Box 1, Dust Bowl, Manuscripts Division, KSHS.

44. This land acquisition program operated only in selected Dust Bowl communities and in Kansas was confined to Morton County, which was the most severely damaged by drought and high winds. For an excellent description of the impact of such a program on a North Dakota community, see Ann Marie Low, *Dust Bowl Diary* (Lincoln, Nebr.: Bison Books, 1984).

45. "Leaders Met to Consider FSA in County," *Elkhart Tri-State News*, Jan. 7, 1938, 1.

46. Population figures from State of Kansas, Statistical Rolls, Agricultural Census, Morton County, Jones and Cimarron townships, 1930, 1935, 1940, Archives Division, KSHS.

47. "Federal Land Buying Program Gets Under Way in Morton County," *Elkhart Tri-State News*, Feb. 11, 1938, 1; "Attack Further Purchases," *Elkhart Tri-State News*, Jan. 13, 1939, 1; "State's Rights Are Again an Issue," *Ulysses News*, Feb. 23, 1939, 8.

48. Letter from Z. W. Johnson to Jess Denious, State Senator, Jan. 6, 1939, Jess C. Denious Papers, Collection 25, Box 3, Correspondence, Jan.–Feb. 1939, Manuscripts Division, KSHS.

49. "The Administration Giving Individualism a Chance," *Ulysses News*, Mar. 16, 1939, 8; "Thousands of Acres of Land on U.S. 'Rest-Cure,'" *Ulysses News*, Apr. 25, 1940, 2.

50. See George S. Atwood, USDA, Forest Service, *History of the Cimarron National Grassland: Land Utilization Project KA-LU-21* (Washington, D.C.: Government Printing Office, 1962), for a description of the history and management of the Cimarron National Grassland. Interestingly enough, the fight over the land buy-out is largely forgotten. Only one of the current residents questioned remembered that there had been any controversy surrounding the creation of the grassland, and he commented that no one he knew felt that the government had coerced them into selling. Interview with Lawrence Smith, Elkhart, June 5, 1989.

51. "Ness County Ramblings," *Ness County News*, Nov. 2, 1939, 5; "Never Yet Has Been Dry Underground," *Ulysses News*, Dec. 21, 1939, 8. For a detailed discussion of irrigation on the southern plains, see Donald E. Green, *Land of the Underground Rain: Irrigation on the Texas High Plains, 1910–1970* (Austin: University of Texas Press, 1973).

52. "Forerunner of New Type of Agriculture, Deep Well for Irrigation Spudded in Today," *Southwest Daily Times*, May 20, 1937, 1.

53. "Irrigation Loans to Be Available Soon," *Garden City Daily Telegram*, Mar. 8, 1939, 53.

54. Only two cautionary notes about irrigation surfaced in the course of my research. The Gray County agricultural agent encouraged his farmers to only irrigate feed crops and livestock, not wheat. Also, S. R. Stebbins, a farmer from Sublette, wrote to Congressman Clifford Hope that irrigation was only a short-term solution, based on limited resources. In the long run, according to Stebbins, it would dry up wells on lower lands and "put them in a dryer land than we have here, and no drinking water." Gray County Agricultural Extension, Kansas Annual Report, 1940, 2; S. R. Stebbins, Sublette, to Rep. Clifford R. Hope, Mar. 26, 1938, Clifford R. Hope Papers, Collection 50, Box 64, General Correspondence, N–Z, Manuscripts Division, KSHS.

CHAPTER SEVEN. FACING A CRISIS OF CONFIDENCE

1. Robert Smith Bader describes the 1930s as a decade of self-denigration, when Kansans developed a "diffident, self-deprecating" attitude toward their state and themselves. I would argue that the rest of the nation may have had a negative image of Kansas, but southwestern Kansans, at least, were anything but diffident and self-deprecating about their land. Their attitude was generally positive to the point of boosterism. *Hayseeds, Moralizers, and Methodists: The Twentieth-Century Image of Kansas* (Lawrence: University Press of Kansas, 1988), 72–85.

2. Great Plains Committee, *The Future of the Great Plains* (Washington, D.C.: Government Printing Office, 1936), 16.

3. John B. Bennett, F. R. Kenney, and W. R. Chapline, "The Problem: Subhumid

Areas," *Soils and Men: Yearbook of Agriculture, 1938* (Washington, D.C.: Government Printing Office, 1938), 68.

4. Hugh H. Bennett et al., *Report of the Great Plains Drought Area Committee* (Washington, D.C.: Government Printing Office, 1936), 6.

5. Bennett et al., *Report*, 10–11; USDA, "Aftermath of the Drought," *Report of the Secretary of Agriculture, 1935* (Washington, D.C.: Government Printing Office, 1935), 51.

6. N. A. Tolles, "A Survey of Labor Migration between States," *Monthly Labor Review* 45, 1 (July 1937): 11; Frances Perkins, Statement, U.S. Congress, House, *Hearings before the Select Committee to Investigate Interstate Migration of Destitute Citizens*, 76th Cong., 3d Sess., pt. 10 (Washington, D.C.: Government Printing Office, 1940), 4122.

7. Chester C. Davis, "If Drought Strikes Again," *Saturday Evening Post* 207 (Apr. 27, 1935): 80.

8. Raymond J. Pool, "White Man versus the Prairie," *Science* 91 (Jan. 19, 1940): 54–57.

9. "The Great American Desert," *Warsaw* (Missouri) *Times*, Apr. 4, 1935.

10. Avis D. Carlson, "Dust Blowing," *Harper's Magazine* 171 (July 1935): 150; Kunigunde Duncan, "Reclaiming the Dust Bowl," *Nation* 149 (Sept. 9, 1939): 269; "Agriculture: 500,000,000 Tons of Dust Cover Kansas and Points East; AAA Moves to Save Nation's 'Bread Basket,'" *News-Week* 5, 13 (Mar. 30, 1935): 6.

11. "Garden of Eden Destroyed When Man Turned the Sod on the Prairies of Kansas," *Topeka Journal*, Apr. 3, 1935; Carlson, "Dust Blowing," 152–153.

12. Margaret Bourke-White, "Dust Changes America," *Nation* 140 (May 22, 1935): 598.

13. Thomas Alfred Tripp, "Dust Bowl Tragedy," *Christian Century* 57 (Jan. 24, 1940): 108–109.

14. Walter Davenport, "Land Where Our Children Die," *Collier's* 100 (Sept. 18, 1937): 12–13, 73.

15. George Greenfield, "Unto Dust," *Reader's Digest* 30, 181 (May 1937): 37.

16. "When Dust Was Dust," *Dodge City Globe*, Mar. 29, 1937; *Topeka Capital*, Mar. 29, 1937; *Topeka Capital*, Oct. 1, 1937; *Arkansas City Traveler*, Dec. 10, 1937. Historian James Malin also argued this point in his articles about dust storms in Kansas, which he wrote to counter the "myth" that Kansans had caused the Dust Bowl by planting too many acres of wheat. He searched newspapers to find stories about dust storms and found that they dated back to the earliest settlement in Kansas, well before farmers had broken large acreages. "Dust Storms, 1850–1890," *Kansas Historical Quarterly* 14, (May, Aug., Nov., 1946): 129–144, 265–296, 391–413.

17. "Plowman's Dust," *Liberal News*, Mar. 25, 1935, 2; "They Can't Take It," *Grant County Republican*, Mar. 28, 1935, 1; "Softies," *Garden City Daily Telegram*, Mar. 21, 1935, 8.

18. "Invitation to Photographers," *Garden City Daily Telegram*, June 6, 1935, 8; "Floods and Dust," *Garden City Daily Telegram*, Mar. 20, 1936, 6.

19. "Despite Winds, Stanton Weather Has Its Benefits," *Johnson Pioneer*, Feb. 9, 1933, 1; "How Big a Mistake to Plow Up the Prairies," *Ulysses News*, Nov. 21, 1940, 1; "Nominations for Any Vacancies in Fame's Hall," *Johnson Pioneer*, June 24, 1937, 2; "They Do It All over the World," *Ulysses News*, Sept. 1, 1938, 8.

20. "A Meager Living in Dirty Hovels for Dust Refugees," *Garden City Daily Telegram*, June 7, 1938, 1, 3; "Welcome Back Home," *Garden City Daily Telegram*, May 26, 1938, 8.

21. "State Junior Chamber of Commerce Raps Dust Storm and Grasshopper Postcards," *Garden City Daily Telegram*, May 14, 1940, 1, 6.

22. "Dust Storm Dilemma," *Garden City Daily Telegram*, Feb. 19, 1937, 8.

23. "Our Biggest Story," *Southwest Daily Times*, Jan. 15, 1939, 2; "Don't Let Dust Photos Describe the Plains to Your Friends Abroad," *Garden City Daily Telegram*, June 16, 1939, 1.

24. "Right Side Up," *Saturday Evening Post* 211 (May 27, 1939): 22; "Arid Farming and Ecology," *Scientific American* 159 (Nov. 1938): 233; Ben Hibbs, "The Dust Bowl Can Be Saved," *Saturday Evening Post* 210 (Dec. 18, 1937): 82; "Creeping Disaster," *Business Week*, July 28, 1934, 36.

25. Harold Ward, "Conquering the Dust Bowl," *Travel* 74 (Feb. 1940), 25; Davis, "If Drought Strikes Again," 76.

26. "Hope in the Dust Bowl," *New York Times Magazine*, July 16, 1939, 21; "Up from the Dust," *American Magazine*, Apr. 1940, 55.

27. Ford County Agricultural Extension, Kansas Annual Report, 1940, 255–256; Morton County Agricultural Extension, Kansas Annual Report, 1940, 3, 118.

CHAPTER EIGHT. TOO POOR TO LEAVE,
TOO DISCOURAGED TO STAY

1. This is based on the questionnaire responses of 80 individuals living throughout southwestern Kansas. They were asked: "If you remained in southwestern Kansas between 1930 and 1940, why did you stay?" Although approximately 125 respondents answered the questionnaire, only 80 actually answered this question or gave a response other than "I was a child and had no choice." The answers fit one or more of six classifications: land ownership; business or job; "no place to go"; no money; attachment to home, area, and family; faith in the land. If answers could be classified in more than one way, they were. See Appendix A for a methodological note about the questionnaire project and a copy of the questionnaire.

2. Questionnaire responses, Ruth Dodge, Kearny County, Fall 1988, and Susie Baker, Morton County, Fall 1988.

3. Questionnaire responses, Laurie Copeland, Ness County, Fall 1988, and Vivian Waterhouse, Ford County, Fall 1988.

4. These five townships are a randomly selected sample of all townships in southwestern Kansas. See Map 8.1 for the relationship of these townships to the area and Appendix B for a methodological note describing data collection and analysis. For the purpose of this study, family linkages were defined by shared surnames within the township. Unfortunately, this did not allow for the tracing of female kin connections, which may very well have been as important to persistence as links between male family members.

5. Kansas Decennial Census, 1925, Highpoint Township, Ness County, vol. 157.

6. All numbers used for descriptions of the five townships are means, unless otherwise noted, calculated using DBase 3, and SPSS/PC+. Family linkages are established through surnames only.

7. All material pertaining to Highpoint Township, Ness County, is drawn from Kansas, Statistical Rolls, Agricultural Census, Ness County, Highpoint Township, 1930, 1935, 1940, Archives Division, KSHS. All information pertaining to land ownership is drawn from Transfer and/or Deed Records, Highpoint Township, Ness County, Ness County Courthouse, Ness City.

8. Kansas Decennial Census, 1925, Ford County, vol. 80.

9. All material pertaining to Pleasant Valley Township, Ford County, is drawn from Kansas, Statistical Rolls, Agricultural Census, Ford County, Pleasant Valley Township, 1930, 1935, 1940, Archives Division, KSHS. All information pertaining to land ownership is drawn from Transfer and/or Deed Records, Pleasant Valley Township, Ford County, Ford County Courthouse, Dodge City.

10. Kansas Decennial Census, 1925, Finney County, vol. 78.

11. All material pertaining to Pleasant Valley Township, Finney County, is drawn from Kansas, Statistical Rolls, Agricultural Census, Finney County, Pleasant Valley Township, 1930, 1935, 1940, Archives Division, KSHS. All information pertaining to land ownership is drawn from Transfer and/or Deed Records, Pleasant Valley Township, Finney County, Finney County Courthouse, Garden City.

12. Kansas Decennial Census, 1925, Meade County, vol. 139.

13. Meade County Historical Society, *Pioneer Stories of Meade County* (Meade, Kans.: Meade County Historical Society, 1985), pp. 40, 143–145. All material pertaining to Logan Township, Meade County, is drawn from Kansas, Statistical Rolls, Agricultural Census, Meade County, Logan Township, 1930, 1935, 1940, Archives Division, KSHS. All information pertaining to land ownership is drawn from Transfer and/or Deed Records, Logan Township, Meade County, Meade County Courthouse, Meade.

14. Kansas Decennial Census, 1925, Hamilton County, vol. 93. All material pertaining to Medway Township, Logan County, is drawn from Kansas, Statistical Rolls, Agricultural Census, Hamilton County, Medway Township, 1930, 1935, 1940, Archives Division, KSHS. All information pertaining to land ownership is drawn from Transfer and/or Deed Records, Medway Township, Hamilton County, Hamilton County Courthouse, Syracuse.

15. Wilfred H. Pine, *100 Years of Farmland Values in Kansas*, Bulletin no. 611 (Manhattan: Agricultural Experiment Station, Kansas State University, 1977), 5.

16. Earl H. Bell, *Culture of a Contemporary Rural Community: Sublette, Kansas*, Rural Life Studies 2 (USDA, Bureau of Agricultural Economics, Sept. 1942), 36. Several of those interviewed for this project mentioned the issue of land values and land sales during the thirties. Brent Gould, then living near Syracuse, purchased a 392-acre farm for $825. If the family that owned the land had waited to sell it until the drought abated, they could have sold it for $10 an acre. Ona Libertus, also of Hamilton County, was forced to sell the 325-acre farm she had homesteaded in the early years of the century for only $300, much to her regret. Interviews with Brent Gould, Liberal, May 3, 1989, and Ona Libertus, Coolidge, June 10, 1989.

17. In his examination of farming on the Canadian plains and prairies, Robert Ankli found that large farms had a significantly greater chance of success than small farms during good or marginal years. During bad years, "no size of farm was adequate unless long-run average yields could be made." "Farm Income on the Great Plains and the Canadian Prairies, 1920–1940," *Agricultural History* 51, 1 (Jan. 1977): 103.

18. For a discussion of the importance of women's subsistence production and the success of farming families in the wheat belt, see Cornelia Butler Flora and John Stitz, "Female Subsistence Production and Commercial Farm Survival among Settlement Kansas Wheat Farmers," *Human Organization* 47, 1 (Spring 1988): 64–68.

19. These definitions of large-scale production of milk and eggs are based upon the standards of the area. That even this level of production would have seemed modest to many other farmers in the Midwest shows that most southwestern Kansans participated in cream, milk, and egg production on a very small scale indeed.

20. Geographer D. Aidan McQuillan in his study of immigrant populations in Kansas found that those farmers with greater investments in livestock had greater persistence rates than those with little or no livestock. He also found greater persistence among farmers with larger holdings. "The Mobility of Immigrants and Americans: A Comparison of Farmers on the Kansas Frontier," *Agricultural History* 53, 3 (July 1979): 593.

21. Donald Worster, *Dust Bowl: The Southern Plains in the 1930s* (New York: Oxford University Press, 1979), 173–177.

22. For a description of the migratory habits of the Mennonites of Kansas, see David A. Haury, *Prairie People: A History of the Western District Conference* (Newton, Kans.: Faith and Life Press, 1981). Interviews with David A. Classen and Elfreda Penner Fast, Hillsboro, Apr. 15, 1989.

23. In an article about the settlement, J. W. Fretz indicated that there was division between the traditionalists in the community and young people who were becoming more evangelical in their faith. "Settlement Folks Are in Oregon," *Meade Globe-News*, May 2, 1940, 1; J. W. Fretz, "The Mennonite Community at Meade," *Mennonite Life* 6, 3 (July 1951): 8–13.

24. Within the five-township sample, nine farmers in Highpoint Township lost their farms; six in Logan Township; four in Medway Township; seven in Pleasant Valley, Finney County (including three Mennonites); and five in Pleasant Valley, Ford County. Among those losing their farms were two women, evidently widows.

25. Transfer and/or Deed and Mortgage Records, Finney, Ford, Hamilton, Mead, and Ness counties.

26. Chattel Mortgage Record, Finney County, vols. 31–38, Office of the Register of Deeds, Finney County Courthouse, Garden City.

27. Nationally, there were an average of 24.7 forced sales per 1,000 farmers during the 1930s. In the region, which included Minnesota, Iowa, Missouri, North Dakota, South Dakota, Nebraska, and Kansas, there were 38.7 forced sales per 1,000 farmers. In Kansas, there were 35.9 forced sales per 1,000 farmers. In this group of five townships, there were only 5.4 forced sales per 1,000 farmers. *Major Statistical Series of the United States Department of Agriculture*, vol. 6, Land Values and Farm Finance, Agricultural Handbook no. 118 (Washington, D.C.: Government Printing Office, Oct. 1957); *Agricultural Statistics, 1941* (Washington, D.C.: Government Printing Office, 1941); USDA, *The Farm Real Estate Situation*, Circulars 150, 354, 548, 662. Transfer and/or Deed Records, Finney, Ford, Hamilton, Meade, and Ness counties.

28. Interview with Eula Reath Wilson, Jetmore, May 11, 1989.

29. All population figures are drawn from U.S. Department of Commerce, Bureau of the Census, *Fifteenth Census of the United States, 1930: Population*, pt. 1; *Sixteenth Census of the United States, 1940: Population*, pts. 2, 3.

30. Hershel Kannier, ed., *Kansas Facts*, vol. 4 (Topeka: Kansas Facts Publishing Company, 1933), 61–63, 163–164.

31. Examination of the sample counties using multiple and step wise regression (using Systat and SPSS PC+) revealed that the variables of farm size, change in population during the 1920s, the mean value of the crop over the course of the decade, and the percentage of foreign-born and second-generation residents explains more than 70 percent (an adjusted squared multiple R of .711) of the variation in population change between counties. (In defining the foreign-born population, Mexican residents were eliminated from the sample because their lack of citizenship created special problems during the 1930s.) Each of these variables was statistically significant at a value of .06 or better (farm size, .037; foreign born, .048; change in

population, .060; value of crop, .002). The presence of the foreign born and the value of the crop showed the greatest influence on the change in total population. While these factors cannot be used to explain the movements of individuals or to predict what happened in other areas, it does help to explain aggregate population changes in these sixteen counties during the 1930s.

32. Kansas State Board of Agriculture, *Biennial Report of the State Board of Agriculture*, vols. 27–32 (Topeka: Kansas State Printing Plant, 1931, 1933, 1935, 1937, 1939, 1941).

33. Two recent studies have shown that immigrant communities often have lower migration rates than old American communities surrounding them. This results from the pecuniary support that community members offer each other, in addition to nonpecuniary support, such as the comfort of family relationships, fellowship, and familiar religious and social traditions. See Jon Gjerde, *From Peasants to Farmers: The Migration from Balestrand, Norway, to the Upper Midwest* (Cambridge: Cambridge University Press, 1985), and Robert C. Ostergren, *A Community Transplanted: The Trans-Atlantic Experience of a Swedish Immigrant Settlement in the Upper Middle West, 1835–1915* (Madison: University of Wisconsin Press, 1988).

34. Worster, *Dust Bowl*, 30.

35. Kansas State Board of Agriculture, *Biennial Report of the State Board of Agriculture*.

36. Ford County Agricultural Extension, Home Demonstration Agent, Kansas Annual Report, 1939, 4; Morton County Agricultural Extension, Kansas Annual Report, 1939, 113–114.

37. For a description of Mexican life in Kansas from 1900 to World War II, see Robert Oppenheimer, "Acculturation or Assimilation: Mexican Immigrants in Kansas, 1900 to World War II," *Western Historical Quarterly* 16 (Oct. 1985): 429–448.

38. "Sugar Company to Aid of the Unemployed," *Garden City Daily Telegram*, June 14, 1932, 1; "Off Relief Rolls to Work in Beet Fields," *Garden City Daily Telegram*, June 12, 1935, 1; "It's the Poor That Worries the Commission," *Garden City Daily Telegram*, July 8, 1931, 1.

39. J. F. Lucey to Clyde M. Reed, Nov. 18, 1930, J. E. Gorman to Clyde M. Reed, Nov. 25, 1930, and Carl R. Gray to Clyde M. Reed, Nov. 28, 1930, Clyde M. Reed, Governor's Papers, Box 3, Unemployed and Mexican Labor File, Manuscripts Division, KSHS.

40. Kansas Commission of Labor and Industry, *Annual Report of the Commission of Labor and Industry, for the Year Ending Dec. 31, 1930* (Topeka, Kansas State Printing Plant, 1931), 63–64; Commissioners' Journal, Kearny County, vol. 6, June 5, 1933, 264.

41. "The Board met with the Welfare Director and decided to send an alien Mexican family back to Mexico. This case has been cleared and O.K.'d by the Mexican government." Commissioners' Journal, Ford County, vol. H, Nov. 29, 1940, 247.

42. Records, Community Congregational Church of Garden City, Minutes of the Ministerial Association, May 4, 1934, 178, Manuscripts Division, KSHS; Oppenheimer, "Acculturation or Assimilation," 445.

43. Kansas Emergency Relief Committee, "Problems of Negro Population and Results of Special Survey," *Public Welfare Service in Kansas, 1934*, KERC Bulletin no. 289, Nov. 1, 1935, 758–759.

44. U.S. Department of Commerce, Bureau of the Census, *Fifteenth Census of the United States, 1930*, and *Sixteenth Census of the United States, 1940*.

45. For a description of an African American farming community in southwestern Kansas and analysis of the problems they faced, see C. Robert Haywood, "The Hodgeman County Colony," *Kansas History* 12, 4 (Winter, 1989/1990): 210–221. Unfortunately for this study, the Kansas agricultural census did not include information about race. Therefore, examination of agricultural census records for townships with African American residents did not yield any usable comparative information.

46. Kansas Emergency Relief Committee, "Problems of Negro Population," 760.

47. Clifford R. Hope to Chester Brown, June 18, 1934, Clifford R. Hope Papers, Collection 50, Box 44, Correspondence A–B, 1934–1935, Manuscripts Division, KSHS.

48. Harvard Sitkoff, in his study of African Americans and the New Deal, reported that "Negroes found it more difficult than whites to get on relief rolls; they usually received less for the work relief they performed than did whites." *A New Deal for Blacks* (New York: Oxford University Press, 1978), 69–70.

EPILOGUE. THE DUST SETTLES

1. Leo M. Hoover, *A Summary of Kansas Agriculture,* Agricultural Economics Report no. 55 (Manhattan: Kansas Agricultural Experiment Station, July 1953), Figure 5.

2. Kansas State Board of Agriculture, *Biennial Report of the State Board of Agriculture,* vol. 33 (Topeka: Kansas State Printing Plant, 1943).

3. Adjusting for inflation, between 1940 and 1950 farmland in Hamilton County rose from $7 an acre to nearly $25 an acre, and farmland in Morton County from $8 an acre to just over $28 an acre. This land more than tripled in value in the course of the decade. Wilfred H. Pine, *100 Years of Farmland Values in Kansas,* Bulletin no. 611 (Manhattan: Kansas Agricultural Experiment Station, Kansas State University, 1977), Table 2.

4. "Families on Western Slope May Return, Says Robertson," *Elkhart Tri-State News,* Feb. 16, 1940, 1.

5. "Industrial Liberal," *Southwest Daily Times,* July 7, 1937, 2.

6. Ford County Agricultural Extension, Kansas Annual Report, 1938, 158; Morton County Agricultural Extension, Kansas Annual Report, 1938, 61–62; Gray County Agricultural Extension, Kansas Annual Report, 1932, 3–5; Grant County Agricultural Extension, Kansas Annual Report, 1930, 25.

7. "The Greatest Need for Southwest Stability," *Ulysses News,* May 9, 1940, 8; "Southwest Needs Farmers," *Garden City Daily Telegram,* Resource Issue, Conservation Section, June 14, 1939.

8. Gray County Agricultural Extension, Kansas Annual Report, 1935, 4; "Never Yet Has It Been Dry Underground," *Ulysses News,* Dec. 21, 1939, 8; "Ness County Ramblings," *Ness County News,* Nov. 2, 1939, 5; "So Near and Yet So Far to What We Need," *Johnson Pioneer,* Apr. 2, 1936, 2.

9. J. C. Hopper to Clifford R. Hope, Feb. 16, 1935, Collection 50, Box 44, Correspondence, 1934–1935, Clifford R. Hope Papers, Manuscripts Division, KSHS; Owen K. Sheldon to Clifford R. Hope, Jan. 7, 1938, Collection 50, Box 64, General Correspondence, N–Z, Clifford R. Hope Papers.

10. "Counties Join to Push Irrigation Project," *Southwest Daily Times,* Sept. 2, 1936, 1; "Thinks Irrigation Practical in Clark County," *Clark County Clipper,* Oct. 1,

1936, 1; H. A. Kinney, Secretary, Liberal Chamber of Commerce, "Water Conservation," *Southwest Daily Times*, Sept. 8, 1936, 2.

11. "Plans Made to Irrigate Ball Farm," *Elkhart Tri-State News*, Jan. 21, 1937, 1.

12. U.S. Department of Commerce, Bureau of the Census, *Fifteenth Census of the United States, 1930: Population*, pt. 1.

13. U.S. Department of Commerce, Bureau of the Census, *Census of Population, 1980: Kansas*, Chapters A–C.

14. U.S. Department of Commerce, Bureau of the Census, *1987 Census of Manufactures: Kansas*, 7–9, 28–35.

15. U.S. Department of Commerce, Bureau of the Census, *Census of Population, Kansas*, 1930–1990.

16. Kansas, Statistical Rolls, Agricultural Census, 1930, 1935, 1940, Archives Division, KSHS.

17. For a discussion of the development of "sidewalk farming" in western Kansas, see Walter Kollmorgan and George F. Jenks, "A Geographic Study of Population and Settlement Changes in Sherman County, Kansas," *Transactions of the Kansas Academy of Science 55*, 1 (Mar. 1952): 1–37.

18. In the 1990 census, population figures for Jetmore were not listed in the general census of population but had to be located in the volume on population and housing. U.S. Department of Commerce, Bureau of the Census, *Census of Population, 1980: Kansas*, and *1990 Census of Population and Housing, Economic and Housing Characteristics, Kansas*.

19. During my visits to these county seats, I was struck by the obvious aging of the population. Visually, it was easy to deduce that young people make up an ever shrinking portion of these towns' populations. The elderly particularly predominate in Clark, Hamilton, Hodgeman, Meade, Ness, and Wichita counties. U.S. Department of Commerce, Bureau of the Census, *1990 Census of Population and Housing, Economic and Housing Characteristics, Kansas*.

20. The people of southwestern Kansas in general do not appear to be impoverished. Ten of sixteen counties have poverty rates at or below the state rate of 8.3 percent. Per capita income tends to be slightly lower than the state average of $13,300, but very much in line with the per capita income of other rural Kansans. *1990 Census of Population and Housing, Economic and Housing Characteristics, Kansas*.

21. Kansas State Board of Agriculture, *Report of the State Board of Agriculture*, vols. 54, 64 (Topeka: Kansas State Board of Agriculture, 1971, 1981); Kansas State Board of Agriculture, *Kansas Farm Facts*, 1991.

22. For an apt discussion of the history and costs of irrigation on the southern plains see John Opie, *Ogallala: Water for a Dry Land* (Lincoln: University of Nebraska Press, 1993), 122–160.

23. Kansas State Finance Council, *Water in Kansas, 1955: A Report to the Kansas State Legislature* (Lawrence: Kansas Water Resources Fact Finding and Research Committee, Jan. 1955), 53–54.

24. Orville W. Bidwell and William E. Roth, "The Land and the Soil," in George E. Ham and Robin Higham, eds., *The Rise of the Wheat State: A History of Kansas Agriculture, 1861–1986* (Manhattan, Kans.: Sunflower University Press, 1987), 4–5.

25. Kansas State Board of Agriculture, *Kansas Farm Facts*, 1991, 16.

26. Interviews with Horace and Elnora Malin, Liberal, Mar. 21, 1989; Elfreda Penner Fast, Hillsboro, Apr. 15, 1989; Leota Swafford Lambert and Elsie Swafford

Riney, Liberal, Mar. 19, 1989; Earl Owens, Liberal, May 3, 1989; Hazel Steenis Shriver, Deerfield, June 14, 1989.

27. David G. Danskin, James M. Foster, and Carroll E. Kennedy, Jr., *The Attitudes and Ambitions of Students at Land Grant Colleges of Agriculture*, Bulletin no. 479 (Manhattan: Agricultural Experiment Station, Jan. 1965).

28. Stevens County History Association, *The History of Stevens County and Its People* (Hugoton, Kans.: Stevens County History Association, 1979), 161; "Tornado, Dust Storms Earlier Challenges," Liberal Centennial Edition, *Southwest Daily Times*, May 22, 1988, 2; Hermes Centennial Edition, *Hugoton Hermes*, July 4, 1985, 2A; H. Don Hazell, *Midnight at Noon: A Pictorial Review of the Dust Bowl* (Kansas City, Mo.: Mindon Cards, 1969).

29. "Fifty Years Can't Erase Dust Bowl Memories," *Wichita Eagle Beacon*, Apr. 15, 1984, 1F; "50 Years Ago: April 14, 1935—Black Sunday," *Southwest Kansas Senior Beacon*, Apr. 1985, 1, 12.

30. William Nikl, a 92-year-old resident of Colby, commented that compared to the storms of the 1930s "this is just, well, it's just a hard wind." "Yellow Haze Rekindles Dust Bowl Memories," *Wichita Eagle Beacon*, Mar. 15, 1989, 6A.

31. *Garden City Daily Telegram*, Mar. 15, 1989, 1–2; *Dodge City Daily Globe*, Mar. 15, 1989, 1; "I Hate to Be the Guy Who Cries Wolf but . . . ," *Hutchinson News*, Mar. 18, 1989, 1.

32. Wichita *Eagle*, Apr. 26, 1872, as quoted by James C. Malin, "Dust Storms Part Two, 1861–1880," *Kansas Historical Quarterly* 14 (Aug. 1946): 269.

33. Vance Johnson, *Heaven's Tableland: The Dust Bowl Story* (New York: Farrar, Straus, and Company, 1947), 275.

34. Gilbert Fite, "The Great Plains: Promises, Problems, and Prospects," in Brian W. Blouet and Frederick C. Luebke, *The Great Plains: Environment and Culture* (Lincoln: University of Nebraska Press, 1979), 198–199.

35. Marc Reisner, *Cadillac Desert: The American West and Its Disappearing Water* (New York: Viking-Penguin, 1987), 455.

36. Donald E. Green, *Land of the Underground Rain: Irrigation on the Texas High Plains, 1910–1970* (Austin: University of Texas Press, 1973), 190–231.

37. Deborah Epstein Popper and Frank J. Popper, "The Great Plains: From Dust to Dust," *Planning* 53, 12 (Dec. 1978): 12–18.

38. "Bull, Most Say, to Suggestion to Return Great Plains to the Buffalo," *Minneapolis Star Tribune*, Sept. 13, 1989.

39. Reisner, *Cadillac Desert*, 469–471.

40. Opie, *Ogallala*, 294.

41. Ibid., 9.

42. Jim Strain of the American Cowman's Association suggested that the region might become a grassland for cattle grazing when questioned about the Poppers' theories. "Bull, Most Say," *Minneapolis Star Tribune*, Sept. 13, 1989.

43. Robert E. Leigh, "Just Plain Wrong," *Planning* 54, 2 (Feb. 1988): 32; Harold E. Willis, "The American Way," and April Rubens, "Close but No Cigar," *Planning* 54, 3 (Mar. 1988): 33–36.

44. Richard Pfister, *Economic Development in Kansas: Water Resources and Irrigation*, pt. 4 (Lawrence: School of Business, University of Kansas, Mar. 1955), 83.

BIBLIOGRAPHY

MANUSCRIPT AND ARCHIVAL RECORDS

Capper, Arthur M. Papers. Collection 12, Box 32, Agricultural General Correspondence, 1918–1939. Kansas State Historical Society (KSHS), Topeka.

Community Congregational Church of Garden City. Minutes of the Ministerial Association of Garden City, 1930–1932. Manuscripts Division, KSHS.

Dean, E. M., and Bertha Carpenter. "Morton County History." N.d. City Library, Elkhart.

Denious, Jess C. Papers. Collection 25, Boxes 1–5, Correspondence, 1930–1940. Manuscripts Division, KSHS.

Epworth Memorial Church. Records of membership and letters to the congregation, 1930–1940. United Methodist Church, Elkhart.

Farmers' Home Administration. Rural Rehabilitation Case Files, Region 7, Ness County, Kansas. Boxes 97–107. Record Group 96. National Archives and Records Administration, Central Plains Region, Kansas City, Kans.

Foster, Lillian. Scrapbook. February–May 1935. Manuscripts Division, KSHS.

Friesen Family. Expense accounts. By permission of Thelma Warner and Verna Gragg, Syracuse.

Friesen, Martha Schmidt. Diary. By permission of Thelma Warner and Verna Gragg, Syracuse.

Hope, Clifford R. Papers. Collection 50, Boxes 44, 46, 52, 53, 64, 69. Manuscripts Division, KSHS.

Huxman, Walter A. Governor's Papers (1937–1939). Correspondence Files, Boxes 1, 2. Manuscripts Division, KSHS.

Kansas. Decennial Census, 1925, vols. 78 (Finney County), 79 (Ford County), 93 (Hamilton County), 139 (Meade County), 152 (Morton County), 157 (Ness County). Archives Division, KSHS.

———. Records of the Secretary of State's Office. Annual Statements, Domestic Corporations. Register, 1929–1930, 1931–1932, 1933–1934. Archives Division, KSHS.

———. Statistical Rolls, Agricultural Census, 1930, 1935, 1940. Finney County, Pleasant Valley Township; Ford County, Pleasant Valley Township; Hamilton County, Medway Township; Meade County, Logan Township; Morton County, Jones and Cimarron townships; Ness County, Highpoint Township. Archives Division, KSHS.

Landon, Alfred M. Governor's Papers (1933–1937). Correspondence Files, Boxes 3, 4, 11, 12, 13. Manuscripts Division, KSHS.

McGill, George. Papers. Collection 43, Boxes 63, 64, 65, 65A, 67. Correspondence. Manuscripts Division, KSHS.

Mennonite Church, Western District. Home Mission Committee Field Files. Boxes 7, 8, 9, 11. Mennonite Library and Archives, Bethel College, Newton.

Ratner, Payne. Governor's Papers (1939–1943). Correspondence Files, Boxes 1, 4. Manuscripts Division, KSHS.

Reed, Clyde M. Governor's Papers (1929–1931). Correspondence Files, Boxes 1, 3. Manuscripts Division, KSHS.

Shriver, Hazel. Expense accounts. By permission of Hazel Shriver, Deerfield.

Stanforth, Edith. Public health nurse, Ulysses. "A Sunday in June," July 1938. Kansas Collection, Spencer Research Library, University of Kansas, Lawrence.

Woodring, Harry H. Governor's Papers (1931–1933). Correspondence Files, Boxes 3, 4. Manuscripts Division, KSHS.

WPA. Central Files, 1935–1944. Box 1374; Box 0295, File 201.31; Box 0296, File 201.32; Box 0297, File 201.33. Record Group 69. National Archives and Records Administration, Central Branch, Washington, D.C.

QUESTIONNAIRE RESPONSES

Clark County: Louise Cauthers Berryman, Doreen Jacobs, Vona Clark Little, Rosa Lee McGee, Paul Randall. Finney County: Preston Burtis, Jr., Mrs. D. V. Douglass, Gaylord Haflich, Lois Stringfield Harmon, Julia C. Roenfeldt, Mamie P. Rooney, Mrs. William G. Witt. Ford County: Carl D. Clare, Elizabeth Dunhaupt, Catherine Evenson Heiland, Oscar V. Heiland, Leila Johnson, Don Kliesen, Hillard Leroy Speer, Arthur Joseph Wadsack, Vivian Waterhouse. Grant County: Maxine Ainsworth, Robert E. Moore. Gray County: Elfreda Penner Fast, Marie Loewen Franz, Marie Kowalski, Loetta Trainer Legg, Daniel Penner, Eileen Phillips. Hamilton County: Pauline Fecht, Letha Ellis Herndon, Ona Libertus, J. Clifford Schmidt, Mrs. Jessie Schroll, Thelma Warner, two anonymous. Hodgeman County: Pansy Mason, Dale Nuss, Louise Schroeder, Iris K. Stambaugh, Eula Reath Wilson. Kearny County: Barbara J. Beymer, Ruth Dodge, Mary R. Jones, Marcella C. McVey, Hazel A. Shriver, Carroll E. Wainwright. Meade County: David J. Classen, Mel Copenhaven, Ora Fletcher, Genevieve Hayden, John I. Schell, Leona Swafford Schell, Vera Waters, Betty E. Wenta. Morton County: Richard L. Akers, Susie Baker, Jeanne F. Daniels, Lois Edgar, Evelyn Heintz Emberton, Hildred Johnson, Louis B. Perkins, Edith K. Rives, Lawrence R. Smith, Lena Smith, Bonna L. Sutton, Vera Thompson, Edgar W. White. Ness County: Opal Musselman Burdett, Laurie Copeland, Lenora Bauer Edwards, Florence Paul Eudy, Edwin Goodman, Leonard Hogsett, Stella McKelvie, Dean McVicker, Alice Williams. Seward County: Ann Bohon, Vaughn Boles, Earl J. Ellis, Mary Isadore Frame, Juddie V. Franklin, Brent Gould, Florence Herring, Minnie Hearn Hoag, Leota Swafford Lambert, Elnora Malin, Earl Owens, Pauline Renick Owens, Elsie Swafford Riney, Ada McGee Sipes, Nellie Wilburn. Stanton County: Milton Earl Burnett, Pearl Josserand, Bernice Trostle, Raymond H. Trostle, Ruby S. Tuggle, Elizabeth Williams, one anonymous. Stevens County: Esther Beasley, Ralph Cutter, Faye DeWitt, Fontell Littrell, Irene Mapp, Helen Marie Sturgeon, Nora Swafford. Wichita County: John K. Glanville, Josie Glanville, Kenneth A. Hooker, Leon H. Minor, Gillies Neyer, Roy W. Smith, Katherine Wilson.

INTERVIEWS BY AUTHOR

Beasley, Esther, and Fontell Litrell. Hugoton, May 22, 1989.
Berryman, Louise. Ashland, July 3, 1989.
Boles, Vaughn. Liberal, May 5, 1989.
Burdett, Opal Musselman. Ness City, May 13, 1989.
Burnett, Milton and Audra. Johnson, June 7, 1989.
Clare, Carl. Dodge City, May 8, 1989.
Classen, David A. Hillsboro, Apr. 15, 1989.
Copeland, George and Laurie. Ness City, May 13, 1989.
Daniels, Jeanne. Elkhart, June 6, 1989.
Dewell, Dorothy. Bucklin, May 9, 1989.
DeWitt, Dutch and Faye. Hugoton, May 21, 1989.
Dodge, Ruth. Lakin, June 15, 1989.
Edwards, Lenora. Beeler, May 12, 1989.
Ellis, Earl. Liberal, May 4, 1989.
Fast, Elfreda Penner. Hillsboro, Apr. 15, 1989.
Glanville, John and Josie. Leoti, June 17, 1989.
Gould, Brent. Liberal, May 3, 1989.
Haflich, Gaylord. Garden City, June 12, 1989.
Harmon, Lois Stringfield. Garden City, June 13, 1989.
Hayden, Genevieve. Plains, July 11, 1989.
Herring, Florence. Liberal, May 3, 1989.
Hoag, Minnie Hearn. Liberal, May 4, 1989.
Jacobs, Doreen and Anna Lee. Ashland, July 2, 1989.
Jenkins, Kathleen. Bucklin, May 9, 1989.
Kliesen, Claryce and Don. Dodge City, May 8, 1989.
Kohler, Robert E. Elkhart, June 3, 1989.
Lambert, Leota Swafford, and Elsie Swafford Riney. Liberal, Mar. 19, 1989.
Libertus, Ona. Coolidge, June 10, 1989.
McGee, Rosa Lee. Ashland, July 3, 1989.
McVey, Marcella. Lakin, June 14, 1989.
McVicker, Dean. Beeler, May 12, 1989.
Malin, H. E. and Elnora. Liberal, Mar. 21, 1989.
Mayers, Betty and O. L. Syracuse, June 10, 1989.
Owens, Earl. Liberal, May 3, 1989.
Owens, Pauline Renick. Liberal, May 3, 1989.
Perkins, Louis B. Elkhart, June 5, 1989.
Patton, Lois, and Fern Patton Royer. Syracuse, June 10, 1989.
Randall, Paul. Ashland, July 2, 1989.
Schmidt, J. Clifford. Syracuse, June 9, 1989.
Schroeder, Louise. Jetmore, May 10, 1989.
Shriver, Hazel Steenis. Deerfield, June 14, 1989.
Smith, Lawrence R. Elkhart, June 5, 1989.
Stambaugh, Iris. Hanston, May 11, 1989.
Sturgeon, Helen Marie. Hugoton, May 21, 1989.
Stutz, W. V. and Margaret. Ness City, May 13, 1989.
Sutton, Bonna L. Elkhart, June 2, 1989.
Swafford, Nora. Hugoton, May 20, 1989.
Thompson, Vera. Elkhart, June 5, 1989.
Trostle, Bernice and Raymond. Johnson, June 8, 1989.

Tuggle, Ruby. Manter, June 8, 1989.
Wainwright, Carroll E. Lakin, June 14, 1989.
Warner, Thelma Dyck. Syracuse, June 9, 1989.
Waters, Vera. Ensign, May 16, 1989.
White, Edgar. Elkhart, June 6, 1989.
Wilburn, Nellie. Liberal, May 4, 1989.
Williams, Elizabeth. Johnson, June 7, 1989.
Wilson, Eula Reath. Jetmore, May 11, 1989.
Wilson, Katherine Scheer. Leoti, June 17, 1989.

LETTERS TO THE AUTHOR

Burdett, Opal Musselman, Ness City, Dec. 9, 1988.
Classen, David J., Hillsboro, Nov. 26, 1988.
Haflich, Gaylord, Garden City, Fall 1988. Writing entitled "The Spring of 1935."
Penner, Daniel S., Hillsboro, Fall 1988.
Waterhouse, Vivian, Jetmore, Nov. 26, 1988.

COUNTY RECORDS

Agricultural Extension Service, Kansas Annual Reports, 1930–1940, for the follow-
ing counties: Clark, Finney, Ford, Grant, Haskell, Kearny, Meade, Morton, Ness,
Stanton, Stevens.
Chattel Mortgage Records for the following counties: Ford, Hamilton, Meade, Ness.
Commissioners' Journals for the following counties: Finney, Ford, Grant, Gray,
Hamilton, Haskell, Hodgeman, Kearny, Meade, Morton, Ness, Seward, Stanton,
Stevens.
Transfer and/or Deed Records. Pleasant Valley Township, Finney County Courthouse,
Garden City; Pleasant Valley Township, Ford County Courthouse, Dodge City;
Medway Township, Hamilton County Courthouse, Syracuse; Logan Township,
Meade County Courthouse, Meade; Highpoint Township, Ness County Court-
house, Ness City.

KANSAS STATE DOCUMENTS

Commission of Labor and Industry. *Annual Report of the Commission of Labor and
Industry, State of Kansas*, 1930 and 1932. Topeka: Kansas State Printing Plant,
1931, 1933.
Council Committee on Soil Conservation. *Soil Drifting: Preliminary Report*. Publica-
tion no. 43. N.p.: Research Department, Kansas Legislative Council Publications,
Nov. 2, 1936.
Danskin, David G., James M. Foster, and Carroll E. Kennedy, Jr. *The Attitudes and
Ambitions of Students at Land Grant Colleges of Agriculture*. Bulletin no. 479. Man-
hattan: Agricultural Experiment Station, Jan. 1965.
Hoover, Leo M. *A Summary of Kansas Agriculture*. Agricultural Economics Report no.
55. Manhattan: Kansas Agricultural Experiment Station, July 1953.
Kansas Emergency Relief Committee (KERC). *Fundamental Policies of the Kansas Emer-*

gency Relief Committee and Summaries of Obligations for Relief, 1924–1936. Topeka: KERC, 1936.

———. *Interpretation of a Social Welfare Program: News Releases April 1, 1934–April 1, 1936*. Topeka: KERC, n.d.

———. *Kansas Relief News Bulletin*, nos. 20–24.

———. "Poor Farms." Topeka: Kansas State Printing Plant, n.d.

———. *Public Welfare in Kansas: A Ten Year Report, 1924–1933*, KERC Bulletin no. 127. Topeka: KERC, Dec. 1, 1934.

———. *Public Welfare Service in Kansas, 1934*, KERC Bulletin no. 289. Topeka: KERC, Nov. 1, 1935.

———. *Public Welfare Service in Kansas, 1935*, KERC Bulletin no. 355. Topeka: KERC, July 1, 1936.

———. *Report: Drought Cattle Operations, The State of Kansas*. Topeka: KERC, May 1, 1935.

———. *Report on Proposed Leather and Wool Program, The State of Kansas*. Topeka: KERC, June 1, 1935.

———. *Social Welfare Service in Kansas, 1936*, KERC Bulletin no. 380. Topeka: KERC, Jan. 2, 1937.

———. *Work Relief in Kansas, April 1, 1934–June 30, 1935*, vol. 1. Topeka: KERC, July 31, 1935.

Kansas State Board of Administration. *Statistics Relating to District Courts, Probate Courts, Poor Farms, Miscellaneous Charity, and Mother's Pensions in Kansas, 1929–1937*. Topeka: Kansas State Printing Plant.

Kansas State Board of Agriculture. *Biennial Report of the State Board of Agriculture*, vols. 27–32. Topeka: Kansas State Printing Plant, 1931–1941.

———. *Kansas Farm Facts, 1989*. Topeka: Kansas State Board of Agriculture, 1989.

———. *Report of the Kansas State Board of Agriculture for the Quarter Ending December 1925*. Topeka: Kansas State Board of Agriculture, 1926.

———. *Report of the State Board of Agriculture*, vols. 37, 45, 54, 64. Topeka: Kansas State Board of Agriculture, 1951, 1961, 1971, 1981.

———. *Soil Erosion by Wind in Kansas*. Topeka: Kansas State Printing Plant, 1938.

Kansas State Board of Health. *Biennial Report of the State Board of Health of the State of Kansas*, vols. 16–20. Topeka: Kansas State Printing Plant, 1932, 1935, 1937, 1939, 1942.

Kansas State Board of Social Welfare. *Report of Social Welfare in 1937*. Topeka: Kansas State Printing Plant, 1938.

———. *The Social Welfare Experience in 1938, 1939, and 1940*. Topeka: Kansas State Printing Plant, 1941.

Kansas State Civil Works Administration. *Review, The Civil Works Program in Kansas, Nov. 1, 1933–March 31, 1934*. Topeka, Kans.: State Civil Works Administration, n.d.

Kansas State College of Agriculture, Agricultural Experiment Station. *Kansas Weather and Climate*. Topeka: Kansas State Printing Plant, 1942.

Kansas State Finance Council. *Water in Kansas, 1955: A Report to the Kansas State Legislature*. Lawrence: Kansas Water Resources Fact Finding and Research Committee, Jan. 1955.

Kansas State Planning Board. *Farm Real Estate Values in Kansas from 1933–1937, Inclusive*. Topeka: Kansas State Planning Board, July 1940.

Meyer, Arthur, State Garden Supervisor. *Relief Garden Program, State of Kansas 1935*. Topeka: KERC, 1935.

Office of the Secretary of State. *Biennial Report of the Secretary of State*, vols. 28, 30, 32. Topeka: Kansas State Printing Plant.

Pine, Wilfred H. *100 Years of Farmland Values in Kansas*. Bulletin no. 611. Manhattan: Agricultural Experiment Station, Kansas State University, 1977.

———. *Mid-Century Farm Tenure in Kansas*. Agricultural Economics Report no. 53. Manhattan: Agricultural Experiment Station, Kansas State University, 1953.

UNITED STATES GOVERNMENT DOCUMENTS

Asch, Berta, and A. R. Magnus. *Farmers on Relief and Rehabilitation*, WPA, Division of Social Research, Research Monograph 8. Washington, D.C.: Government Printing Office, 1937.

Atwood, George S. USDA, Forest Service. *History of the Cimarron National Grassland: Land Utilization Project KA-LU-21*. Washington, D.C.: Government Printing Office, 1962.

Bell, Earl H. *Culture of a Contemporary Rural Community: Sublette, Kansas*. Rural Life Studies, vol. 2. USDA, Bureau of Agricultural Economics, Sept. 1942.

Bennett, Hugh H. et al. *Report of the Great Plains Drought Area Committee*. Washington, D.C.: Government Printing Office, 1936.

Clawson, Marion, Davis McEntire, and C. P. Heisig. "The Migrants: 'Stump Ranching.'" *Land Policy Review* 3 (May–June 1940): 32–38.

Commissioner of the General Land Office. *Annual Report of the Commissioner of the General Land Office for the Year 1885*. Washington, D.C.: Government Printing Office, 1885.

Cronin, Francis D., and Howard W. Beers. *Research Bulletin: Areas of Intense Drought Distress, 1930–1936*. Washington, D.C.: WPA, Division of Social Research, 1937.

Edwards, A. D. "Influence of Drought and Depression on a Rural Community: A Case Study in Haskell County, Kansas." Social Research Report no. 7. Washington, D.C.: USDA, Jan. 1939.

Farnham, Rebecca, and Irene Link. *Effects of the Works Program on Rural Relief*. WPA, Division of Social Research, Research Monograph 13. Washington, D.C.: Government Printing Office, 1938.

Federal Emergency Relief Administration, Division of Research, Statistics, and Finance. "Rural Problem Areas Survey Report No. 9: The Short Grass–Winter Wheat Area, Hodgeman County, Kansas." Oct. 19, 1934.

———. "Rural Problem Areas Survey Report No. 35: The Short Grass–Winter Wheat Area, Meade County, Kansas." Dec. 3, 1934.

Federal Writers' Project of the Works Progress Administration. *Kansas: A Guide to the Sunflower State*. New York: Viking Press, 1939. Reprint edition, *The WPA Guide to 1930s Kansas*. Lawrence: University Press of Kansas, 1984.

Gaer, Joseph. *Toward Farm Security*. Washington, D.C.: Government Printing Office, 1941.

Great Plains Committee. *The Future of the Great Plains*. Washington, D.C.: Government Printing Office, 1936.

Heisig, Carl P. "The Migrants: New Farms on Newly Irrigated Lands." *Land Policy Review* 2 (Nov.–Dec. 1939): 10–16.

Henson, Edwin R. "Borrowed Time in the Dust Bowl." *Land Policy Review* 3 (Oct. 1940): 3–7.

Janow, Seymour, and Davis McEntire. "The Migrants: Migration to California." *Land Policy Review* 3 (July–Aug. 1940): 24–36.

Kifer, R. S., and H. L. Stewart. *Farming Hazards in the Drought Area*. WPA, Division of Social Research, Research Monograph 16. Washington, D.C.: Government Printing Office, 1938.

Link, Irene. *Research Bulletin: Relief and Rehabilitation in the Drought Area*. Washington, D.C.: WPA, June 1937.

Lively, C. E., and Conrad Taeuber. *Rural Migration in the United States*. WPA, Division of Social Research, Research Monograph 19. Washington, D.C.: Government Printing Office, 1939.

Luten, Wilhelmina. *An Analysis of Employment of Women on Works Progress Administration Projects, December 1935 through May 1936*. Washington, D.C.: WPA, 1936.

McEntire, Davis, and N. L. Whetten. "The Migrants: Recent Migration to the Pacific Coast." *Land Policy Review* 2 (Sept.–Oct. 1939): 7–17.

McMillan, Robert T. "Farm Families in the Dust Bowl." *Land Policy Review* 1 (Sept.–Oct. 1938): 14–17.

Rowell, Edward J. "Drought Refugee and Labor Migration to California in 1936." *Monthly Labor Review* 43 (Dec. 1936): 1355–1363.

Selby, H. E. "How Many Acres Do We Require?" *Land Policy Review* 3 (Sept. 1940): 8–11.

Taeuber, Conrad, and Carl C. Taylor. *Research Bulletin: The People of the Drought States*. Washington, D.C.: WPA, March 1937.

Taylor, Carl C., Bushrod W. Allin, and O. E. Baker. "Public Purposes in Soil Use." *USDA Yearbook, 1938*. Washington, D.C.: Government Printing Office, 1938.

Taylor, Carl C., Helen W. Wheeler, and E. L. Kirkpatrick. *Disadvantaged Classes in American Agriculture*. Social Research Report 8. Washington, D.C.: USDA, FSA, and Bureau of Agricultural Economics, Apr. 1938.

Taylor, Paul S., and Tom Vasey. "Drought Refugee and Labor Migration to California, June–Dec. 1935." *Monthly Labor Review* 42 (Feb. 1936): 312–318.

Tolles, N. A. "A Survey of Labor Migration between States." *Monthly Labor Review* 45 (July 1937): 3–16.

Troxell, Willard W., and W. Paul O'Day. "The Migrants: Migration to the Pacific Northwest, 1930–1938." *Land Policy Review* 3 (Jan.–Feb. 1940): 32–43.

U.S. Congress. House. *Hearings before the Select Committee to Investigate Interstate Migration of Destitute Citizens*. 76th Cong., 3d Sess., 1940–1941. Washington, D.C.: Government Printing Office.

U.S. Department of Agriculture. *Agricultural Situation*, vols. 16–25.

———. *Agricultural Statistics: 1941*. Washington, D.C.: Government Printing Office, 1941.

———. *Climate and Man: 1941 Yearbook of Agriculture*. Washington, D.C.: Government Printing Office, 1941.

———. *Crops and Markets* 8, 8 (Washington, D.C.: Government Printing Office, Aug. 1931): 293.

———. *Crops and Markets* 8, 9 (Washington, D.C.: Government Printing Office, Sept. 1931): 360–361, 403–404.

———. *Farmers in a Changing World: Yearbook of Agriculture, 1940*. Washington, D.C.: Government Printing Office, 1940.

———. *The Farm Real Estate Situation*. Circulars 150, 354, 548, 662.

———. *Major Statistical Series of the United States Department of Agriculture*, vol. 6.

Land Values and Farm Finance. Agricultural Handbook no. 118. Washington, D.C.: Government Printing Office, Oct. 1957.

———. *Report of the Secretary of Agriculture*, 1935, 1936, 1939. Washington, D.C.: Government Printing Office, 1935, 1936, 1939.

———. *Soils and Men: Yearbook of Agriculture*, 1938. Washington, D.C.: Government Printing Office, 1938.

———. *Yearbook of Agriculture*, 1937. Washington, D.C.: Government Printing Office, 1937.

U.S. Department of Commerce, Bureau of the Census. *Fourteenth Census of the United States Taken in the Year 1920*, vol. 2, pt. 1, Agriculture.

———. *Fourteenth Census of the United States Taken in the Year 1920*, vol. 3, pt. 1, Agriculture.

———. *United States Census of Agriculture*, 1925, 1, The Northern States.

———. *Fifteenth Census of the United States, 1930: Manufactures, 1929*, vol. 3, Reports by States.

———. *Fifteenth Census of the United States, 1930: Population*, vol. 3, pt. 1.

———. *Fifteenth Census of the United States, 1930: Population*, vol. 3, pt. 6, Families.

———. *United States Census of Agriculture*, 1935, 1, 1, The Northern States.

———. *Final Report on Total and Partial Unemployment, 1937*, vol. 2, Reports by States, Iowa–New York. Washington, D.C.: Government Printing Office, 1938.

———. *Sixteenth Census of the United States, 1940: Manufactures, 1939*, vol. 3, Reports for States and Outlying Areas.

———. *Sixteenth Census of the United States, 1940: Population*, vol. 2, pt. 3.

———. *Sixteenth Census of the United States, 1940: Population, Internal Migration, 1935–1940*.

———. *Sixteenth Census of the United States, 1940: Agriculture*, vol. 1.

———. *United States Census of Agriculture*, 1945, 1, 13, Kansas.

———. *Census of Population, 1980: Kansas*. Chapters A–C.

U.S. Department of the Interior, Census Office. *Statistics of the Population of the United States at the Tenth Census*. Washington, D.C.: Government Printing Office, June 1, 1880.

———. *Tenth Census of the United States, 1880: Population*. Washington, D.C.: Government Printing Office, 1883.

Wells, Oris V. "How Many Farmers Do We Require?" *Land Policy Review* 3 (Sept. 1940): 3–7.

Works Progress Administration. Division of Social Research. *Areas of Intense Drought Distress, 1930–1936*. Washington, D.C.: Government Printing Office, January 1937.

Zimmerman, Carl C., and Nathan L. Whetten. *Rural Families on Relief*. WPA, Division of Social Research, Research Monograph 17. Washington, D.C.: Government Printing Office, 1938.

OTHER PUBLISHED PRIMARY MATERIALS

"Agriculture: 500,000,000 Tons of Dust Cover Kansas and Points East; AAA Moves to Save Nation's 'Bread Basket.'" *News-Week* 5, 13 (Mar. 30, 1935): 5–6.

Bourke-White, Margaret. "Dust Changes America." *Nation* 140 (May 22, 1935): 597–598.

Carlson, Avis D. "Dust Blowing." *Harper's Magazine* 171 (July 1935): 149–158.

"Creeping Disaster." *Business Week*, July 28, 1934, p. 36.

Davenport, Walter. "Land Where Our Children Die." *Collier's* 100 (Sept. 18, 1937).

Davis, Chester C. "If Drought Strikes Again." *Saturday Evening Post* 207 (Apr. 27, 1935).

"Diaries of Iman C. Wiatt." Kearny County Historical Society. *History of Kearny County, Kansas*, vol. 2. North Newton, Kans.: Mennonite Press, 1973.

"Documented Dust." *Time* 27 (May 25, 1936): 47–48.

"Don't Bet on the Bad Lands." *Collier's* 98 (Oct. 3, 1936): 62.

"Drought Strikes Home." *Business Week*, July 28, 1934, p. 5.

Duncan, Kunigunde. "Reclaiming the Dust Bowl." *Nation* 149 (Sept. 9, 1939): 269–271.

Greenfield, George. "Unto Dust." *Reader's Digest* 30, 181 (May 1937): 37–38.

Henderson, Caroline A. "Letters from the Dust Bowl." *Atlantic Monthly* 157 (May 1936): 540–551.

Hibbs, Ben. "The Dust Bowl Can Be Saved." *Saturday Evening Post* 210 (Dec. 18, 1937).

Kains, M. G. *Five Acres and Independence: A Practical Guide to the Selection and Management of the Small Farm.* New York: Greenberg, 1935.

Mueller, Patricia, ed. *Kansas Author's Club Bulletin Year Book, 1934*, vol. 10. N.p., n.p., 1934.

"Our Point of View: Arid Farming and Ecology." *Scientific American* 159 (Nov. 1938): 233.

Ploughe, J. S. "Out of the Dust." *Christian Century* 52 (May 22, 1935): 691–692.

Pool, Raymond J. "White Man versus the Prairie." *Science* 91, (Jan. 19, 1940): 53–58.

Popper, Deborah Epstein, and Frank J. Popper. "The Great Plains: From Dust to Dust." *Planning* 53, 12 (Dec. 1978): 12–18.

"Right Side Up." *Saturday Evening Post* 211 (May 27, 1939): 22.

Sears, Alfred B. "The Desert Threat in the Southern Great Plains: The Historical Implications of Soil Erosion." *Agricultural History* 15 (Jan. 1941): 1–11.

Svobida, Lawrence. *An Empire of Dust.* Caxton, Idaho: Caxton Printers, 1940. Reprint edition, *Farming the Dust Bowl: A First-Hand Account from Kansas.* Lawrence: University Press of Kansas, 1986.

Tripp, Thomas Alfred. "Dust Bowl Tragedy." *Christian Century* 57 (Jan. 24, 1940): 108–110.

Ward, Harold. "Conquering the Dust Bowl." *Travel* 74 (Feb. 1940).

NEWSPAPERS AND PERIODICALS

Arkansas City Traveler
Bazine Advocate
Bucklin Banner
Clark County Clipper
Dodge City Daily Globe
Elkhart Tri-State News
Fowler News
Garden City Daily Telegram
Grant County Republican
Hugoton Hermes
Hutchinson News

Johnson Pioneer
Kansas Social Welfare Journal
Kansas Social Welfare News
Leoti Standard
Liberal News
Meade Globe-News
Minneapolis Star Tribune
Nation's Business
Ness County News
Planning
Southwest Daily Times
Southwest Kansas Senior Beacon
Syracuse Journal
Topeka Journal
Ulysses News
Warsaw (Missouri) *Times*
Wichita Eagle Beacon

SECONDARY SOURCES

Adams, Ruby Winona. "Social Behavior in a Drought-Stricken Texas Panhandle Community." M.A. thesis, University of Texas–Austin, 1939.
Armitage, Katie. *Making Do and Doing Without: Kansas in the Great Depression.* Lawrence: University of Kansas, Division of Continuing Education, 1983.
Arrington, Leonard J. "Western Agriculture and the New Deal." *Agricultural History* 44 (Oct. 1970): 337–353.
Bader, Robert Smith. *Hayseeds, Moralizers, and Methodists: The Twentieth-Century Image of Kansas.* Lawrence: University Press of Kansas, 1988.
Barron, Hal S. *Those Who Stayed Behind: Rural Society in Nineteenth-Century New England.* New York: Cambridge University Press, 1984.
Beddow, James B. "Depression and New Deal: Letters from the Plains." *Kansas Historical Quarterly* 43 (Summer 1977): 140–153.
Bender, Thomas. *Community and Social Change in America.* New Brunswick, N.J.: Rutgers University Press, 1978.
Blouet, Brian W., and Frederick C. Luebke, eds. *The Great Plains: Environment and Culture.* Lincoln: University of Nebraska Press, 1979.
Bonnifield, Paul. *The Dust Bowl: Men, Dirt, and Depression.* Albuquerque: University of New Mexico Press, 1979.
Bremer, Richard G. *Agricultural Change in an Urban Age: The Loup Country of Nebraska, 1910–1970.* Lincoln: University of Nebraska Press, 1976.
Carman, J. Neale. *Foreign Language Units of Kansas, I, Historical Atlas and Statistics.* Lawrence: University Press of Kansas, 1962.
Cohen, Lizabeth. *Making a New Deal: Industrial Workers in Chicago, 1919–1939.* New York: Cambridge University Press, 1990.
Easterlin, Richard. "Population Change and Farm Settlement in the Northern United States." *Journal of Economic History* 36, 1 (March 1976): 45–75.
Fearon, Peter. "From Self-Help to Federal Aid: Unemployment and Relief in Kansas, 1929–1932." *Kansas History* 13, 2 (Summer 1990): 107–122.

Fink, Deborah. *Agrarian Women: Wives and Mothers in Rural Nebraska, 1880–1940.* Chapel Hill: University of North Carolina Press, 1992.

————. "Sidelines and Moral Capital: Women on Nebraska Farms in the 1930s." In Haney, Wava G., and Jane B. Knowles, eds. *Women and Farming: Changing Roles, Changing Structures.* Boulder: Westview, 1988, 55–70.

Fite, Gilbert. *The Farmers' Frontier, 1865–1900.* New York: Holt, Rinehart, and Winston, 1966.

Fitzgerald, Daniel. *Ghost Towns of Kansas: A Traveler's Guide.* Lawrence: University Press of Kansas, 1988.

Flora, Cornelia Butler, and John Stitz. "Female Subsistence Production and Commercial Farm Survival among Settlement Kansas Wheat Farms." *Human Organization* 47, 1 (Spring 1988): 64–68.

Floyd, Fred. "A History of the Dust Bowl." Ph.D. diss., University of Oklahoma, 1950.

Foreman, W. James, and Robert S. Eckley. *Economic Development in Southwestern Kansas,* pt. 5, Agriculture. Lawrence, Kans.: School of Business, Bureau of Business Research, Aug. 1, 1951.

Fretz, J. W. "The Mennonite Community at Meade." *Mennonite Life* 6, 3 (July 1951): 8–13.

Fuller, Wayne E. "Changing Concepts of the Country School as a Community Center in the Midwest." *Agricultural History* 58, 2 (Spring 1984): 423–441.

Goodrich, Carter, et al. *Migration and Economic Opportunity: The Report of the Study of Population Redistribution.* Philadelphia: University of Pennsylvania Press, 1936.

Green, Donald E. *Land of the Underground Rain: Irrigation on the Texas High Plains, 1910–1970.* Austin: University of Texas Press, 1973.

Gregory, James N. *American Exodus: The Dust Bowl Migration and Okie Culture in California.* New York: Oxford University Press, 1989.

Guither, Harold D. *Heritage of Plenty: A Guide to the Economic History and Development of United States Agriculture.* Danville, Ill.: Interstate Printers and Publishers, 1972.

Gulliford, Andrew. *America's Country Schools.* Washington, D.C.: Preservation Press, 1984.

Ham, George E., and Robin Higham, eds. *The Rise of the Wheat State: A History of Kansas Agriculture, 1861–1986.* Manhattan, Kans.: Sunflower University Press, 1987.

Haury, David A. *Prairie People: A History of the Western District Conference.* Newton, Kans.: Faith and Life Press, 1981.

Haywood, C. Robert. "The Hodgeman County Colony." *Kansas History* 12, 4 (Winter 1989/1990): 210–221.

Hazell, H. Don. *Midnight at Noon: A Pictorial Review of the Dust Bowl.* Kansas City, Mo.: Mindon Cards, 1969.

Hewes, Leslie. *The Suitcase Farming Frontier: A Study of the Historical Geography of the Central Great Plains.* Lincoln: University of Nebraska Press, 1973.

Hope, Clifford, Sr. "Kansas in the 1930s." *Kansas Historical Quarterly* 36, 1 (Spring 1970): 1–12.

Hudson, John C. *Plains Country Towns.* Minneapolis: University of Minnesota Press, 1985.

Hurt, R. Douglas. *The Dust Bowl: An Agricultural and Social History.* Chicago: Nelson-Hall, 1981.

———. "Letters from the Dust Bowl." *Panhandle-Plains Historical Review* 52 (1979): 1–13.

———. "Return of the Dust Bowl: The Filthy Fifties." *Journal of the West* 18, 4: 85–93.

Jellison, Katherine. *Entitled to Power: Farm Women and Technology, 1913–1963.* Chapel Hill: University of North Carolina Press, 1993.

Johnson, Vance. *Heaven's Tableland: The Dust Bowl Story.* New York: Farrar, Straus, and Company, 1947.

Kannier, Hershel, ed. *Kansas Facts,* vol. 4. Topeka: Kansas Facts Publishing Company, 1933.

Kraenzel, Carl Frederick. *The Great Plains in Transition.* Norman: University of Oklahoma Press, 1955.

Low, Ann Marie. *Dust Bowl Diary.* Lincoln, Nebr.: Bison Books, 1984.

Luebke, Frederick C. "Regionalism and the Great Plains: Problems of Concept and Method." *Western Historical Quarterly* 15, 1 (Jan. 1984): 17–38.

McCoy, Donald R. "Alfred M. Landon, Western Governor." *Pacific Northwest Quarterly* 57, 3 (July 1966): 120–126.

McDean, Harry C. "Federal Farm Policy and the Dust Bowl: The Half-Right Solution." *North Dakota History* 47 (Summer 1980): 21–31.

———. "Social Scientists and Farm Poverty on the North American Plains, 1933–1940." *Great Plains Quarterly* 3 (Winter 1983): 17–29.

McNall, Scott G., and Sally Allen McNall. *Plains Families: Exploring Sociology through Social History.* New York: St. Martin's Press, 1983.

McQuillan, D. Aidan. "The Mobility of Immigrants and Americans: A Comparison of Farmers on the Kansas Frontier." *Agricultural History* 53, 3 (July 1979): 576–596.

Malin, James C. "The Adaptation of the Agricultural System to Sub-Humid Environment." *Agricultural History* 10 (July 1936): 118–141.

———. "Dust Storms, 1850–1900." *Kansas Historical Quarterly* 14 (May, Aug., Nov., 1946): 129–144, 265–296, 391–413.

———. *History and Ecology: Studies of the Grassland.* Lincoln: University of Nebraska Press, 1984.

———. "The Turnover of Farm Population in Kansas." *Kansas Historical Quarterly* 4 (Nov. 1935): 339–372.

———. *Winter Wheat in the Golden Belt of Kansas: A Study in Adaptation to Subhumid Geographical Environment.* New York: Octagon Books, 1973.

Martin, Robert F. *Income in Agriculture, 1929–1935.* New York: National Industrial Conference Board, 1936.

Mays, William E. *Sublette Revisited: Stability and Change in a Rural Kansas Community after a Quarter Century.* New York: Florham Park Press, 1968.

Miner, Craig. *West of Wichita: Settling the High Plains of Kansas, 1865–1890.* Lawrence: University Press of Kansas, 1986.

Neth, Mary. "Building the Base: Farm Women, the Rural Community, and Farm Organizations in the Midwest, 1900–1940." In Haney, Wava G., and Jane B. Knowles, eds. *Women and Farming: Changing Roles, Changing Structures.* Boulder, Colo.: Westview, 1988, 339–355.

———. "Preserving the Family Farm: Farm Families and Community in the Midwest, 1900–1940." Ph.D. diss., University of Wisconsin–Madison, 1987.

Opie, John. *Ogallala: Water for a Dry Land.* Lincoln: University of Nebraska Press, 1993.

Oppenheimer, Robert. "Acculturation or Assimilation: Mexican Immigrants in Kansas, 1900 to World War II." *Western Historical Quarterly* 16 (Oct. 1985): 429–448.

Ostergren, Robert C. "Kinship Networks and Migration: A Nineteenth-Century Swedish Example." *Social Science History* 6, 3 (Summer 1982): 293–320.

Osterud, Nancy Grey. *Bonds of Community: The Lives of Farm Women in Nineteenth-Century New York.* Ithaca, N.Y: Cornell University Press, 1991.

Perkins, Ralph. "Relief Work in a Dust Bowl Community." *Sociology and Social Research* 23, 6 (July–Aug. 1939): 539–545.

Pfister, Richard. *Economic Development in Kansas: Water Resources and Irrigation,* pt. 4. Lawrence: School of Business, University of Kansas, Mar. 1955.

Reisner, Marc. *Cadillac Desert: The American West and Its Disappearing Water.* New York: Viking-Penguin, 1987.

Riney-Kehrberg, Pamela. "From the Horse's Mouth: Dust Bowl Farmers and Their Solutions to the Problem of Aridity." *Agricultural History* 66, 2 (Spring 1992): 137–150.

———. "Hard Times, Hungry Years: Failure of the Poor Relief in Southwestern Kansas, 1930–1933." *Kansas History* 15, 3 (Autumn 1992): 154–167.

———. "In God We Trusted, In Kansas We Busted . . . Again." *Agricultural History* 63, 2 (Spring 1989): 187–201.

———. "Separation and Sorrow: A Farm Woman's Life, 1935–1941." *Agricultural History* 67, 2 (Spring 1993): 185–196.

Rohrer, Wayne C. *A Century of Migration of the Kansas Population,* Kansas State University Economics and Sociology Report no. 1. Manhattan: Kansas Agricultural Experiment Station, May 1961.

Rubright, Lynnell. "Development of Farming Systems in Western Kansas, 1885–1915." Ph.D. diss., University of Wisconsin–Madison, 1977.

Saloutos, Theodore. *The American Farmer and the New Deal.* Ames: Iowa State University Press, 1982.

———. "The New Deal and Farm Policy in the Great Plains." *Agricultural History* 43 (July 1969): 345–355.

Schuyler, Michael W. "Drought and Politics in 1936: Kansas as a Test Case." *Great Plains Journal* 15 (Fall 1975): 3–27.

———. "Federal Drought Relief Activities in Kansas, 1934." *Kansas Historical Quarterly* 42 (Winter 1976): 403–424.

Schweider, Dorothy, and Deborah Fink. "Plains Women: Rural Life in the 1930s." *Great Plains Quarterly* 8 (Spring 1988): 79–88.

Sears, Paul B. *Deserts on the March.* Norman: University of Oklahoma Press, 1947.

Shi, David E. *The Simple Life: Plain Living and High Thinking in American Culture.* New York: Oxford University Press, 1985.

Sitkoff, Harvard. *A New Deal for Blacks.* New York: Oxford University Press, 1978.

Stein, Walter J. *California and the Dust Bowl Migration.* Westport, Conn.: Greenwood Press, 1973.

Tweton, D. Jerome. *The New Deal at the Grass Roots: Programs for the People in Otter Tail County, Minnesota.* St. Paul: Minnesota Historical Society Press, 1988.

Ware, James Wesley. "Black Blizzard: The Dust Bowl of the 1930s." Ph.D. diss., Oklahoma State University, 1977.

Wessel, Thomas R., ed. *Agriculture in the Great Plains, 1876–1936.* Washington, D.C.: Agricultural History Society, 1977.

Westin, Jeane. *Making Do: How Women Survived the '30s.* Chicago: Follett Publishing Company, 1976.

Worster, Donald. *Dust Bowl: The Southern Plains in the 1930s*. New York: Oxford University Press, 1979.
Zickefoose, Paul W. *Economic Development in Southwestern Kansas*, pt. 2, Population and the Labor Force. Lawrence, Kans.: School of Business, Bureau of Business Research, July 1953.

LOCAL HISTORIES

Centennial Book Committee, Bucklin. *Century of Stars: A History of the City of Bucklin, Kansas, and Its Surrounding Community*. Shawnee Mission, Kans.: Kes-Print, 1986.
Family Heritage Society. *Family Heritage Album of Ness County, Kansas*. McPherson, Kans.: Family Heritage Society, 1976.
Finney County Historical Society. *History of Finney County, Kansas*, vols. 1, 2. N.p.: Finney County Historical Society, 1950.
Grant County Historical Commission. *Grant County, Kansas*. Dallas: Taylor Publishing Company, 1982.
Kearny County Historical Society. *History of Kearny County, Kansas*, 2 vols. Dodge City, Kans.: Rollie Jack, 1964 (vol. 1); North Newton, Kans.: Mennonite Press, 1973 (vol. 2).
Meade County Historical Society. *Pioneer Stories of Meade County*, 4th ed. Meade, Kans.: Meade County Historical Society, 1985.
Millbrook, Minnie Dubbs. *Ness Western County, Kansas*. Detroit, Mich.: Millbrook Printing Company, 1955.
Morton County Historical Society. *Morton County, 1886–1986*. N.p.: n.p., 1986.
Stevens County History Association. *The History of Stevens County and Its People*. Hugoton, Kans.: Stevens County History Association, 1979.
Sullivan, Frank S. *A History of Meade County, Kansas*. Topeka, Kans.: Crane and Company, 1916.
Toland, Pauline, ed. *Seward County, Kansas*. Liberal, Kans.: K.C. Printers, 1979.
Wichita County History Association. *History of Wichita County, Kansas*, vol. 1. North Newton, Kans.: Mennonite Press, 1980.

INDEX